BRIAN JACKS

the MINDSET OF A CHAMPION

With MARC GINGELL

GN00759427

First Published in 2017 by Brian Jacks

Updated in September 2018 by Brian Jacks

ISBN 978-981-11-4079-2

Foreword

By Brian Blessed

What a privilege to write a foreword for a book about such a remarkable man as Brian Jacks. How does one appraise such a character?

The story began for me in 1956 when I was accepted into the Bristol Old Vic Theatre School. We were taught voice work, singing, movement, the classics, acting, fencing and judo. Our judo teacher was a black belt called George Brandt who had a great hairy chest and had the physique of a young gorilla. He and I had some right old tussles. I was in prime condition having just finished my National Service in the parachute regiment. Before that in my early teens in Yorkshire I had done a lot of Catch-as-catch-can wrestling but it was judo that intrigued me, I studied every book on the subject.

In 1962 I was cast as a tough policeman PC Fancy Smith in the popular BBC series Z Cars. At that time I was introduced to the two brothers Joe and Doug Robinson who ran a vibrant judo club called The Judo Kan in Orange Street, London. Doug was a light heavyweight and Joe a heavyweight. They were unbeatable. Doug was a 7th Dan and Joe an 8th and they were also successful actors in numerous films and television programs. Joe in addition was World Cumberland Wrestling Champion, World Catch-as-catch-can champion and European Professional Wrestling Champion. The atmosphere at the Judo Kan was electric. To have the famous Robinson brothers as instructors was miraculous, they gave me private training and had me contesting everywhere. The result was that I frequently turned up for filming in Z Cars hobbling like an old man, but that didn't stop me loving the place.

People from all walks of life trained there from white belt to black belts. Bodies flew around the room like confetti. One day emerging through the throng of sweating bodies was the grinning face of a young lad called Brian Jacks. Laughing his head off, he used to be all over me like a rash, never in all my life had I ever come across such a joyful devotee of sport. What an inspiration he was! He was a young lion, fearless in every way. He had no vices, no vanity. You know my love of live is enormous and with Brian I met a kindred spirit. Young and old sought his advice and instruction. He gave people hope and belief. "You can all be champions, there is nothing in this world you can't achieve if you set your mind on it" he shouted and he was sixteen years of age.

The Robinson brothers continued to be his proud teachers and it was fascinating to see his rapid progress. He proudly told me one day that he had perfected a technique that had destroyed half of his opponents. If he saw anybody slacking in training he would quickly grab them and lift them onto the mat with a good natured "Come on lazy bones".

Over the next 2 years he developed into a powerful, fast and brilliant judoka, he seemed to sail thought the various grades at a rate of knots ultimately attaining international status. Brian became a British, European and World contender representing Great Britain in the European Championship, World Championships and Olympic Games. He won Britain's first medal at a World Championship in 1967

I remember him showing his medals to us on one occasion and within minutes he was on the mat teaching a white belt bank manager how to hold his balance. The man was fat, stiff and he was dreadfully frightened yet Brian patiently encouraged him and treated him as if he was a budding world champion. At the end of the lesson he allowed the gentleman to throw him flat on his back, I was profoundly moved, I had never witnessed such kindness. In the early years before he was champion we would go at it hammer and tongs, even then his superior technique was obvious. I countered it with every dirty trick I could think of, such as treading heavily on his toes and grabbing other sensitive areas of his body.

Years later I met him at Television Centre, the BBC was celebrating Eamonn Andrews 'This Is Your Life'. He magnanimously said to my daughter Rosalind "It was bloody awful doing judo with your dad. He was like trying to throw a tank". Rosalind was astonished at how huge his hands were. That's Brian Jacks all over; huge hands, huge talent and huge heart and soul. His achievements are legendary.

Following his retirement from judo he became the nation's favourite achieving international status for his outstanding performances on the BBC program 'Superstars'. Brian dominated the British and European version of the contest winning 4 titles.

I could go on and on about Brian but it would require a book as large as Shakespeare's plays. Adventure is the key to the new millennium and Brian has always encouraged people to fulfil their dreams. For me, he is one of the greatest athletes of all time. His life is a celebration; this book is a celebration. I urge everyone to beg and borrow left right and centre to buy it.

Brian is like a shining beacon showing the way. I salute him.

Brian Blessed

Brian with Brian Blessed – Boxing at Langhams!

To my fantastic wife Lek.

And my amazing son Philip, his beautiful wife Nam, and my wonderful granddaughter Millie.

A million thanks - Brian Jacks.

Errol Field – A Special Dedication

In the acknowledgements and pages of my book you will read about a special person who helped me so much throughout my career. Errol Field. He was my brick and I regarded him as a member of my family. He became the God Father to my only granddaughter Millie. Very sadly, on the 13th September 2017, Errol passed away. Thank you for all your special help Errol and there is not a day goes by when I don't think of you.

Brian Jacks September 2018.

Millie with her Grandfather and God Father Errol Field

Acknowledgements

Many people have played a part in telling my story and my thanks to all of them. From my early days at the London Judo Society with Ted Mossom, Mick Leigh and John Waite. In Japan, the excellent Kisaburu Watanabe really influenced me as did the hundreds of Japanese students who used me as a 'rag doll.' It hurt but I learned from them. Nobuko also helped. She provided something I needed and helped me to focus during quite a difficult time. Back in England, Trevor Leggett helped enormously as did Alan Petherdridge and Colin Draycott. For Superstars, I received expert help from many people with my very good friend, my brick, Errol Field playing a leading role. In Thailand, my beautiful wife Lek has been a fantastic support. I couldn't manage my business without her.

Many people have helped with the writing of my book and firstly I have to thank my son Philip for driving me crazy to start putting pen to paper. If it were not for him and my wonderful granddaughter Millie I would never have started. Other people who have helped include, Stephanie Leigh, John Bowen, Christine Wildman, Eddie Mullen, Robert Mewitt, Tony Underwood, Chantal Davies, David

Finch, and Marc Gingell. Plus of course, all of my family who always supported me so well. Especially Mum and Dad.

Brian Jacks September 2018

Stage 1

SAT ON THE BANK

1

SAT WITH THE sick kids on the bank I watched dejectedly as school sports day unfolded with a lump in my throat and a pain in my heart. What was wrong with me? Why couldn't I be out there with them? In my mind, I knew I could do it. I knew I could compete. But my body just couldn't take it.

Unable to participate in the normal playground activities such as football, played with a tennis ball during the winter, or cricket played with the same tennis ball during the summer. Plus missing out on general kids playground fun stuff had been bad enough. But now I had to sit and endure all the healthy kids taking part in this. School sports day and family fun day festival all rolled into one. Kids were being applauded and cheered and winners were presented with trophies which meant even more applause. On top of all this, which made things even worse, a sizzling hot sun shone down on a beautiful sunny day in July 1951. Everywhere I looked people seemed happy. They smiled, chatted, and kids excitedly played games. Teachers, dressed in casual short-sleeved shirts for the day, mingled with parents many of who'd taken the afternoon off work to enjoy this spectacle with their kids. School sports days always reminded me of fabulous East End, good old knees up, street parties with this one no exception. My parents were always there and they smiled along with everyone else. I looked at my Dad. He loved all sport and as we were a close-knit East End London community he knew many of the other parents plus their kids taking part. He cheered, like everyone else, even though he had no one to cheer for because I, as with previous years, sat on the bank with the sick kids. My spot and a place I knew I had to accept. Some kids were fit and healthy and they could do as they pleased. But not me and I'd now become resigned to a life of sat on the bank.

I'd always wanted to run around in the garden with Dad and kick and throw balls. We tried but I just couldn't do it. He had a bicycle and liked to take long rides. I know he would have loved me to join him. Again we tried. Again I couldn't do it. At school, my friends would tell me how they had fun wrestling with their dads on their living room floors. I'm sure Dad and I could have had fun doing this. We tried. I think you know the outcome!

During that afternoon he looked in my direction several times with an anguished expression on his face that seemed to say to me. 'Brian, what is wrong with you? Why aren't you out there with the other kids? I can help you.' I could only stare back with a sad and depressed expression on my face that said. 'Sorry, Dad. I can't do it.'

At the end of the day, our headmaster gave a short speech. He thanked everyone for coming and for those who took part. Again Dad looked in my direction where I sat on the bank with the sick kids.

2

I entered the World on the 5th of October 1946 and right from the start I did one thing very well. My parents both said they'd never seen, or perhaps I should say heard, anything quite like me before and they both came from big families. Dad had three brothers and three sisters and Mum, four sisters and six brothers. Many of them visited me in London's Whitechapple Hospital during the first few days with both sets of Grandparents. They, like my parents, all said the same thing. Grandad Jacks had actually been born in Poland and christened Abraham Ruben Jackovich. History's proved that he hadn't picked the best time to be born there and at the tender age of seventeen he stowed away on a cargo ship bound for England. He didn't speak any English and travelled alone. After docking in Southampton he made his way to London where he settled in London's East End. He picked up the English language as quickly as he could and soon joined the armed forces where he registered himself as Alfred Jacks. As a keen boxer, he boxed whenever he could and later became the combined armed forces heavyweight boxing champion. It must have taken monumental courage for him to leave Poland knowing that he might never see any of his family again and as far I know he never did.

My Dad, Albert Jacks, born on the 29th of August 1923, became the third of seven of Grandad's children and they all lived in a tiny house which meant sharing beds with his brothers. I think they slept four to a bed and had one outside bathroom. None of this bothered Dad whose two great loves were boxing and carpentry. At fourteen he left school to begin his carpentry apprenticeship but his dream job became a nightmare two weeks later when he handed his first pay packet to his Mum. With a big family, she didn't feel this contained enough money and she urged, or possibly ordered, Dad, to find a better-paid job. Not long after that Dad found himself sat on the back of a horse-driven milk cart where he'd run back and forth, from door to door, delivering milk for a few extra shillings each week. He'd found his better-paid job which made his Mum very happy. Dad had a saying that he always used with us. He said. 'Out of bad comes good.' When I questioned him about the good, from the bad of having to give up carpentry ambitions, he replied that it kept him fit running around all morning.

In 1941, at the age of eighteen, Dad received his call-up to go to war. He joined the Royal Navy and soon found himself on board an HMS rescue motor launch vessel that rescued British and German air force pilots all around the British Isles. Later he served on full rescue alert in Cornwall and Jersey before he eventually found himself stationed at St. Mary's in the Isles of Scilly. At this point in time, Dad had already met my Mum, Lillian May Shepherd, who'd had a similar East End upbringing as Dad with a big family, living in a small house, and sharing beds with her sisters. During Dad's call-up they communicated by telegrams and they met whenever Dad could take leave. At the end of World War Two, they were married and I came along soon after.

Mum said the second I came into the world I cried and cried and cried and I never stopped. She said I was a real screamer and she'd never heard anything like it. In the hospital there were other newborn babies who cried as well but they had no chance against me. I cried them all into submission. Mum also said it seemed like I'd entered some kind of crying game competition. If for some reason I stopped and another baby started, I would soon be at it again.

At home, one hundred and twenty-four Whitehouse Road, Stepney, things were just the same and Mum bit her fingernails down to the bone as she worried about what to do with me. She said the crying continued even though there were no other babies for me to compete with. I'm sure I must have driven her close to tears many times. In addition to crying, I felt sick a lot, had severe stomach pains, and didn't have anywhere near the amount of energy other babies had. Mum took me from doctors to hospitals, back to doctors and back to hospitals. Everywhere she went medical staff brushed her aside with the advice for me to get some rest and I would be okay in the morning. At least I'd stopped crying but my stomach pains were more intense and walking became the next problem. I waddled and I had no power to lift anything heavy. Mum became a total wreck.

Prior to the war Dad quit his job with the milk company and taken a position at Smithfield's Market where he worked in the poultry section plucking chickens. He followed this up with a short spell as a barber but he had another dream.

Anyone visiting London will know that it's almost virtually impossible not to notice the famous London black Hackney carriages. They are all over London and their drivers are just as famous due to their tremendous in-depth knowledge of London's road systems. Wave down a London taxi and you can be guaranteed that the driver will know the shortest and best way to get you to your destination. Street names, famous landmarks, hotels and basically anywhere you like. But these guys don't just turn up one day, jump in a black taxi, and speed off. They need a special licence which means they have to undertake a rigorous training programme. This is commonly referred to as 'The Knowledge' and is considered to be one of the hardest tests in the world to pass. It can take two to four years to learn depending on how much time a person can put in.

The knowledge took Dad seven months and three weeks to pass which at that time might have been a record, or close to it, and he did this with pedal power. Every morning he'd wake up at six a.m. and rode and rode his bike around London until dusk. As he did he picked up information and made notes. I think he got through about twenty notebooks. One day he had a good chat with me about exactly how he'd managed it so quickly. He explained to me about preparation and how vitally important preparation should be with everything I did. He had another one of his sayings that he would bring out from time to time. He would say to me. Brian. Fail to prepare and prepare to fail. Then he said. Look at this wall. He pointed to a wall in our home and then said. Imagine North, East, South, and West. He pointed to each direction as he spoke. This gives you your major points for North, East, South, and West. Now pinpoint on the centre of one location and use a picture in your mind to remember each one. I'm not exactly sure if I got it there and then but that's how he did it. He embedded a chart of London in his brain by using his pictures, key points, as a device to help him remember all he needed. This would have included over two hundred and fifty different routes, more than twenty thousand streets, and a similar amount of landmarks. It worked for him and I fully understood the importance of preparation.

3

MY SISTER BARBARA arrived two years after me and we'd already moved into a large flat in Leyland Buildings Shoreditch. Mum spent most of her time looking after us. She cooked fantastic food and often took on part-time work to bring in extra cash. She cooked, cleaned and tended people's gardens. I particularly loved Mum's pie and mash and liquor sauce.

At school, my teachers soon identified me as someone with special needs who needed to sit out games and sports. During these times they gave me pens, pencils, and paper and sat me with other kids who'd also been excluded from sports. We sat on a bank and watched as other kids ran around and enjoyed themselves. We drew stuff, they played, but I really wanted to get down from the bank and join in. But I remembered what Dad had said. Out of bad comes good. As much as I felt bad about not being down there I learned to draw well, performed quite well in drama classes, and had a talent for making people laugh. This proved Dad's theory correct although I still wanted to be out there on the field with the fit kids. Dad wanted me there as well.

Growing up in the East End I really believed it must have been the best place in the world to live. The people were extremely friendly and it all seemed so open with a huge amount of trust. You could walk down the streets where both my grandparents lived and let yourself into anyone's house. Each house had its front door key attached to a piece of string and anyone could pull a key out of any letterbox and walk straight in. People used to sit outside their houses, chat with each other, and play card games. Everybody seemed to know each other which created a nice friendly atmosphere and there never seemed to be any danger. We were such a tight-knit East End group. People were friendly, they cared, and you could virtually go anywhere and do anything.

We didn't stay long in the flat and lived in a few short-term places before we settled into a council house on Thriffwood Estate, Silverdale, Sydenham. Thriffwood had twenty-two houses and we moved into number twelve located in the inner section of Thriffwood, facing Mayow Park and two blocks of flats. To the left of the flats, just across Dacres Road, we had Forest Hill Secondary School at that time under construction. There were six houses in the inner section facing our way, six behind us, and ten in the outer section facing the railway lines. This felt much better for us as since the arrival of Barbara we were getting a bit cramped. Now we had a big house and a garden. Plus, right on our doorstep, we had three 'adventure playgrounds' to explore. The woods, railway lines and the park which had a huge, manor type house sat in one corner with an orchard full of apples, pears, and plum trees.

This whole area must have been at least three acres and represented so many opportunities for the kids living nearby. Trees to climb, woods to explore and hide in, hills to slide down on whatever kind of sliding object we could find. Many kids on the nearby estates used to congregate there and we played all sorts of games. We used to build camps in the woods and even had campfires. But we had to be careful the park keepers didn't catch us. We used to call them Parkies' and they had one who wore a black patch over his left eye. Of course, we called him Patcheye, Patcheye the Parkie,' and we thought he must have been at least a hundred years old. Although looking back now I know that sounds ridiculous. He may have only been about sixty. But we feared him most.

In the park, the woods and even around the railway lines I don't think we did bad things. We just wanted to be outside and have fun. We didn't have radios or televisions then and of course, there were no mobile telephones. We never had a television until I was twelve and then it was just a small box, with black and white pictures, that were sometimes very difficult to see.

Dad always encouraged me to make things with wood. His first love and I followed him with this passion. Whenever I spoke with him about making something he said to get on with it and see how it turned out. Then, if it didn't work, I would go back to him and we would work out where I'd gone wrong. Sometimes he watched and if he could see me making a mistake he would talk me through it. He really wanted me to try and mistakes were inevitable. But they educated me and Dad didn't want to do everything for me as he knew I would never have learned to do anything.

On one particular day in the woods, we played our Robin Hood game and we made these bows from branches that we'd cut down from a Yew tree. We were meticulous and made sure they were as perfect. Our arrows were canes used for flowers and again we were careful with our preparation. But we had something special to use for our arrowheads as one of our gang had turned up with darts. We cut off the flights and shafts and attached the dart barrels, the lethal pointy bits that stick into dart boards, to the end of our arrows. After about two hours we had five set of bows and arrows which were quite lethal and could travel fifty to sixty yards. We split into two teams and took it in turns to fire and run, or in my case waddle, between two base camps that we'd set up about fifty yards apart. During my attempt, I heard this voice shout 'Look out Brian.' I froze, looked up, and this arrow went right up my nose. It penetrated so hard we couldn't pull it out. Blood went everywhere and one of the Parkies' came running to investigate. He soon realised how bad things were and called for an ambulance.

After that, our parents got together for a bit of pow-wow which resulted in a short ban from the woods for a few of us. I spent two nights in the hospital while they sorted things out and observed me. Mum again pleaded with doctors to try and find out exactly what was wrong with me as my stomach pains were getting worse. A few gathered around my bed, asked questions, prodded my body and asked me where I felt pain. Again I told them, as I had many times, that I felt incredible pain in my stomach. They, like so many others, went into a huddle and came out telling me to get some rest and everything would be okay. I went home, rested for a few days, and absolutely nothing changed.

AS A POOR East End family we couldn't afford holidays so we, like many East End families, went hop picking in Kent. And when I say we I don't just mean my family. I mean most of my family plus hundreds of other East End families. I think we must have resembled some kind of pilgrimage as we evacuated London's East End to head for Kent each year. But it really had to be one of the most exciting times of the year and always took place during the school holidays towards the end of August. These were magical days and I think most East End kids, who escaped to Kent's fields for a month, would say the same thing. Especially with a hot sun that always seemed to burn down on my back. I suppose there were times when it rained but I can't remember those. Just long, very hot, magical summer days.

Most years we ended up on the same farm as we'd always left a good impression with the farmer who owned it. He, like most hop farmers, sent out invitation cards to all the families he wanted to work for him. Mum always seemed especially excited when her card dropped through our letterbox. But she had a lot of preparation to do. She had to make sure we took enough cans of food to see us through hop picking. Baked beans, soups, corn beef and stuff like that. Old cooking pots, blankets and warm clothes for cold summer nights were all packed neatly for our departure. Plus all kinds of other bits and pieces that she believed might come in useful which included an old pram. We usually left in a bit of a convoy and I remember I travelled in Uncle Harry's truck. As we drove out of London I always enjoyed the transformation from London's drab buildings to Kent's green fields.

Looking back now we might not have had the best living conditions. Basically, we were in a small hut, with enough room to sleep six, with no water or electricity, plus a big bed with a straw-stuffed mattress. Mum would never let us enter until she'd given it a good spring clean which normally took her half a day as it hadn't been lived in for a year. So we played in the fields which we did a lot as there was nothing to do in the hut apart from sleep. We would wake up at 7:00 a.m. and pick hops, almost straight away, until about 5:30 p.m. Well I didn't, I couldn't in my condition, but I had a special job. I took responsibility for the old pram which I used to push to the nearby store to collect water. I think most of the younger kids only had to fill one basket before they could go and play and I spent a lot of time on a makeshift swing, made with a plank of wood and some thick rope, which dangled down from a huge acorn tree. My cousins pushed me and they ran about playing all kinds of games. It would have been nice to have been able to join in.

At the end of the day, Mum and a few Aunties, cooked food on a big open fire outside our huts and we would all sit around the fire, chat, listen to a few old family stories, play cards and watch the sun go down. On more than one occasion we had a good old East End cockney sing song where Uncle Ronnie took centre stage. He had a great voice, sounded a bit like Nat King Cole, and he also sang in many East End pubs. That was our day and if it doesn't sound that glamorous now it certainly was then. It also proved a great way to unite families.

Back home again in the woods and a few of us were having another Robin Hood day. This time without bows and arrows as we'd promised our parent's we'd never make them again. Instead, we made swords. We found suitable pieces of wood, again cut down from Yew trees, and shaped them into fine looking swords. I remember it was a Sunday morning and we played until around lunch time without any problems. I felt proud of my sword and decided to take it home to show Dad. I found Mum in the kitchen cooking Sunday lunch and when I walked in she had a carving knife in her hand. Automatically I said on guard Mum! We playfully touched weapons and were about to try a second time when Mum slipped and unfortunately her carving knife cut through my tendons on the back of my right hand. Blood went everywhere including all over Mum's roast chicken that she'd just taken out of the oven. Mum looked devastated. Not about the chicken, about me, and the ambulance soon turned up on our doorstep yet again.

'OUT OF BAD comes good.' Remember Dad's saying? Well, that certainly couldn't apply to me as I lay in bed with my right arm suspended in the air. At least at other times, when stuck in the hospital, I had my right-hand functioning so I could doodle and draw pictures. Now I couldn't do anything except stare up at the ceiling. The days went by so slowly and yet the hospital staff continuously woke me up at 6:00 a.m. every morning. What was the point of that when I still needed sleep? I asked Dad when he came to visit me later that day and he knew I felt depressed. I'd only been there three days but it felt like three weeks. Dad remained upbeat and said it again. 'Out of bad comes good.'

That night, around 3:00 a.m., the stomach pains that had dogged me since birth really kicked in and bad just got a whole lot worse. I'm not sure why as I'd just laid there doing nothing for more than three days. I had to call a night nurse who tried to help me as best she could. She gave me painkillers and by about 5:00 a.m. my pain eased and I finally slept. But the morning crew soon woke me an hour later when they started banging around. I looked up at the ceiling as I could do nothing else. At seven years old I'd just been through the worse night of my life and I really needed my parents.

Mum arrived at noon and she'd already heard about my problems from one of the nurses. She looked worried and tense as I explained more about my nightmare. As I finished a doctor appeared to check on my hand. Mum let him do his job and he seemed pleased and mentioned I should be able to go home soon. Mum thanked him for that before she raised the problems I'd had during the night. He looked at my charts, where the nurse must have recorded something, and he asked a few questions as he prodded me as I'd been prodded so many times before. He then rubbed his chin with his index finger and asked Mum if she would meet him in five minutes outside the ward as he needed to check on something. Mum, so used to being blown away by doctors seemed amazed that someone might be taking my problem seriously. She managed a smile but I could see the worry in her eyes.

About twenty minutes later Mum reappeared with the same doctor and another doctor. The new one, whose name I found out later was Professor Ian Aire, asked me more questions. Some I'd been asked before and a few new ones. He also prodded me around a bit before he went with the thoughtful, thumb and index finger, rub on his chin. It must have been a rub on the chin, thumb and index finger day, as I think I even started doing it. But he soon reached his conclusion which he explained to us. I actually had no idea what he was talking about and neither I think did Mum. But we both understood that he might have some ideas about how my problem could be fixed and for the next two days time flew by as a succession of medical people arrived at my bed to take notes. I had to hop in and out for a number of tests and they made me drink a horrible thick creamy yellow liquid that nearly made me sick. Apparently, this fluid went into my intestines and could pinpoint the position of any kind of rupture on x-rays. They also gave me an injection that made me cold. In the end, they decided they would open me up.

On the morning of the operation, Mum and Dad were both there when Professor Aire appeared. He seemed fresh and ready for action but advised my parents to go home and return again at 2:00 p.m. We had a quick hug before a pretty young nurse held my hand and led me away. I couldn't look back. She took me to a place where I put on a special gown and waited with me for about thirty minutes before another group of people arrived, including Professor Aire, all dressed in green robes with masks covering their faces, and what looked like shower caps covering their hair.

Sometime later I woke up with the pretty young nurse still holding my hand. She explained that the doctors had opened my stomach and fixed the problem inside. I felt drowsy and in pain. She understood and said that was normal and that she would get me something for that later.

I stayed in intensive care for two days and my parents visited many times. I couldn't move and felt pain when I coughed, pain when I laughed and it was impossible for me to sit up. After two days they switched me back to the children's ward and I stayed in the hospital for another three weeks before they allowed me to go home.

At home, I still had to take medication and couldn't yet return to school. Mum took great care of me and as more time went by I found I had more energy than ever before and I could walk a lot better. The operation seemed to have worked and with my new found power I knew I'd soon be back at school where I'd be able to run down from that bank and join the fit kids. With this in mind, I started to push myself a bit more. In the garden, I practiced running around in circles. I'm not exactly sure how I looked but I found it fantastic that I could now move with almost the same freedom as the other kids. I couldn't wait to get back to school and two months after my operation I returned to Kelvin Grove Primary School a new man, well a new boy, approaching eight years and three months old.

I didn't take my usual place on the bank! I came down and joined in with the fit kids. I knew I had to take it easy, which I did for a few days before I let myself go. I'd wasted enough time and now my moment had arrived. I'd show them.

Around six months later I sat on the bank with the sick kids again. Because, after two months of being down with the fit kids, something happened. Something inside me seemed to burst. My friends who drove the ambulance picked me up and everyone at Sydenham General Hospital welcomed me back. Professor Aire and his team, after more thumb and index fingers thoughtful chin rubbing moments, operated again. It was like take two of my first operation and I returned to school two months later. But I had a warning not to do anything too strenuous for three months. Mum, worried about my rush to join the fit kids, kept a very close eye on me. Dad, who wanted me out with those fit kids as well, spoke to me about the need for my body to recover from two major operations. At school, the teachers watched me, as did the kids on the bank, and the fit kids as well. I felt strong and I needed to do something. Dad, who sensed this, spoke with me and we agreed on a programme of exercises. Nothing too strenuous, mainly gentle jogging, skipping and some long walks with him around the local woods and wasteland as he wanted to monitor my progress. This gentle build-up proved a perfect formula and soon we incorporated thirty-minute bike rides into our routine. I loved this quality time with Dad who seemed to know exactly what I needed, when to push me harder, and when to ease off. Just after my ninth birthday, I went back to see Professor Aire who really believed I'd made a complete recovery.

What happened to me and how did it happen? Well, I had something called a hiatus hernia. A hernia is something people get when an internal body organ pushes into an area it doesn't belong. The hiatus is an opening in the diaphragm, the muscular wall separating the chest cavity from the abdomen. Normally, the esophagus, the food pipe, goes through the hiatus and attaches to the stomach. In a hiatus hernia, the stomach bulges up into the chest through that opening. Anyway, that's the technical blurb. All I can tell you is that it's very painful and I wouldn't wish it on my worst enemy. How it happened is not clear but there were two schools of thought. I could have been born with it. Or I could have created it myself with my intense crying during my first few days and weeks after being born. Mum and Dad both believed it could have been self-inflicted.

But it felt absolutely fantastic to be like the other kids and Mum and Dad were so pleased for me. A year later at primary school, when everything had healed, I joined in with sports and soon began to excel in all kinds of activities. I also took part in the annual summer sports day and even won the fifty-yard sprint. Mum and Dad were there, as they had been before, but this time there we no worried looks from Dad in my direction. He looked so pleased and he'd even helped me with preparation for that particular race. He encouraged me with his preparation quote. 'Fail to prepare then prepare to fail. We'd prepared, I did well, and I took the applause that came my way. I looked up at the sick kids on the bank and waved to them. After all, I used to be one of them. They remembered me and I remembered them. I would never forget.

As for Professor Aire, he didn't actually belong to the Sydenham General Hospital. He arrived the day after my severe night of stomach pains to present a lecture to a number of senior doctors. He took a special interest in my case. He ordered all the intensive tests, experiments and performed my operations. I remember after the second one he spoke with Mum. He put his hand on her shoulder and said that she could stop biting her nails now.

'Out of bad comes good' proved right again. By that, I mean the incident with Mum in the kitchen. This triggered my visit to the hospital, followed by my night of severe stomach pains, which eventually resulted in my problem reaching the attention of someone who could help. Out of bad definitely came good!

6

ON SUNDAY THE 4th of September 1956, I distinctly remember the date as it was about a month before my tenth birthday, Dad said he had something important he wanted to discuss with me. He looked serious and I actually thought I'd done something wrong. My mind quickly flashed back to the previous week but I couldn't think of anything that deserved a telling off from Dad. I followed Dad outside into the garden where we sat on the grass with our backs against the base of the apple tree. A position we'd taken many times during the last few months as we discussed my fitness. Dad remained quiet for at least a minute and I didn't want to say anything to break the silence. Whenever Dad had something to say I knew it had to be important.

Eventually, Dad asked me how I felt and I told him that I'd never felt better or stronger. It had been over a year since my second operation, my stomach tissue had healed, and I could run around a lot more than I ever had before. At a recent check-up at the hospital, I'd passed all tests and my doctors were very pleased. Dad knew this already. He then asked if I'd like to try judo as I seemed to be getting on my feet for the first time in my life. At that time I didn't know anything about judo or had ever spoken to anyone with any judo knowledge. But Dad went on to explain that he'd tried judo and that he'd been training for nine months. Dad then spoke passionately about judo for the next hour and he surprised me with his in-depth knowledge of this sport.

He explained that a man called Jigoro Kano, born in 1860 in a place called Mikage, Japan was the 'Father of Judo.' At the age of fourteen, when Kano was five feet two inches tall and weighed ninety pounds, he wanted to find a way to defend himself. He spoke to Nakai Baisei, a family friend, and also a member of shogun's guard. Nakai suggested that jujitsu might be the way for Kano to go as he'd studied this before even though it was getting out of date. He showed the young Kano a few moves which were aimed for smaller men to take out larger and stronger opponents. Kano decided he would try this despite reservations from his father who wanted him to try a more modern sport instead.

In 1877, when Kano attended Tokyo's Imperial University, he started to look for jujitsu teachers. In time he found Fukuda Hachinosuke who taught in a ten mat room close to his University. There Kano had to learn how to take fall after fall after fall from his teacher and senior students. This enabled him to learn the mechanics of techniques.

Fukuda would provide Kano with a brief outline of a technique and then let him practice in order to learn from experience. Later, when Kano had acquired some basic skills, Fukuda taught him some traditional forms. No special mats were around at this time so when Kano fell he landed on straw mats laid over wooden floors.

Fukushima Kanekichi, a senior at the school, provided a stern test for Kano. Kano, who knew he had to think of something outside of the box to beat him, decided to try some other techniques. First, he tried sumo but that didn't work. He then looked at something called a 'fireman's carry,' which he found in a book about western wrestling, and it worked.

In 1879 Fukuda died and Iso Masatomo, then sixty-two and exactly five feet tall, took over as Kano's instructor. Due to Kano's intense training, and solid grounding installed in him by his father and Fukuda, he soon became an assistant at Iso's school. But whenever Kano came across an opponent he couldn't beat he'd look for ways to improve himself so he could beat him. He trained harder as well as smarter. At this point Kano realized that to reach the level he wanted, which was to be the best, he had to combine the finest of several elements of different martial arts. He looked around for teachers who could provide him with these elements. In 1881 Iso died and Kano began training with Iikubo Tsunetoshi and mastered different techniques from him. At this point in his life, Kano became so skilled that he exchanged places with his teacher. Kano became master and Iikubo his student. Iikubo explained that there was nothing more he could teach Kano.

Kano had looked at and studied many different forms of martial arts, and when he believed he found the best of everything, plus a few of his own inventions, he packaged them together to form judo. In 1906 judo began being introduced into Japanese public schools and Kano became known as the 'Father of Judo.' He opened his own training centre which he called the Kodokan and this became known as the 'Spiritual Home' of judo in Tokyo. Kano oversaw the development of this. In 1882 he had ten students and twelve mats. But by 1911 he had more than a one thousand Dan graded students. That means they were black belts. In 1890, in need of more space, Kano found a location with room for sixty mats. But he didn't remain there long and by 1894 he'd moved to a larger space located in Tomizaka-cho, Koishikawa-cho. The Kodokan continued to move locations to cope with the higher number of pupils who wanted to train. By 1934 Kano relocated to a 510 ten mat facility. In

1958, twenty years after Kano's death, the Kodokan moved to its current location with space for over 1,200 mats.

At this point, Dad asked if I was okay and if I wanted him to continue. I quickly nodded twice and Dad picked up his thread.

He said Kano, an idealist, had broad aims for judo. He believed judo encompassed self-defence, physical culture, and moral behaviour. So we have physical exercise, judo the martial art, and the cultivation of wisdom and virtue. Physical exercise meant that people who trained, would develop their bodies in an ideal manner to enable them to be outstanding in matches, and by improving their wisdom this would improve their daily lives. Within a few years, judo became Japan's number one practiced martial arts sport and Kano achieved a doctorate degree in judo. He also worked hard with the development of athletics and Japanese sport. In 1935 he was awarded the Asahi prize for his outstanding contribution to the organizing of sport. At this point, Dad looked at me again and I nodded for him to continue which he did.

Judo has a competitive element as well where the aim of both players is to either throw or take down their opponent to the ground. Where they try to force a submission. He then talked about the belt system. From the lowest ranking white belt right up to black followed by a Dan for each step up from black. Dad explained there were six levels to achieve before reaching a black belt. White, yellow, orange, green, blue and brown. Dad had his blue belt which made him two steps down from his black. At this point in time, Dad didn't speak in detail about Dan grades and he concluded my brief introduction into judo's history with one last comment about Kano. Dad said that Kano didn't agree with weight categories. He was small but he could throw people a lot bigger than him. He wanted everyone to come together and show how being highly trained and skilled meant that size didn't matter.

Dad had taken up judo with three things in mind. He thought he might need some form of self-defence, in case he had a problem late at night driving his taxi, plus he wanted to lose weight which he'd gained by sitting in a taxi all day. For the third reason, he wanted to get fitter. With three, for the price of one, Dad had a bargain and he always liked one of those. To me, this sounded great and I was fascinated that Dad had been training for nine months without telling me. Soon we went back inside and he showed me his white judo kit. Loose fitting white trousers with a similar white jacket.

He put it on and looked like a real warrior with his blue belt holding everything in place.

The following Wednesday Dad took me with him to the London Judo Society (LJS) where he trained. I only went to watch and get more of a feel about judo. The LJS building had three floors and the more you progressed in judo the higher up you went. Beginners were on the first floor, intermediates on the second, and higher ranking players were on the third. I remember walking into this hall, roughly three quarters the size of a tennis court, where eight grey mats covered most of the floor area. A few wooden chairs were placed just to one side of the mats, and a selection of judo pictures, in frames, were attached to areas of the walls. Dad introduced me to Mr. George Chew, the President of the club, and a Scotland Yard policeman. He wore a very smart suit and looked a formidable character. Rather like a headmaster which made me nervous. 'Brian. Take your hands out of your pockets.' Were the first words he said to me! I followed his orders. Dad had already advised me that protocol here meant I had to ask Mr. Chew if I could train at the LJS. Not that evening of course because I didn't have any kit yet and Mr. Chew would never let anyone near his mats unless they were properly dressed. Nervously I made my request with my hands down by my sides and stood to attention. He, although at that time the LJS junior club hadn't started yet, agreed. Mr. Chew had a partner called Mr. Eric Dominy and he wore a similar smart suit. One of the first sounds I heard was a man crashing on to the mat after being thrown by a much smaller woman. A large gong sat in one corner of the hall with a mallet. From time to time someone banged the gong which signaled that players had to change partners. I watched Dad on the mat. He bowed to his training partner who bowed back. They then gripped each other's jacket's which I knew meant they were grappling. They were only practicing a few moves so neither of them ended up on flat on the ground.

Driving home Dad asked me how I felt about judo and if I still wanted to give it a try. He didn't push or demand. He never did. With Dad, he encouraged me to try things and helped when I needed help. His attitude was that he wanted me to learn and he believed the best way to do this was to let me try.

With judo now very on my mind, and before I could get to the LJS, Dad asked if I wanted to watch him in a competition at the Chelsea Town Hall. London's taxi drivers' had a judo team and they had a match against London's metropolitan police. I sat in the front row of a crowd of around two hundred people and I couldn't wait for Dad's contest. Luckily he came on first.

There he was, my Dad, all five feet eight inches of him and I felt so proud. Soon his opponent joined him. A huge unit of a man who must have been about six feet two inches tall and twice as heavy. I felt so nervous and frightened for Dad. This looked like a real David and Goliath contest and most of the crowd must have had their money on the giant to win.

They bowed and within five seconds Dad had swept his feet away and the policeman went smack down on his back. The referee called a full point and that was it. Dad had won. I'll never forget the sound the mat made when the giant's back connected with it. The thud and the shocked, pained expression on that policeman's face, as he realised he'd been beaten. The crowd also seemed stunned before they were all on their feet applauding. I think I was up first and applauded loudest and longest. I didn't want to stop. At the end of the day, the taxi drivers were well beaten but they were still presented with plaques by the metropolitan police. Both teams showed immense respect for each other and I still have my Dad's plaque today. I think that day, even though I'd never actually been on a mat, is where my judo career started. I was so enthralled and engrossed watching those men, normal taxi drivers and normal policemen, taking part in this amazing competition. It was a fantastic opening for my wanting to begin judo. A magical point in my life and as if a light had suddenly switched on in my head. Seeing Dad with his trophy meant so much to me. It had to be the most inspirational moment in my life. I wanted a trophy. I WANTED TO WIN.

Dad later explained how he mentally approached his contest and his 'big' three D's philosophy. He knew his opponent would be a lot taller than him and much heavier. But that didn't matter. In his mind, he kept repeating: 'The bigger they are the harder they fall. The bigger they are the harder they fall. The bigger they are the harder they fall.' He said he spent five minutes, looking in the dressing room mirror, and repeating the same sentence over and over again. This psyched him up and then he focused on his three Ds. Dedication, Determination, and Domination. For dedication, he knew he'd put in a huge amount of effort to reach his blue belt level in nine months. This coupled with determination helped him reach this level. As for domination, apart from the mandatory bow before the contest, he'd gone out of his way not to let his opponent catch him watching him during the warm-ups. He wanted this giant policeman thinking what

I have done to this little taxi driver and why is he angry with me?' Dad adopted a tactic used by many fighters to try and catch their opponents off guard. A kind of kidology approach and it certainly worked in this case. Although Dad had covertly checked him out during his warm up. Dad knew that after he bowed he made two steps to the right. To counter this Dad moved one step to his right, grabbed his sleeve and threw him. But at the end, Dad helped his opponent up and made sure he was okay.

7

AS MY FIRST LJS session approached I wanted to find out more about the club and the people who started it. So Tuesday, after tea, I asked Dad what he knew. He explained.

Shortly after the Second World War, the South London Judo Society formed due to an overflow of players training at the Budokwai Judo Club in Kensington, London. The reason for this attributed to the end of the war because a number of people, that included Mr. Dominy, had spent time in German prison camps, and they wanted to learn self-defence. Later the founder members dropped south from the name.

Mr. Dominy had been incarcerated in a high-security German prison camp as a result of an earlier escape. There he met a man called Mr. Percy Sekine who'd also suffered the same fate. They had adjoining cells, with a hole in the dividing wall, which allowed them to communicate together. They discussed many subjects including sport. Mr. Dominy had been a successful runner and Mr. Sekine had practiced judo and he planned to start a judo training class in the camp gym very soon. Mr. Dominy would have joined had the Germans not stepped in with a new plan. They were fed up with prisoners trying to escape so they moved all those who they felt might try to a large hut in the centre of the camp. From this location, they believed it would be impossible to dig a tunnel. But they were wrong and this resulted in a mass breakout by those who'd relocated to the 'hot' security hut and a temporary delay in the judo class. This eventually started after they were recaptured. Mr. Sekine took on the role of instructor with Mr. Dominy a student.

Judo jackets were made from mail bags in the theatre workshop. Mr. Sekine instructed for about a year with six to eight students before being moved on. At this point, Mr. Dominy trained on, without an instructor, with one other person although they had to stop when a shortage of food forced the medical officers to ban all sport. Soon after that, Mr. Dominy escaped and this time made it home to England safely. He joined the Budokwai and later visited Mr. Sekine's parents where he heard about a man called Mr. George Chew who'd been stationed in India as a parachute instructor. Mr. Sekine made it home after his camp had been overrun by Russians and soon Mr. Chew returned from India where he met Mr. Dominy at the Budokwai. They became great friends. Gunji Koizumi, the founder of the Budokwai, suggested that Mr. Chew and Mr. Dominy should form an overflow club and soon the South London Judo Society started.

Now I had a good understanding of the Japanese roots of Judo, how my club had started and the people behind it. I felt ready to begin my first session. I woke early on Wednesday and I had to think about why I felt so excited. Then I remembered it was judo Wednesday. Of course, I had to get through school unscathed, which I did, and I made it home without taking any risks in the park or the woods. Mum gave me some tea, which I didn't really want before I sat looking out of the living room window waiting for Dad to arrive. Just after 6:00 p.m. he parked outside and I noticed he had a brown package under his arm as he closed our front gate. Before he could unlock the front door I'd opened it for him. Dad smiled and made a move as if he wanted to hide the package behind his back before he passed it to me. I ran upstairs and returned two minutes later wearing my first judo kit. Now I felt like a real warrior and Mum and Dad looked at me with smiles on their faces. I felt proud but I still had an hour to wait before we would leave for training so I played in the garden, trying out by myself a few of the moves I'd recently seen, and made a few of the noises. Eventually, the hour, which seemed like two, passed and I sat next to Dad on a box in his taxi as we pulled out of Thriffwood and made our way to St. Oswald's Place in Kennington.

During the thirty minute drive my emotions went from one extreme to another. Having witnessed Dad, whip the feet away from the metropolitan police officer, I wanted to be like him. Dad had been fearless, strong and moved with such speed. I knew I could be like him and in my mind, it all seemed so easy. Then a few seconds' later seeds of doubt entered my head as I recalled how other taxi drivers, had battled on the mat, for what seemed an eternity to me as a nine year old. All kinds of different judo techniques were used and I had absolutely no idea what they were.

My thoughts were also about the judo mat and again they were like a yo-yo. Up and down. Up and down. Would it be hard? Would it be soft? Would it be easy? Would it be difficult? One minute I had it all worked out and I believed it would be easy. Then the next I thought about being thrown and getting hurt just like some of those taxi drivers who were smashed on their backs at the Chelsea show. Would I suffer as they had? Also, and slightly more concerning for me, I thought about my stomach. Would my body really let me do something like this? Or would judo be pushing it too far and result in another body shut down that would land me in hospital. I tried to banish this thought. Doctors had given me the all clear and if anything now I'd reached a stage where I considered myself stronger than a lot of kids my age and even some kids who were older than me. This thought soothed my anxiety and I returned to thinking about whipping my opponents' feet away for a quick and easy win just like Dad. But I really didn't know. I didn't have a clue.

We arrived and fortunately for me, Mr. Chew and Mr. Dominy were nowhere to be seen. Those were two who had been through a lot, particularly Mr. Dominy, and I felt quite apprehensive about seeing them again. Especially if I totally failed. So for me, if it turned out I couldn't do this and I made a complete idiot of myself, I preferred to do so not in their presence. We entered an office where Dad paid my training fee before he went to get changed. I waited and thought more about my entrance on the lowest floor level that I would join very soon. How soon could I progress to the middle floor and how much longer to the top floor?

Dad entered level one with me as his class started a bit later. There were about fourteen other people in this class and a few were enormous. Their ages ranged from eighteen to fifty. I felt slightly hesitant at first but Dad reassured me with a comment about Jigoro Kano and I know he meant no disrespect by this. He said Kano had only been a small man, knee-high to a grasshopper, and yet he'd taken on people of all sizes and weights and worked out a way beat them. Now he said to me you are Kano, you are knee high to these grasshoppers, and you will work out ways to beat them.' Dad smiled and looked like he wanted to say more but we were interrupted by a shout from a small man who'd just limped into the room.

Dad moved away from the mats and I observed my first judo coach, Mr. Ted Mossom, who could have been in his late fifties. First, he warmed us up with ten minutes running on the spot, twenty straight toe touches with our left hands and right hands touching our left feet and right feet at the same time, twenty swing toe touches where with our legs apart we touched our left feet with our right hand and vice versa. Twenty press ups followed next before we ended this session with two minutes of faster running on the spot. For me, this felt quite strange as I'd never worn a judo kit before and everything became quite loose. My jacket, belt, and trousers. Mind you I had been wearing it for nearly two hours by now. Mr. Mossom, who must have spotted this, called me over to him where he ordered me to stand to attention. He also instructed me to keep my hands by my sides and to get ready to bow. Which I did of course as he didn't seem the type of person who would take kindly to anyone disobeying him! Especially a nine year old. He then questioned me about my belt which I knew had fallen almost down to my ankles.

A few of the class sniggered but Mr. Mossom wouldn't have any of that. He ordered the rest of the class, including me and Dad who had nothing to do with this class, to do another twenty press-ups. We did and as I stood up again he said he would show me the correct way to tie my belt. As quick as a flash he did it and I had no idea how. Mr. Mossom asked me if I got it and of course, I said yes. I didn't want to run the risk of another twenty press-ups for me and possibly the rest of the class. Later I would ask Dad exactly what happened.

At that point, he sent me back to the line and we were instructed to do forward rolls. Very easy for me as I could do them in my sleep. A few of the bigger members of our class had difficulties but with my size, which meant I had a low centre of gravity, it was very easy. I'd also started gymnastics at school which included work on the trampoline so that helped as well. I think I probably showed off a bit. I dived in the air and pretended to roll over imaginary objects. Really the things I'd been doing at school for the last few months and I knew I wouldn't hurt myself. Not like some of the older students who really struggled. I looked at Dad on the side and he could see me showing off. But he probably knew this would change when I faced more difficult tasks.

Dad disappeared upstairs and we continued with tumbling practice. One of our class had to sit in the centre of the mat, on his hands and knees, curled up in a kind of ball position. The rest of us had to dive, in a kind of forward roll motion, over the top of them. Right up my street as it really mirrored the exercises I'd been practicing at school. Again my classmates, who'd struggled with forward rolls, had problems with this. They were landing on their knees, their arms and it must have been quite disconcerting for the man in the middle when he saw them approaching. But he knew with me he didn't have to worry as I felt quite confident that I could have dived over five or six people with no problem at all.

We learned how to fall down sideways and practiced something called a break-fall with one arm. Standing up, I had to put my right leg in front of my left leg, and take it right the way across as if I wanted to make a sweeping action across my body. Then I had to fall down on my right-hand side and bang the mat with the flat of my right hand.

When my session finished I went up to level three to watch Dad training and this looked a totally different judo game. Dad had taken his position on the mat with yellow, orange, blue, brown and black belts. A real mixture of standards and they performed totally different exercises. Downstairs I'd been taught to move forward and throw my opponent back. But on this level, they were moving in to throw their opponents forward, over their shoulders, over their hips, and over their legs.

I sat in a corner and watched Dad practice. He bowed to his partner and they grabbed hold of each other whilst they moved around the mat. One of them would try to throw the other and the other would try to avoid being thrown. They were executing free practice and this looked much more fun and wanted to jump straight to level three. But I'd only learned one throw and one hold down. Driving home Dad said I had to pay my dues downstairs, learn techniques correct the way, and then move up the floors. Although, with Dad on level three already, this represented a perfect opportunity for me to gain extra knowledge every week by just watching him. This I'm certain gave me a huge edge over the people in my class who didn't hang around once our session had finished. I mentioned to Dad that I didn't really enjoy the press ups and he explained that in judo strength counted a lot as did fitness. To succeed I needed to be strong and fit.

Before we arrived home I asked Dad about Mr. Mossom and Dad explained that he'd been born with polio which left him with one leg three inches longer than the other. This is why he limped. But instead of wallowing in self-pity he used this disadvantage as an advantage when it came to judo as this defect enabled him to perform some techniques in a far better way than a person with legs the same length. Dad also mentioned that he'd achieved his third Dan, had become a well-respected figure in the judo world, and that he was a man who pushed his students very hard. This sounded very interesting to me. A man, who hadn't had the best start in life, but who'd bounced back and forged a very good judo career. We had something in common and I hoped this would be a good sign for me at the start of my judo career.

8

MY LJS BEGINNERS' CLASSES finished at the end of 1955 and I felt I'd learned a lot from Ted Mossom and from my time spent watching senior players upstairs. Although as much as I enjoyed watching, and learning, I would have much preferred more mat opportunities with them. Dad kept telling me to be patient. Ted Mossom proved a fantastic coach and a great inspiration. He also coached senior classes and had become well known in judo as a groundwork guru. Any players who needed to improve their groundwork would invariably end up at the LJS for extra tuition with Ted.

I learned some very important early lessons from Ted during my introductory course. He taught me about legwork on the ground and how to control my opponents that way. I learned how to dominate people inside my legs and how to fake a release that would lull opponents into a false sense of security. One second I would have them in a position where they tried for all their worth to hold on. Then I would fake a slight release, they would relax, and at that point, I would go in big and force them into a submission. I also obviously understood that the quicker I could get someone on his back the quicker the contest finished. I knew I had to watch people, as Dad had watched to perfection at Chelsea's show, how they stepped back and to their sides early in contests. Very early on I would always look to find ways to get my opponents on their backs as fast as possible because if I could win a fight quickly it meant I had more rest time before my next fight.

As I began competitions I think I really focused on five ways to win contests early.

1. I looked for ways to throw opponents on their back just after they'd bowed.

2. I used great groundwork.

3. I used left handed techniques.

4. I cut off opponents' blood supply using neck holds.

5. I used choke submissions by pushing on their Adam's apples.

At the start of 1956, Dad spoke to me again about judo. He could see that I had some talent for this sport and, coupled with the fact I'd now totally recovered from my operations, he could sense that I'd started to become a more confident person. However, I'd also acquired a reputation for being a tenacious little so and so and this is what Dad wanted to speak to me about. He knew about my intensity and he wanted to make sure I controlled this side of my character. He understood that being determined would help me in certain situations. But he stressed that I must confine all my judo to the correct time and place. By this, he meant the mat and I knew that the basic principles of judo were about control of the mind and body.

As we moved through the early part of 1956 the LJS junior class began to really kick off. Alf Stoddard, the son of another taxi driver and two years my senior, became the second junior and by April we were up to six. I think I must have been the youngest but I had more experience which gave me an advantage. This created one drawback for me as a rule had to be put in place that stopped juniors from joining in on the third floor.

At school, my new found confidence had also been recognised and I joined in with all kinds of sports and became one of the best at school at almost everything. I really enjoyed PE and we used to set a gym up in the main hall as we didn't have a real gym. Other kids, who hadn't really paid me any attention before, now looked up to me and I seemed to get on well with nearly everyone.

As I passed through Forest Hill, where I remained in the in crowd, I have to admit that I had absolutely no interest in academic work. In my experience classrooms seemed to be three types of students. Group one sat at the front and hung on to every word teacher's said. Group two sat in the middle and they couldn't quite decide if they wanted to be in group one or three. They were middle of the road types and seemed happy to drift in and out of everything. I sat at the back of the class with group three and we were in a totally different world. We didn't hang on anything the teacher said or drift between groups one and two. We were at school for one thing and one thing only. To have fun! We might have pushed a few teachers to their limits with our behavior. Kids in group one never looked back and those in group two sometimes joined in. I lost count of the number of times I had my knuckle rapped by a few exasperated teachers. One, in particular, geography teacher Mr. Ashby, seemed to spend more time down the back of the classroom, with his cane, than he did up the front!

With my gym work at school, my judo improved with our first junior coach called Mick Leigh who I learned a lot from him. I found out later that quite a few adults didn't believe a junior class would take off. But this negativity proved totally incorrect as within a few months more junior classes had started. Mick helped mould us into the best junior team in London and under him, we won the Peter Sellers cup. Sellers, the actor and comedian, who many people remember for his appearances in the Goons with Spike Milligan, Harry Secombe, and Michael Bentine, and for his superb performances as Inspector Jacques Clouseau in Blake Edwards' classic Pink Panther films, used to practice judo at the LJS and became president of the society in 1962. I used to see him around the club quite a lot but I never really took any notice as I didn't really understand much about what he did at that time. Later I realised what a special talent he had.

But I had my own talent now and if I had to measure how much my life had changed, between nine and fourteen, I think it would be impossible. If I said a million percent this would not be an exaggeration. I'd gone from the bank to become one of the most decorated sportsmen in my school. Plus I'd also become a very good judo player. One of the best for my age in Great Britain. I'd won competitions, medals and been crowned English junior champion. But despite this, I remained injury prone which might have been down to the intense effort I put into everything I did with the exception of academic work. With any game or sport, I never held anything back.

Stage 2

SAT ON THE PLANE

9

MONDAY 2ND OF October 1961. I'd gone from sat on the bank to sat on the plane and it had all happened so quickly. I really didn't know why, how, what or anything. But somehow I'd ended up on this small, British Overseas Airways Corporation (BOAC) plane, destined to arrive in Japan in about two days' time. Flights, from England to Japan at that particular time, did take a long time to reach their destinations. The previous Wednesday Dad had sold his car and the next day he purchased my air ticket. This meant Friday became my last day at school. I didn't get to sit any final exams, which could well have been a blessing because I knew, as did probably everyone else, that my results would have been appalling.

That Friday night I didn't know how I felt. I'd left school and, at least for now, I wouldn't be spending any time in a garage, carpentry shop or on Marmite's factory floor. But what would the next five years have in store for me?

During the weekend, of which I spent most of my time indoors as Mum didn't want me outside risking injury, I didn't get a lot of time to think about anything. Our house became an open house as a succession of family and friends dropped by to offer their best wishes. Sunday afternoon, it must have been around 4:00 p.m., Dad and I finally had time for a chat in our usual place. He spoke about his special three D's which of course started with discipline. He knew how well I'd controlled myself but he also knew I'd face challenges in Japan that required more discipline. He'd witnessed my determination many times and urged me to stay focused at all times. He mentioned Jigoro Kano and how he'd learned the hard way from his first coach Hachinosuke Fukuda, but he stayed determined and reached a stage where he'd swapped places with his third coach Iikubo Tsunetoshi. As for domination, he'd also seen this many times with me and he urged me to continue to try and dominate my opponents although he knew they would be far tougher than any I'd met so far. Dad also promised that he would visit me even if he had to walk halfway around the world.

Despite all the weekend excitement I didn't feel apprehensive about anything and slept very well especially Sunday which, for me, could have been just a normal school night if Mum hadn't made such a fuss and prepared a special tea. Pie and mash with liqueur sauce. She mentioned that it might be a while before I had that again and offered seconds. I refused.

Monday morning we were all up at 5:00 a.m. and Mum seemed to be having a bit of a flap and asking me questions that didn't really seem important. Had I washed behind my ears? Did I need to cut my fingernails? Had I been to the bathroom? And did I want more to eat? Dad sat in his chair and calmly read the morning newspaper. Finally, we left for Heathrow Airport, in Dad's taxi, at about 6:30 a.m. Mum, Dad, Barbara and my brother Shayne who must have been three years old at that time.

As we pulled out of Thriffwood I stared at my house, the park, Forest Hill School, the woods and the railway line. The thought that I wouldn't be back here again for five years felt unreal to me. At Heathrow, where we had a bit of a send-off committee that included Uncle Lenny, Aunty Doris plus a few other family members and friend. I checked in with my suitcase and then that dreaded moment arrived. I took a deep breath, to keep my emotions in check, and hugged Mum and Dad in a joint hug. Barbara joined in and I felt Shayne's small hands around my legs. I looked at Mum and her bottom lip quivered. She had her handkerchief out and brushed away a tear that ran down her right cheek. Dad seemed all stiff upper lip and gave me a huge handshake followed by a massive hug. As he did he whispered into my ear that I should go now and not look back. But his very last words to me were that he would be out to see me within two years and that was a promise.

As I walked towards departures it felt just like the time at Sydenham hospital when the pretty young nurse held my hand as we walked away from my parents for my operation. This time I didn't have anyone to hold my hand but I disobeyed Dad and looked back at the four members of my family as they stared at me. They waved, I waved, and as soon as I knew they couldn't see me I let my emotions go. I think for anyone, at any age let alone fourteen, who has to say goodbye to their parents for possibly five years, and fly halfway around the World, it might be an extremely emotional moment. Tears flowed.

On the plane the air hostesses, as they were called back then, took very special care of me as I began to think, possibly for the first time, about what to expect. I tried to draw comparisons between that night I sat in Dad's taxi and we drove me to my first session at the LJS. At that time my mind had been like a yo-yo with positive and negative thoughts about judo. Now I found myself in a similar situation although I felt confident enough about my judo ability. I believed I could handle that side of things. But how would I cope in Japan with the language and everything else related to living in a foreign country? At least I knew I had one friendly face waiting for me, Bobby, who'd already been there for over a month.

The flight dragged on and on and on and I just sat there bored out of my mind. There were no in-flight movies to watch, as there are these days, and the only interruptions were for food and when we landed to drop people off and refuel. I tried to brush up on my Japanese language skills. About two months before Dad, who may have sensed something might be happening, encouraged me to learn Japanese. Just basic polite words such as good morning, good evening and thank you. With the help of a Japanese dictionary, I wrote them down and tried to remember them.

We stopped five times in Austria, Turkey, Kuwait, India, and Burma. Each time we were allowed off and I think India left the greatest impression on me. I couldn't believe the poverty there and the grimy looking people begging all over the place. I'd never seen anything like this before. India really worried me as we flew the last leg of our journey from

Burma to Japan and this might have been when reality hit me. Especially as I didn't know if Japan would be just like India? My thoughts, yet again, were mixed, to say the least. By this stage, I'd not seen my parents for more than thirty-six hours and I missed them. I missed the woods, the park, the school and I missed the East End that I'd grown up with and loved. Realization, when it hit, hurt, and I blinked away a few more tears.

I'd regained my composure by the time I met Bobby and felt eager to speak to him about his Japanese experiences so far. Although we were never friends at the LJS, as we were in different junior classes, I really expected us to become best friends now. But at first, he seemed reserved about answering any of my questions. I asked about Mr. Hatta and he didn't really answer although I thought he said he hadn't seen him for a long time. I knew Mr. Hatta travelled a lot but I'd kind of expected to see him quite often. I also believed he would be my Japanese Dad, my mentor, and that he might have a chauffeur lined up to take me everywhere in the same way that Dad had been there for him. As the English junior champion, I thought I might have warranted that. But at least Mr. Hatta had arranged for a taxi to transport us to his home.

Bobby did speak about where we were headed and mentioned the streets were very narrow with only just about room for two cars to pass. He didn't speak anymore. He just looked out the window with a depressed expression on his face which startled me. I have to admit that the few alarm bells, which had started to ring during my epic flight, had now grown in force. Especially seeing him like this all white-faced and withdrawn. What had I let myself in for!

10

OUR TAXI PULLED up outside a wooden elevated house on the outskirts of Tokyo that Bobby had managed to explain to me had been built like that to withstand earthquakes. Mr. Hatta, as I'd already expected, had left Japan on business. His wife had also left town and his two sons were at university in America. This left two other people staying at the house. Mr. Hatta's Mother and his mother in law.

They must have both been in their seventies, probably less than five feet foot tall, and wore typical Japanese kimonos.

In the small kitchen, they served us Japanese green tea, served in small V-shaped cups, which I didn't take to at first. The tea. Not the cups! Tea without milk and sugar just didn't taste right. They also served rice biscuits. As snacks go there were a number of things I would have preferred but these women were trying very hard and I appreciated their effort. Soon they left us alone which gave me a chance to talk with Bobby who seemed more relaxed now that we were in the house. He mentioned that his experiences on Japan's trains were not that great and he'd had many problems getting to the Kodokan. He explained the train network. A huge circular line where trains went around in a big circle. He also mentioned how complicated he found understanding Japans stations where all signs were written in Japanese. As for the Kodokan, he said there were sometimes 400 to 500 people training there.

With Japan time at four p.m. on Wednesday the 4th of October, this meant seven a.m. back in England with the nine hours' time difference, I felt desperately in need of sleep. I'd just travelled for nearly forty-eight hours and I needed a bed. Bobby, who'd completed the same journey six weeks before, fully understood and he showed me to a small room on the second floor. I remember I felt so weary and slightly depressed as I climbed those wooden steps with my suitcase. I also felt hungry and my thoughts switched back to England and Mum's pie and mash. I definitely regretted my decision to refuse an extra portion during that last supper with my family.

My room had a sliding door that Bobby opened for me and I stumbled in. He helped me prepare my bed, a futon mat, which had been rolled up and sat in one corner of my room. Without speaking he unrolled it, laid it in the centre of my room and pointed to a small black object that looked like a block and the size of a shoebox. My pillow! Bobby looked at me with a serious frowned expression on his face before he shrugged his shoulders again and walked out. Despite my incredible fatigue I would have liked him to have stayed for a few minutes and given me more insights as to what his life had been like so far in Japan. I still felt positive about being in there but I could sense something had happened to Bobby and I couldn't quite put my finger on what. I hoped to discuss more with him later. Now the time had arrived for me to hit the sack or in this case this rather flimsy futon, which felt a lot like lying on the floor.

Before I left England I knew I wouldn't have a bed, like my Thriffwood one, or a comfortable pillow to rest my head. At that time I didn't think anything about it. Now, as reality bit again, I did. I wanted to sleep so hard. I felt desperate for it. Never in my life could I remember wanting sleep so much. But I found it difficult as I felt so uncomfortable on the floor and my mind bounced all over the place. I laid there and stared at the ceiling. I could have been in hospital again and even, for a few moments, wished I could have been there. At least Mum and Dad would have been there and that pretty young nurse might have held my hand. Then I thought back to those special moments with Dad, sat in the garden with our backs to the base of our apple

tree, and the discussions we had about life and judo.
be strong and not wallow in self-pity.

Something seemed to be holding me down by my ankles. In fact, it felt like my ankles were set in cement. I tried to wriggle free but nothing happened. This cement started to slowly climb up both my legs to my knees. I started to panic as it began to grip my thighs and my waist. I could do nothing as my arms and upper body soon became immersed. As it reached my neck I couldn't breathe. At this point, I knew my time had come and I felt ready to be totally immersed in cement. I felt calm. But, at the very last moment, I felt a sudden rush of adrenalin that travelled from my toes, right through my entire body, and up to my head. This enabled me to burst through the cement as if it was confetti. Slowly I raised my perspiration soaked body from my futon mat that also felt wet from my body heat. As I sat I stared around my strange small room as if seeing it for the first time. My adrenalin cement dream, that I had a few times before, had returned again and I took the timing of this as a sign that nothing would stop me here in Japan. No challenges were going to break me. Kano had done it and so would I. I would become the master.

I checked my watch, still on UK time, which said 4:30 p.m. and I knew it had to be 1:30 a.m. in Japan. I found a light which didn't really illuminate my nine square metre room much. I had a cupboard for my clothes and that was basically it. I felt hungrier than I ever had before but I had no idea how to get food and I didn't know the location of Bobby's room. I found a bathroom where I washed and looked at my face in the mirror. A few days before, when I'd looked at my face in the bathroom mirror at Thriffwood, I'd been a fourteen year old boy without a care in the world. Now I'd just reached fifteen, a boy alone, who would have to grow up very quickly in a totally strange world. I felt like an alien who'd suddenly been transported to a different planet.

11

THE FOLLOWING MORNING a knock on my door at 6:00 a.m. woke me. I opened it to find a worried looking Bobby standing outside. I asked him what had happened and he said nothing but that I should try and get downstairs for breakfast in ten minutes. This sounded like music to my ears so I quickly dressed and joined him. The old women were in the kitchen and this time I tried my best Japanese greeting for good morning. They looked at me, then at each other, and said nothing as they carried on with what they were doing. I looked at Bobby, sat opposite me, who looked away. One of the old ladies placed a small bowl of rice in front of me with a raw egg. She gave the same combination to Bobby who began picking at it with his chopsticks. He motioned for me to copy and kicked me under the table. I did. It tasted horrible. As birthday breakfasts go it had to be the worst I'd ever eaten. I'd never tasted anything so terrible in my life. Bobby continued to pick at his and eventually finished it. I wanted to speak but I believed a kitchen code of silence must have been in place because nobody had spoken since my attempt at Japanese for good morning.

After breakfast, Bobby mentioned that he had a few things to do and that he would be back later that night to talk more about life in Japan. I asked him what I should do and he just said to relax and recover from my long flight. Nobody expected to see me at the Kodokan until the following Monday. I mentioned to him that it was my birthday and he very kindly wished me a happy birthday. He disappeared and left me sitting in the kitchen staring and picking at my breakfast. The old ladies kept looking at me and I sensed they wanted me to finish up so they could get out of the kitchen. I did as best I could.

Still famished I climbed the wooden stairs to my room where I found my bunch of birthday cards in my suitcase. There must have been ten, mostly from family, and under normal circumstances, I would have had a lot more. My swift departure must have caught a few people by surprise. I shuffled them around and recognised the handwriting on many. I soon found Mum and Dad's and decided to put that on the bottom of the pile. I wanted to save that one until last. I checked my watch, nearly 7:30 a.m., and made a decision to open one card every thirty minutes. That meant I had something to do for the next five hours as I had absolutely no idea how I would spend the day.

It turned out to be more like thirty-six as I drifted in and out of the weirdest sleep patterns I'd ever experienced. I opened a card, read it, placed it by the side of the bed and then I couldn't keep my eyes open. The effort of opening a card, reading it, sent me back to sleep where I dreamt the strangest dreams I'd ever dreamt. I seemed to be on a dream world mystery tour that transported me from being chased in Thriffwood Woods by Patch Eye The Parkie, to the hop fields of Kent and the homemade swing with the wooden seat, back to Thriffwood and being chased by dogs in the old ladies' orchard and back to school sitting on the bank. I opened another card, read it, placed it with the other one and then seemed to go through the whole weird sleep thing again. I'm not sure if this happened due to jet lag, homesickness, having to sleep on the floor or feeling depressed about spending my birthday in that room.

At around 8:30 p.m. Bobby knocked my door and asked if I felt hungry. I thought what a stupid question. I followed him downstairs, where we sat in exactly the same places, and the old ladies served us breakfast again but just slightly bigger portions. I thought what the hell is this? Bobby, who must have read my thoughts, motioned for me to keep quiet. I felt so hungry but also very tired. I couldn't eat. My head started to rock backward and forwards and I had to shake myself awake. Bobby recognised the signs and helped me back upstairs to my room where I felt so relieved to see my futon mat. I collapsed on it and had no recollection of anything until Bobby knocked my door again for breakfast.

Now I felt a lot better, I must have been so tired, and dreamt out, that I'd slept for a good nine hours uninterrupted. I had a massive appetite and could have eaten a horse. But sadly no horses were on the menu as the old ladies served what looked exactly the same as they had the previous morning and evening. Bobby picked at his and I picked at mine. The taste had not improved. In fact, this dish, that seemed to have a few other bits floating in it, tasted ten times worse. Bobby said he had things to do again but promised that he would show me around during the weekend. This left me in my room again for my second full day in Tokyo.

I felt so lonely and lost. I wanted to sleep again and wake up at home with Mum and Dad. What had happened to me? How could a nightmare be so real? I buried my face in my shoebox pillow and silently cried my heart out for a good ten minutes until I remembered the rest of my cards. They would cheer me up.

A few of the birthday wishes made me smile and soon I reached my last card from Mum and Dad. I held it for a while and tried to imagine what must have been going through Mum's mind when she wrote it. Mum always wrote the cards. As I opened it and saw Mum's handwriting, my tears welled up again.

'Happy fifteenth Birthday Brian! Sorry, we can't be with you for this one. We miss you. We love you. Take care. Love Mum, Dad, Barbara and Shayne xxx'

But this time Dad had written something.

'Brian. I imagine this will be a very different birthday for you but don't worry it's a sacrifice we all have to make. We will have many birthdays together in the future. I promise you we will be there within two years even if I have to drive the taxi. Show them what you've got son. Love you. Take care. Dad x. P.S. Buy something nice for your birthday.'

Dad had enclosed a £5 note and a few more tears welled up. Dad had already sacrificed so much for me to make this trip and I knew another £5 wouldn't have been easy. I suppose I read the card for the next thirty minutes before I decided to get myself together. I placed all my cards around my room and unpacked my suitcase. I then did something I'd never done before. Wrote Mum and Dad a letter.

'*Dear Mum and Dad, Thank you for my card. I've not spent the money yet so I can't tell you what I've bought. Tomorrow, Saturday, I think Bobby will take me to a few places and I will see if I can buy something then. Please thank everyone for their cards and nice wishes. My flight took a long time and I felt quite bored. I also found it hard to sleep sitting up. I tried to practice Japanese and a Japanese Air Hostess saw me and helped me. She was very nice. There are lots of cars on the roads in Tokyo and many look familiar. I think they must have been exported from England. Also, the car we travelled in had a back door that opened automatically. Mr. Hatta has a very nice house that is made of wood. It looks quite small from the outside but it's a lot bigger inside. Mr. and Mrs. Hatta are not here right now so their mothers are taking care of us. They are very nice and making me feel very welcome. I don't have to go to the Kodokan until Monday. That's all really for now. I will write again soon. Miss you. Love Brian xx*'

I didn't mention the food as I didn't want to worry Mum and I didn't say anything about Bobby 's reserved behavior although without him being there I don't know what I'd have done.

Bobby knocked my door again, this time a bit later than usual as it must have been 7:30 a.m. and once we'd finished with our routine breakfast, more of the same, we were out on the road to explore parts of Tokyo. A fantastic feeling for me as I'd begun to feel claustrophobic cooped up in that house for nearly three days. The strange sounds of Tokyo puzzled me. I suppose they would have just been the same as London or quite similar apart from food being prepared on the street. They had all kinds of food, right there on the street, and this intrigued me. Of course the Japanese language and all the street and road signs, written in Japanese, completely baffled me.

We had about a twenty minute walk to the station and all along the street vendors were trying to get people to buy their food. Some of the aromas were really quite interesting and I questioned Bobby about one of them that looked like a chicken on a skewer. This turned out to be called yakitori and chicken had been grilled by this mobile food vendor on his portable charcoal grill. Bobby asked if I wanted one. Did I want one! Of course, I wanted one and ended up with three. I savoured this delicacy as if I hadn't eaten for a week which was pretty much true. I just wished he'd spoken to me about it sooner.

As we walked we talked and I asked Bobby how he really felt about Japan and his life so far. Of course, he shrugged his shoulders but I asked him to be honest with me because if he had problems I wanted to know as I might face similar situations to him. I wanted to be prepared. Plus life for him should have been so much easier as he had the benefit of a Japanese sponsorship. Bobby looked me in the eyes and said the daily travel to the Kodokan had started to depress him and that the Japanese students were a bunch of tough nuts who took a lot of pleasure from throwing an English man around the mat. I laughed at that and replied that we were there to learn and what better way to do so than with people who were better than us? As for the travel, I didn't see how sitting on a train for a few hours a day could be such a big deal. Again he shrugged his shoulders.

I followed Bobby and although there were a lot of people at the stations I didn't see how travel could be a problem here. He seemed to have no problems buying our tickets and we relaxed on the trains. It all seemed so easy although most people looked at us as if they hadn't seen two young English guys on a train before.

After about ninety minutes we arrived at the Kodokan and I couldn't believe I'd arrived at the spiritual home of judo. The buildings looked far bigger than I'd imagined. We couldn't enter at this particular time but Bobby explained the layout of the two buildings facing us. A low rise three stories on the left and a higher rise eight-story on the right. They were connected. The lower rise had training halls on the first floor that included private areas for different levels of judo players. The big arena on the second floor contained one big mat area about the size of five tennis courts. The third floor had a viewing gallery all around it. The higher rise building had a basement with changing rooms, a restaurant, a reception on the first floor, the second floor had an entrance to the viewing area, the third and fourth floors were offices, and the fifth to seventh included accommodation for people training who needed a place to stay. We didn't stay long but before we left I made sure we had pictures taken with Kano's statue at the front of the building.

At this point in time, I felt hungry again and Bobby suggested we visited a place called the Ginza where we should be able to buy decent food and other things. The Ginza's well known for being one of Tokyo's best shopping districts and can be compared with New York's Times Square and London's Oxford Street. We had a very nice afternoon and attracted a lot of attention from the locals who might have thought we actually were aliens from outer space.

More than once a few brave locals spoke with us and some even touched my blonde hair. Maybe they were checking to make sure it was real. We looked in a few stores that included the Ginza Wako, where we couldn't afford anything, and the Mitsukoshi store where the prices were more realistic and we ate in a nice restaurant.

I had a massive steak and left absolutely nothing on my plate. By 6:00 p.m. that evening we were back at Mr. Hatta's house as Bobby had said we needed to be home early so as not to disturb the old ladies. They, as you might expect for old ladies, slept early and we had to respect this and do our best not to bother them. As much as I understood this, and appreciated Mr. Hatta for letting me stay there, it constrained me. I liked to have fun and a laugh and a joke which I always had with Mum and Dad. But now I found myself almost tiptoeing around the house and whispering to Bobby. Admittedly we were there to train and we needed to focus on that. But we were teenagers, not quite ready to live in a temple, which is how Mr. Hatta's house felt sometimes even though I'd only been there a few days.

At least we'd eaten well that day with a full breakfast, lunch and, as we walked back to the house from the station, more yakitori. I didn't actually feel hungry but forced it down as I didn't know when my next decent meal might be. Well, we were in for a shock as the next decent meal appeared about thirty minutes later. As we sat in the kitchen and expected to go through the motions of trying to eat the not so tasty dinner the old ladies served, they pulled a rabbit out of the hat that completely surprised us. No, not with a real rabbit, they served us sukiyaki which had been boiled in a hot pot. The ingredients were a mixture of thinly sliced beef, bean curds, green onions, cabbage, mushrooms, and some special rice noodles. They'd also added some sauce, similar to soya sauce, but much sweeter. The old ladies showed us how to take a piece of food with chopsticks, dip it into some raw egg and eat. It really tasted very good but obviously not on the same level as Mum's pie and mash. Although, I have to say it did excite my taste buds, and I think this might have been the moment in my life when I realised that there might have been more to life than pie and mash. I also felt completely stuffed.

12

FOR THE FIRST twenty minutes I think I might have behaved like a kid a in a chocolate factory without chocolate. On the second floor, in the big arena, I must have skipped, jogged and walked around the huge mat ten times soaking up the electric atmosphere as I observed and listened to the unmistakable customs and sounds of judo. Although a few routines were different from the styles I'd witnessed at the LJS. I watched as judo players bowed together before free practice. I noticed how players gripped each other and I watched their patterns of movements around their particular areas of the huge mat. The whirlwind speeds of lightweights compared to the more measured and slower movements of heavyweights. The sounds were so similar to the LJS, although on a much grander scale, and with obviously most of the chatter in Japanese. However, I heard some English being spoken. Coaches, some of who could have been in their late seventies, were on hand and ready to step in with some valuable advice, engage in a practice, or take time out to explain and demonstrate certain techniques. There could have been 400 people in this massive arena, all dressed in white judo kits, and nearly all tied with black belts.

A few people stared at me and must have wondered why this young kid had ventured into their sacred space wearing a brown belt. But as English junior champion I felt I belonged there. I'd found my place and I didn't care about them. I noticed Bobby as he hovered around the sidelines not really doing anything. I went up to the gallery where I stared at the action below. It all seemed magical to me and I so wanted to be part of this action. I needed to be part of it. I had to show them I could do it and, given time, I knew I could not only be just as good as them but I would be better. Brian Jacks had arrived, not some lightweight on a jolly making up numbers, and I would take this place by storm and own my spot on that huge mat. I could taste it. I went down to level one and peered into each of the six private smaller training rooms on this level. These were about 100 square meters and were where special classes were held for beginners, intermediates, ladies, break fall training and special techniques. They also had a gymnasium with all kinds of weights.

Earlier that day, Monday the 9th of October 1961, I'd presented myself at the Kodokan with my two letters of introduction. One from Mr. Hatta, my Japanese sponsor although this didn't include any sponsorship grants, and the other from the LJS. They were expecting me and we completed the registration formalities. They said they needed a few days to process my forms and that I'd receive my membership card then. But I could use the Kodokan during this process period.

Before I'd left England I'd been awarded my brown belt, one down from a black, but in Japan, they wanted to reassess me. I'm not sure if this had anything to do with my age or if they had some concerns with Bobby as I knew he hadn't been assessed when he arrived. Bobby, with a black belt already from the LJS, had been allowed to use the big arena from day one. But from what I'd seen of him he didn't seem to be making much of an effort. Perhaps they were now concerned that they'd accepted him without assessing him based on their standards and now they might not have considered him a real black belt by Japanese standards. This meant they didn't want to make the same mistake with me. The Kodokan's standards were higher than the LJS at that time. Two six Dan grade instructors, who didn't speak English very well, performed the assessment and decided to relegate me to one of the smaller training rooms downstairs. At the same time, they downgraded me from a brown belt to a blue belt in terms of British belt structures.

Japan's belt system worked in a different way to the UK. In their structure beginners are classed as red belts, followed by the sixth, fifth and fourth levels, who all wear white belts. The next three levels, third, second and first, wear brown belts. Dan rankings follow and first to sixth receive black belts. Seventh to eight belts are red and white blocks and ninth to tenth are red. So a first Dan is a black belt with one bar and so on and so forth. Kano had plans to go up to a twelfth, which would have been a red belt, but he passed away before this could be completed. Out of respect for him, Japan's Judo Federation decided to scrap this idea. So in Japan, all players start with a red belt and, if they perform to the highest levels, they end up with a red belt again. This means they have completed the circle of knowledge and learned all there is to know about judo. All this takes time and meant my assessors had actually extended the amount of time it would take me to complete the full circle. I have to admit that being downgraded hurt especially as I didn't really rate Bobby as a better player than me. Yes, he'd beaten me during the all-important contest to win the sponsorship. But I felt we were at least on the same level. I needed time to process this news.

Even though I didn't have Dad there to lean on I knew he'd have encouraged me to do the right thing and not go into a strop. With that in mind, I decided to get down there and go for it with all I had. They'd challenged me and I accepted it although I didn't really consider it much of a challenge once it started. After my downstairs sessions, I spent a lot of time watching what happened in the main arena. I wanted to see how tough the Japanese students were and how Bobby coped with it. I think the first year students were at least eighteen which meant there were a lot of players on the mat aged between eighteen and twenty-two. Were they tough? Oh yes, they were. They were as hard as nails and they'd probably been practicing judo for a minimum of ten years already. As for Bobby, I noticed that he seemed to keep his distance and only spent the minimum of time on the mat. I'm not sure if he would have agreed with me but I think he tried to hide. He never jumped to the front of the queue when other players were looking for someone to practice with. He seemed to shy away and never volunteered for anything.

As for me I'd practiced judo for more than five years and become English junior champion. I think I'd moved on quite a bit from beginner and intermediate levels and didn't need to go through this again downstairs where the classes were far too easy for me. I knew, as did the other students, and within two weeks so had my teachers. They decided to re-assess me and turned up with Japanese students around the same age as me. This meant that with them being Japanese they were smaller than me and after practicing with bigger boys they were very easy for me to handle. I had contests with them, which were absolutely no problem at all for me, and the assessors asked me to demonstrate different techniques which I did very well. I'd impressed them enough to promote me back to my original brown belt level which allowed me to join the action in the main arena again.

Prior to this three things happened. I received my Kodokan foreign membership card, membership number 2,820, and at the same time my locker key. A few days after I received my card I met Mr. Kyuzo Mifune who officially welcomed me to the Kodokan. Dad had mentioned Mifune many times and advised me to show the maximum amount of respect I could should I ever meet him. He'd been one of Jigoro Kano's first students and considered by many as one of the greatest judo technicians ever.

In my next letter to Dad, I explained that I'd met Mifune, which he knew already as I'd enclosed a picture, and that I had my locker. I also advised that I'd become much better at break-falls. But I also had to explain about my short-term downgrade and how things had shaped up for me since being permitted access to the main hall. Or perhaps I should say how things were for me as I flew through the air and landed on the mat because that's exactly how I spent most of my time. Bobby had been correct in his assertion that these Japanese boys were tough and they had absolutely no qualms about banging me around the mat. I felt like a rag doll, cannon fodder to them, but I may have brought this on myself with a serious error of judgement.

During my first session back in the big time I felt up for it and ready for some action. My boldness soon caught the attention of an older Japanese teacher, Mr. Shoichiro Sato, an eighth Dan, who could have been seventy-five. He flapped his hands and waved with his palms down in my direction. A clear signal that he wanted to practice with me. Confidently I took my place opposite him. Now, you must remember, I'd just been promoted back upstairs and I wanted to make a good impression. So I took being on the mat with this man as a signal and a perfect opportunity for me to make a big statement of intent. I gave him, sixty years my senior, a torrid time. I went at it like a bat out of hell and I tried whatever I knew to throw him on his back. He didn't know what had hit him and I knew I'd shaken him. As we moved around I sensed more eyes focused on us. Other players stopped what they were doing. They were taking notice and must have been impressed with me. I'd made it and now they knew. Or so I believed! But I didn't realise that I shouldn't have tried to throw the old man around! Nobody had advised me about that Kodokan etiquette which said I had to let the old boy throw me around and, as I learned later, this old boy loved making the most of his esteemed position. I'd made a huge misjudgment and might just as well have flashed a red flag in front of a bull.

The Japanese black belts were not impressed and many lined up to have a crack at me. They smashed me around the mat. Especially students from the university that this old man represented. They were incensed that someone like me had dishonored their mentor. They really ganged up on me and gave me a hard time. It felt like a tag contest, where one would spend two minutes working me over then tag his mate, who did the same thing and this continued. But I had no one to tag to relieve me. The one person who might have helped, Bobby, had disappeared. I just had to stay there and be thrown and thrown and thrown.

Many Kodokan students were from Tokyo's universities on judo scholarships. They would have practiced judo at their high schools and if they reached black belt level this meant they automatically qualified for a judo scholarship. Top students were headhunted by the big universities who wanted their judo section to be number one in Japan. Rather like most young talent in any sport these days where big clubs come in and put them in their academies at a very early age. They also wanted their students to make Japan's teams for the Olympic Games and other important competitions. A university, with an Olympic Gold medalist on their campus, would be a major attraction and add great prestige for that university. Students with scholarships only had to think about judo. Although I'm sure a few of them must have had some interest in academic work. They trained at their universities for four hours a day and then another two at the Kodokan in the evening. These Japanese students were very good, fast, strong, fit and they moved around the mat as if they owned it. I soon realised which players would pick on me and the ones who wouldn't. Now and again I managed mat time with a bit of a tall skinny type of student and this always excited me. I knew I had a chance to get these guys down but it always took a huge amount of effort.

I explained all this to Dad in my letter and mentioned that Bobby must have taken the same kind of treatment before me, which might have explained his current lack of effort at now. Or maybe lack of effort is an unfair description as he might just have had enough of being thrown about like a rag doll. I know that a person can only take so much.

One other point that Bobby had mentioned during my first few days in Japan had been travelling. My first experience of Japanese trains had taken place during a weekend when fewer people must have travelled. But the following week, when I experienced Japan's rush hour that seemed to go on all day and night, I fully understood his comments. Stations were packed and on the trains, we were squashed in like sardines. I stuck as close to Bobby as I could and even held on to his jacket because I didn't want to lose him. He knew where to get off. He had the knowledge. I had no idea although I'd tried to pay attention and understand the Japanese writing for the signs at the stations I needed. But I really needed him. Then he got sick, I had to go solo, and I wished I paid more attention. I knew I could walk to the station, no problem, but the trains were pure hell. There were just so many people all pushing and pulling and I didn't like being shoved onto trains by the mass of people behind me. They squashed me into this train and I didn't even know if it would take me where I wanted to go. I hated travelling alone in those early days and many times it turned out to be an absolute nightmare. Several times I missed my station because I couldn't read the Japanese writing, and I ended up in exactly the same place as I'd started due to the circular network.

This challenged me, as did being thrown around at the Kodokan and living with the old ladies at Hatta's house. When I first met Bobby he'd mentioned problems with travel and how Japanese students at the Kodokan had treated him. I'd kind of laughed it off. But now I'd seen things first hand and I really understood the full extent of the problems.

13

BOBBY HAD WORKED out a train system although he said it had taken him about a month. Somehow he remembered all relevant Japanese signs in his head. He had a picture in his brain that triggered key points for him. A similar system used by Dad to pass the knowledge. I didn't feel quite as confident as Bobby so I used a notebook to record all important data. I also took this one stage further by writing down important information on large sheets of paper. I used key points, sometimes just one Japanese character, which I made sure I could read from some distance away. Then I stuck the sheets to my ceiling in my bedroom which enabled me to study in bed. This way I had three points of study. My notebooks, my room ceiling and the actual stations where the real signs were. This is the method I used to try and pass my knowledge as I knew I couldn't rely on Bobby for the next five years. In fact, there were times when I thought I wouldn't be able to rely on him for the next five days.

The Kodokan came next and my thoughts were about how I could solve my problems there. I'd made a rod for my own back by trying to throw old Sato and by perhaps being overconfident at times. At the LJS I'd been top dog and the same more or less applied at school. Now I'd upset the locals who were hell-bent on extracting revenge at every opportunity. I considered a few options. I could lay low for a while with a fake injury until they'd forgotten. I knew that wouldn't work as I would have had to lay low for five years. They would never forget. I could request to go back downstairs for another month but this felt like running away. I'd never run away from anything and I didn't want to start now. I could also play Bobby's game. Turn up, hide in shadows, and come out when the coast looked clear. None of these options, which I knew Dad would have been ashamed of me if I'd even considered, were acceptable. I knew that. I thought back to Kano who during his early days with his coach had to take fall, after fall, after fall to enable him to learn the mechanics of techniques. Now I found myself in the same place as Kano although at least I had a kinder mat to fall on.

For the next two weeks, despite mine and Bobby's efforts with the old ladies, nothing changed. I'd been with them a month and they'd only pulled one rabbit out of the hat. We'd bought them presents and given them yakitori skewers as we believed they'd understand the unsaid message that we wanted yakitori on our menu with the occasional sukiyaki. Unfortunately, this communication must have been lost in translation as they continued to serve up the same terrible stuff as they had before. Our presents, really sukiyaki bribes, had fallen on deaf ears. I couldn't believe it and felt angry. They knew how to prepare good food so why didn't they do it! The old women tried to be friendly, they now always said good morning, and I tried to speak more Japanese to them. I wanted to build some kind of relationship with them and a friendship. Initially, I thought they might have been shy with no real understanding of how to deal with foreigners although I had no idea really. But I just couldn't handle this soggy rice diet for breakfast, lunch, and dinner. Trains, which some days I caught with Bobby and some days I didn't, remained a complete mystery to me and a nightmare. Plus at the Kodokan things got worse. I think my reputation seemed to grow daily as other students, who might not have been there during that Sato day, must have heard about it through Japan's university grapevine, and they wanted their five minutes of fame with me as well. After the first month, I had enough and I have to admit I shed a few tears in my room as I wrote my next letter.

'Dear Dad, I've had enough. I can't take this anymore. The sheer culture shock of everything is too much for me. The culture shock of the food they are serving me in the house. It's terrible. I can't eat it. The culture shock of

travelling from one place to another. The culture shock of the trains that are nearly impossible to get on and then, when I do get on, I don't know when to get off as all the signs are in Japanese. It takes me ninety minutes to get to the Kodokan and sometimes a lot longer if I get lost. Then the culture shock of the Kodokan where the Japanese students are ganging up on me and throwing me all over the place. It's too much Dad. I miss you, Mum, the woods, the park, the East End, the LJS and even my old school. I can't do this. It's too much for me. I have to worry about eating, worry about travelling and worry about training. I'm missing everything about my wonderful life in England and I don't care if I come back and end up working on Marmite's factory floor. I'm sorry Dad. I know you've sacrificed so much for me and I've let you down. But don't worry. I will work and pay you back every penny you have spent on this trip. Love Brian'

I put the letter in an envelope, sealed it, addressed it and cried some more. I fully understood how Bobby must have felt when he met me at the airport. I, like him, had been tormented to a point where I'd been broken. Japan had beaten me and I couldn't take anymore. From sat on the bank, to the plane, and now smashed on the mat. The Japanese system had beaten me. I had to get out of there.

14

SAT AT A table for three in Kobe's Steak House I focused on my T-bone steak and didn't pay much attention to the conversation my dinner partners were engaged in. Most of the time they spoke in Japanese so I didn't understand anyway. It had been almost a month since I'd seen any decent food on my plate and I wanted to make the most of it. They could have been talking about aliens invading the planet for all I knew but it wouldn't have made any difference. I needed food. Good decent food that I could relate to and I'd found it at this Ginza steakhouse. I'd heard that Kobe cows were bred on special diets that included beer to make them hungry. They were also kept in first-class pens and massaged regularly in an effort to produce more tender beef. I might not have believed that until this minute, with a Kobe steak on my plate, which I could almost cut with my fork. My cow must have received a special amount of tender loving care to produce steak this tender. They also served dripping sauces, crispy garlic chips, and some amazing vegetables. But my steak, oh my god, after that soggy rice this felt like steak heaven. It just melted in my mouth and you know sometimes, you have a moment when you want to lick your plate clean? This had to be one of those. But I didn't think my dinner partners, still more focused on talking than eating, would approve. Trevor and Kisaburo chatted on, sometimes they looked at me and I looked at them, but they chatted on and I continued eating.

Trevor Pryce Leggett, born in London in 1914, had been a big name in judo for a very long time. TP, as he became known, started judo in secret as his father didn't approve. He studied law at London University and graduated in 1934. He'd joined the Budokwai two years prior to this where he studied under Yukio Tani. Tani, a strict disciplinarian, used the old samurai school approach and ingrained this type of attitude into TP. In 1939 he went to Japan and immediately embraced the challenges set by the locals who had this way about them which suggested they were superior to anything and anybody from the UK. TP soon gained his fifth Dan which went some way to shut them up. After one session TP found himself in a cold shower next to a Japanese student. Almost an hour later they were both still standing in their showers as freezing cold water rained down on their heads. They'd found themselves in an 'I'm not leaving until you leave' situation and vice versa. Eventually, so that neither of them lost face, they left together.

By the time Japan entered the Second World War in 1941 TP had already attached himself to the British Embassy in Tokyo which meant he, along with other embassy staff, were interned. Later he left Japan as part of an exchange with London based Japanese embassy staff. Although during his internment he continued to practice judo with his Japanese guards. Between 1943 and 1945 he served in India with Britain's South East Asia Military headquarters where his fluency in Japanese proved a great asset.

TP began teaching at the Budokwai in 1945 and made senior instructor in 1954. He split his time between England and Japan after he joined the BBC external service. In 1950 he became programme organiser for the Japanese section. TP influenced a generation of British judoka with his disciplined approach installed in him by Tani. He became well known for never resting during training and encouraged his students to follow him. TP had a special Sunday class and anyone lucky enough to be selected always felt honoured to attend. He became known as an English master of judo who liked to teach his students to strangle their partners into unconsciousness and then revive them. Annually he held a resuscitation class where all black belts had to go down to a lower training area. There he would show them how to render opponents unconscious and how to revive them. His teaching methods were respected and feared and he had a talent for knowing what students dreaded. He would make them confront their fears in an effort to help them overcome them. Anyone not focused during training with him would be slammed into the mat with a colossal throw.

I'd spotted Kisaburu Watanabe, born in Nigata in 1936, during one of my first visits to the Kodokan. Not only had I noticed him but after just over a month in Japan, I think I might have been more impressed by him than any other player I'd ever seen. He had superb style and a wide range of throwing techniques. I'd even spent some time on the mat with him, and his coach, which helped me understand more about judo. He had five favourite techniques which he performed equally well both on the left-hand side and the right-hand side. I also knew he could throw people no matter how heavy they were. At five feet nine inches tall and just under thirteen stone he could throw people who were eighteen stone and more. He'd proved this by winning Japan's open championships.

The purpose of this dinner, other than the opportunity for me to gorge so much food that I felt sick, had been for TP to interview me for a newspaper article that would be published back in Britain. I think Dad, with help from people in the judo world, had arranged this. He still hoped that someone, somewhere, would sit up and take notice and come up with an offer of a belated sponsorship. But really it seemed to provide TP and Watanabe a chance to bond together as I think they were already good friends. TP asked me a few questions about school, the LJS, Japan in general and what I thought of making Britain's team for the 1964 Olympic Games in Tokyo. I gave him some general answers related to his England questions. For Japan I daren't say anything about how I really felt with the great Watanabe, who spoke very good English, sitting beside me. As for the Olympic Games, which would be the first time that judo would ever be included, I told him I didn't expect to make the team as there were many British players around who were better than me.

Just in case you're wondering what happened to my letter! When I woke that morning I still had it in my hand. I looked at it, remembered the contents, and looked at it again. I went to the bathroom where I had a good look at my face in the mirror and asked myself a big question. Did I really want this Japanese jungle to swallow me up, spit me out, and disappear into obscurity on Marmite's factory floor? I thought about what my Grandad might have done and my Dad. I knew they were fighters. They wouldn't have given up so how could I! I would stay and fight and fight and fight. So what if the Japanese fighters treated me with disdain. I couldn't change their upbringing or their culture. But I knew I could prove myself worthy and earn their respect. I tore the letter up into as many tiny pieces as I could manage.

15

MY DINNER WITH TP and Watanabe proved a huge breakthrough and probably much more than I realised at that particular time. TP had been around the Japanese scene for more than twenty years and been accepted by locals as one of their own. He'd broken down cultural, social and whatever other barriers needed breaking down. Being from London also gave us a common bond and he seemed great mates with Watanabe currently one of Japan's top players. I knew if I could get Watanabe in my corner life at the Kodokan might improve. I did and it did. He spent time with me to explain different techniques, often put his hand on my shoulder, and laughed out loud at some of my comments. My tormentors stood on the perimeters of the mat, looked on open-mouthed. I could just imagine their thoughts. Why would a Japanese superhero be wasting his time with some kid from England?

Dad telephoned about once a month, on a Sunday, as back then transatlantic telephone calls were very expensive and apart from the postal service there were no other ways to communicate. I never mentioned how bad things were in Mr. Hatta's house although he might have sensed something in my tone. However, during one of Mr. Hatta's rare stays, he took us out for dinner where we tried to explain that we weren't happy with the food we were being served. He seemed genuinely concerned and said he would try to do something to help.

Whatever he had in mind came too late for Bobby who, completely out of the blue one day, announced he'd had enough. He packed his bags and left Mr. Hatta's house. He also quit judo although he stayed in Japan and switched his attention to karate. He tried to convince me to change as well and out of curiosity I went along a few times and had a look. I soon realised that karate didn't create the same excitement factor for me as judo. But Bobby seemed happier than I'd seen him for a few months which might have been down to not being thrown around on a mat. That didn't happen in karate.

1962 started with an improvement in my standing at the Kodokan and Tokyo's jungle became less of a puzzle. There'd also been an easing down of aggression with some of my fellow students although I knew a few hardliners would never ease off. I had Mr. Hatta's promise that he would try to do something to improve the food at his house plus another development at the Kodokan which helped to turn my life around. I mentioned before that during my first day I heard a few English speaking voices. Those voices, even though not all of them were native English speakers, belonged to foreign students and there must have been ten of them. Bill Backhus, an ex-American marine, had introduced himself to me and we'd become quite friendly.

William Eugene Backhus, ten years my senior from Philadelphia, had served in the US Marine Corps before he settled in Tokyo to practice judo. He said he'd exhausted all facilities and expertise in his own country had and now wanted to test himself in Japan. He joined a shifting population of about fifty Americans and Europeans who'd arrived in Tokyo to study at that time. Not all of these people followed judo.

I'd now worked out the trains and gained a lot more confidence in the Kodokan. This only left the food issue to be resolved at Mr. Hatta's house. Despite that, I think I'd almost regained my old confident spark, the cheeky cockney, always up for a laugh and a joke. Maybe Bill recognised this and he kind of took me under his wing. He became like a big brother to me and in some ways a father figure. Bill even suggested I moved into the Kodokan or found my own place.

I soon began to wonder if Mr. Hatta had taken my comments about food seriously as nothing much had changed in Mr. Hatta's kitchen. I thought that with just me to feed they might have been able to come up with something more acceptable. But they didn't and things climaxed one day when they served me a bowl of soggy rice with salt for breakfast. It tasted horrible. I couldn't eat it and even accused them, in their language, of trying to poison me. They didn't like that and I stormed out of the kitchen.

That day I left the house, picked up a few yakitori skewers during my walk to the station, and reflected on how things were going. Particularly money. I didn't have enough money to keep buying food like this. Dad sent £12 a month and I knew I couldn't ask for any more. But to enable me to train I needed good food. Well food that I called good and not the inedible stuff they were serving me. This bugged me all day and I didn't have a good session at the Kodokan. I couldn't focus. Bill sensed my problem and we had a quick chat followed by a meal together in the Kodokan's restaurant. Again Bill suggested that I should get my own place and I replied that I couldn't even afford dinner let alone my own place. Bill very kindly paid for my dinner and even lent me some cash to help until the end of the month. He also spoke to a pretty young waitress there called Nobuko who he knew I liked. Bill, who spoke fluent Japanese, put in a good word for me. Nobuko blushed as she walked away.

I dreaded returning home that night and facing the old ladies again. But when I did they were like a reception committee waiting for me with Mr. Hatta. He didn't seem angry and maybe he understood my situation better than I thought. Fortunately, Mr. Hatta had a plan B and I just had to pack my bags and meet him in his car in twenty minutes. I looked at the old ladies, who smiled. I don't think they hated me. Although at their time of life I don't think they wanted to deal with a teenager again. Particularly an English one.

Plan B turned out to be the house of Mr. Yunosuke Aoki, a samurai descendant, and his wife Katsu Aoki. They had four sons, in their late teens and early twenties, who practiced wrestling. After Yunosuke and Katsu married they opened a jazz coffee shop named Ellington after their favourite jazz musician Duke Ellington. During the Second World War Yunosuke switched to sweets and specialised in desserts. Later he met a talented chef called Fujisake, opened a full-service restaurant, and this is when I walked in. But it wasn't just a regular Japanese restaurant that only served Japanese dishes. They specialised in western food as well and served things like barbeque chicken and pork. I'd moved from 'Hell's Kitchen' to 'Dream Kitchen World' and it felt fantastic. I just had a basic room, very similar to Mr. Hatta's house, but that didn't matter as they had food, glorious food, that I could actually eat. Yunosuke named his restaurant Benihana after a red safflower he found in Tokyo's war-torn rubble.

This for me proved a fantastic breakthrough and obviously meant no more soggy rice. I could eat, more or less, what I liked and I even tried many different kinds of dishes that I know I'd never have eaten in England. Many times I watched as Fujisake cooked and I could see the genuine love he had for what he did. I even thought that one day I could be a chef. But not at this place as Fujisake would never let me go anywhere near preparations of his meals. I could look but not touch. I just served meals, waiter Jacks, which proved a novelty as at that time I don't think there were any other teenage British waiters working in the Ginza. I served, washed dishes, and chatted to customers which gave me a perfect opportunity to practice my Japanese language skills which were coming on quite well. I became quite close friends with Hiroaki Aoki, at twenty-three, the eldest son of the Aoki family and nicknamed Rocky. Rocky became a big name in Japanese wrestling and captained his University wrestling team. He also made Japan's 1960 Olympic squad. I only knew him a short time as later he moved to America where he became a big success and started the Benihana chain that later became a worldwide brand.

Life for me at this point had improved immensely and I felt quite comfortable at the Aoki house, travelling and with the way things were going at the Kodokan. I no longer felt depressed about Japan's jungle and didn't want to get out of there anymore. At the Kodokan I could always discuss things with Bill and Watanabe seemed to have a kind of soft spot for me. I remember sitting on the mat with Watanabe's coach one day, he must have been about eighty-three, and he spoke about being thrown. He said that the only way to learn is to get thrown around and, whilst being thrown, try to think of ways to get out of that situation. How to stop a throw and how to get to my opponent before he threw me. As we were speaking he asked me to close my eyes which I did and I could hear all the noises around me. He asked me to keep my eyes closed and blank out those noises. He said to think of nothing. Think blank. I sat for five minutes and eventually everything seemed to blank out. Then he started talking again and he said imagine you are walking through a field and there is grass all around you about five feet tall. As you walk through this grass there is nothing else there except for one huge oak tree right in the middle of the field. Look around you, he said, but keep your eyes closed. Look around and walk towards the big oak tree. As you're walking the wind starts to blow. It blows so hard that your clothes and hair blow forward. That wind is also hitting the oak tree. It's hitting it so hard that it bites the branches off the tree and they are flying everywhere. Then he said stop and he asked me to tell him what the strongest thing I saw was. I immediately said the oak tree as trees are big and strong. But he said no. He said where is the grass? I said it's up past my waist where it had been before the wind blew. There you are he said. You have to practice judo in the same way. You have to give way, come back, and give way again. Don't stand rigid like an oak tree and get broken up and thrown. I think that might have been one of the biggest lessons I learned during my early days in Japan.

16

MR.HATTA'S BENIHANA plan B turned out to be a perfect fit for me. I loved the food and being able to train with Aoki's sons. I also enjoyed the restaurant where I did anything they asked to help pay for my keep and extra food. But despite plan B's obvious advantages I still had the annoying daily grind of travelling to and from the Kodokan. Also, with Aoki's house in a different location to the restaurant, this added to my daily travel time. I think most days I spent four hours travelling. I spoke with Bill again about this and he mentioned that he'd heard about a room available at the Kodokan, on the top floor, close to the fire escape. I would have to pay about £7 pounds a month. I looked at Bill with my 'how the hell can I afford that?' kind of face and he said don't worry as I'd save money on travel and that he another idea that might help to make this work. He convinced me to give this a try and I had a long chat with Dad about it during our next monthly call. Dad agreed and two months after moving in with Aoki's I moved out and into the Kodokan. I only had one problem, an old caretaker, who ruled the place with an iron fist after his big bosses had gone home. Officially lockdown should have been 10:00 p.m. but he'd always done this by 9:30 p.m. and disappeared. No one could get in or out after he left.

As I said Bill played a bit part in my decision to move into the Kodokan which proved a masterstroke as it completely cut out my hours of daily travel which really helped to improve my training. Bill always took time out to talk and eat with me and had this clever ability to get people to do things for him, and help him, even complete strangers. I'd never met anyone so shrewd, streetwise and intelligent. Some people were a bit suspicious of him. They couldn't understand how someone, who they thought did nothing, always managed to have money in his pocket. He also drove a nice car and lived in an expensive apartment. I knew, although I never bothered to explain to other people, that it came down to those three points. There were rumours that he had links with the CIA, FBI and the KGB and I laughed whenever anyone mentioned that around me. I knew Bill, when not training at the Kodokan, sold insurance. His customers were mostly Americans from American army bases that were in and around Tokyo at that time. Many times we visited Meiji Army Base even if Bill didn't have an appointment. With an appointment, the armed guards signed him in as they had Bill on their list. They ignored me sat next to him. With no appointment, he just flashed an ID card, which he might have forged, and the same thing happened.

No one really questioned Bill about anything and later he also managed to get me a card.

If Bill had some business, he would take care of that first, whilst I waited in his car and looked around in wonder at this massive army place, with loads of houses, all occupied with army personnel, and their families who just waited for Bill to sell them insurance. Or that's how it seemed as he never left a house without his customer's signature on the dotted line. I loved being on those bases and they opened up another new world full of opportunities. I could get decent food and they had a big shop there full of American clothes which you couldn't buy in Japanese shops in 1962. I ended up buying some fantastic cheap American clothes that I really needed at that time. A Harris tweed jacket, scarf, cravat, bow tie, corduroy trousers, beetle-crusher shoes with thick crepe soles, a hat, and even a pipe. Bill, who'd helped me select these items, believed I really looked the part.

We had a third member of our team, who also trained at the Kodokan and he regularly joined us in the downstairs restaurant. Ronald Cory, from Las Vegas, who we always referred to as Cory. He must have been around the same age as Bill and being from Vegas meant he'd studied the art of playing cards and become a master. He discovered ways to beat the house, by that I mean Las Vegas casinos, and once they realised how he did it they banned him. For Bill and I, plus a few others who joined us from time to time, Cory would always have a pack of cards close by and he could perform all kinds of tricks. Cory would arrange games with a few of us and he gave the cards a good shuffle before he dealt five cards to each person. Cory won every game as he seemed to know exactly what cards everybody had. Which I found out later he did. He wore a silver ring, on his little finger of his right hand, which had a mirror on the inside that no one could see. As he dealt he looked in this mirror so he knew exactly which card everyone had even before they did. Cory had a few other tricks that didn't include cards which he showed me. I practiced these and I became quite proficient as well. I found Cory a fascinating character and he introduced me to the world of magic which I'm still very interested in.

As for Bill well he helped me in another direction as well. Girls. I've already mentioned that he put in a good word for me with Nobuko and living at the Kodokan meant that most days I went down to the restaurant to see her. I remember watching the clock as it ticked down towards the end of a session and as soon as I received the all clear I sprinted down to the changing rooms making sure as I ran that I caught a quick glimpse of Nobuko as she served. I knew she saw me but I didn't care. I just wanted to see her. I quickly showered, dressed and took my seat in the restaurant a few minutes later. I felt excited about seeing her and spent a lot of time during the day thinking about her and trying to work out some smart Japanese things to say. Despite this, I remained fully focused on my judo and in a way I think she helped me improve. I'd been at the Kodokan for more than six months and people were talking about me. I believed the more I improved, the more people would talk, and this would get back to Nobuko who'd be impressed as well.

Nobuko, six months older than me, came from Tokyo and lived near Senkawa railway station. She attended Tokyo's Ikebukuro High School and worked part-time as a waitress at the Kodokan. Most nights I ate there and Bill and Cory often joined me. Obviously, they hadn't sprinted from training and showered at breakneck speed. Eventually, after a great deal of persuading from Bill who thought it might be good for me to have some female company in my life, Nobuko agreed to a date. But this had to be on a Sunday and we planned for Sunday the 1st of April. This gave me six days to prepare some clever Japanese phases.

Before moving into the Kodokan Bill had mentioned a couple of points that would help me. One being the obvious reduction in my monthly travel expenses and his other idea involved me making extra money by working for a living. Although he didn't mean menial restaurant work or anything like that! Bill always looked at life on a much grander scale and he had big plans for me. At that time in Tokyo, many people wanted to learn English and local newspapers were full of advertisements. I explained to Bill that I didn't feel this would be right for me as I didn't have the best English vocabulary and couldn't spell to save my life. Bill just laughed this off and said I had a much better idea than the Japanese who wouldn't really know how well I spoke or if I had appalling spelling. With Bill's help, I applied for many jobs, which offered great money, but they kept rejecting me because of my age. Bill, being Bill, wouldn't have this and this is why we made some serious additions to my wardrobe which I mentioned before. For my next interview, I wore my army base collection of clothes that you might have wondered why a fifteen year old would buy. This included my Harris Tweed jacket, Beetle-Crusher shoes that made me look two inches taller. Plus I'd tied my rather nice silk cravat around my neck and had my pipe in hand for effect. With this look, I managed to pass myself off as a nineteen year old

English teacher and got a job. The following week I would start work for the Ce-Eto Company who hired me to teach English to their employees' children. At £8 an hour, this represented a huge boost for me even if it was only a few hours a week. I really had to thank Bill again for providing me with an ID card that said I was nineteen as well.

Towards the end of March, I found myself almost broke again and in desperate need of food. I hadn't seen Bill for a couple of nights and I knew he had some urgent business somewhere. With my big date looming I thought it best to not visit Nobuko, without money in my pocket, as she might have reconsidered our date if she knew the sorry state of my financial affairs. After training, I managed to scrounge a few rice biscuits that one of the Japanese students had discarded. I hoped this would be enough to see me through the night. Unfortunately, around 10:00 p.m., my hunger pains kicked in big time and I needed food. With the time, well-passed lockdown, I had to activate a plan that Bill and I had discussed. A kind of escape from the Kodokan and scrounge food operation that Bill had been drilling me about for two weeks. Bill called this his 'singing for his supper plan' that he said he'd used successfully in many parts of the world when he struggled with cash flow problems. For my first challenge, I had to escape from the Kodokan. To do this I opened my window, climbed on to the window ledge, held on to a shaky old drain pipe as I stretched my right foot across to a railing, then with one foot in place, I released my grip on the drain pipe and stretched my other foot on to the railing. With both feet, precariously perched on those railings, I jumped ten feet down to a rusty old fire escape and then ran down the fire escape where at the bottom a ten feet high wall greeted me. I ran up the wall, jumped down on the other side, and that completed my great escape from the Kodokan without triggering any alarms or disturbing armed guards. Eric Dominy would have been proud of me. Okay, there were no alarms to trigger and of course no guards.

Stage two of this plan meant I had to find a little bar type place, which that also served food, where a few Japanese middle management businessmen had stopped for a few drinks after work. Once inside I would order one drink, which I just about had enough money to pay for, and wait. Rather like people on the trains Bill believed these businessmen would be infatuated with me and try to speak with me. At first, upon Bill's instructions, I had to play it cool and act rather shy. After all, for this stage, I'd reverted back to being a fifteen year old boy who'd just left school. As the whisky and sake flowed I had to accept their offer to join them at the bar which Bill had predicted. Obviously, I couldn't join them in their sake toasts but they very generously shared any food they had and even ordered more for me. They also paid for my drink. Like most Japanese at this time they regarded me as a bit of a novelty and to have me sit with them seemed like an achievement for them. Plus I gave an Oscar-winning performance. I corrected their mispronunciations and made sure I added new words to their English vocabulary. I even performed a few tricks that I'd picked up from Cory. Mr. Best, my old English teacher at Forest Hill Comprehensive, might have turned in his grave if he hadn't still been alive! But these Japanese businessmen loved it making it a win, win, win situation for everybody. At the end of the evening, full and still with the money I had for my one drink in my pocket, I returned to the Kodokan where I executed my Ninja Warrior thing again to get back into my room.

17

ON FRIDAY, BEFORE our big date, I saw Nobuko just to confirm that she'd be at our agreed meeting point. But I hadn't sprinted out of the arena at the end of the session and showered in less than a minute. I now tried to play it cool even though I felt excited inside. I also felt quite nervous and I didn't really know what we would do. I needed another chat with Bill to try and come up with some kind of plan. Bill just laughed and told me not to worry about it. He had a plan for Saturday with Cory, which included me. He didn't go into details, except to explain that it involved Meiji army base and any plans which included Meij were always fine with me. I loved it. It felt like how I imagined an American village would be apart from soldiers running around in uniforms. I didn't have to sing for my supper that night as payday had arrived and I had cash in my pocket.

At lockdown, I remained in my room where I tried to plan next month's budget. It hurt when I ran out of money and I couldn't afford to buy food. I had to find a way to get by until the end of the month and still have money in my pocket. Although I knew I would have extra income in April to play with. I met Bill the next day at his apartment and as I walked in a stunning Japanese girl walked out. I didn't know what she sold but doubt if it had anything to do with insurance. Bill, upon seeing my flummoxed look, smiled and told me not to worry my time would come.

We left in Bill's big black right-hand drive Buick car and drove a short distance to pick up Cory. He, in a similar fashion to Bill, appeared to be saying goodbye to another gorgeous Japanese girl who could have been Bill's date's sister. Cory joined Bill in the front but we didn't get far before we ground to a halt at the back of a huge Tokyo traffic jam. We didn't move for five minutes and Bill soon had enough of this. He switched on his in-car loudspeaker system, which I'd never seen before, and announced in perfect Japanese that we were the police and we had an emergency. Cars in front of us began to move to one side and we slowly edged forward. Bill continued making announcements, other drivers created space, and very soon we'd left the chaos behind us. At Meiji Bill and Cory flashed their identification cards as I waved mine from the back. Again I had to admire Bill's ingenious methods for breaking through Tokyo's gridlocked traffic and our incredibly easy access to Meiji again. But this is how Bill lived his life. Nothing flustered him and he just seemed to make his own rules for every situation. Being part of Bill's inner circle meant I usually benefited as well so I stopped thinking about how he managed to pull off these types of stunts and accepted them as normal.

We were at Meiji and we were there for a reason. Although Bill didn't have his usual insurance briefcase with him. He had Cory instead and they had another plan. After a quick snack, we crossed the camp to another location that I hadn't noticed before where Cory's eyes lit up like he'd won the jackpot as we entered Meiji's casino. This could have been any casino in Las Vegas as it had slot machines, blackjack, roulette, craps and poker tables. To be honest I didn't want to be there and I'd had have been perfectly happy to wait in the car. Plus I'd spent most of the previous evening planning my monthly budget that didn't include an expenditure column called gambling! Although my tune soon changed when free food and drinks appeared. They found a table and I watched. I knew they had this idea about how they could beat red and black on the roulette wheel as they'd discussed their plan a few minutes ago. I didn't take much notice but I remember they kept speaking about red and black. Six hours later, and I must admit I'd become bored in there waiting for them, they left the table with a few more dollars than they'd started with.

As we drove out Bill switched his attention to me and my big date the following day. He wanted to know where and what time we were meeting, which I explained, and he also wanted to know how I felt. I talked about my mixed emotions, excited and nervous, and Bill made a joke with Cory as they probably remembered their early teenage dates from years ago. That's how our return journey went. The usual kind of jokes you get between blokes, and a young teenager, about to begin a journey into the mysterious world of the opposite sex. Well, that's how we started until, in the middle of nowhere, one of Bill's warning lights flashed to indicate we'd run out of fuel. Bill pulled over and I thought oh no as we were making good time and I expected to be home long before lockdown. I had left my window open, just in case I had to break in again, but I never really enjoyed having to do that as there were risks involved.

I had no idea how Bill would resolve this problem and even half expected to have to spend the night in his car. Not ideal preparation the night before my big date but I should really have known better. Bill activated another one of his ingenious master plans. He stopped another car as it approached and explained his problem to the driver of this car. Obviously, he had to do this in Japanese as the chances of stopping another American were not that great in 1962.

The Japanese driver, probably quite surprised that he'd met an American so fluent in Japanese, listened to Bill and agreed to help. Bill went to the boot of his car where he just happened to have a five-gallon container and a plastic hose about three feet long. He put one end of this tube in the other motorist's fuel tank and the other end in his mouth. He then sucked enough fuel to generate a flow of fuel up the plastic pipe which he quickly moved from his mouth to the container. Bill, after he'd spat out a mouthful of fuel, reengaged the quite stunned looking Japanese motorist in conversation. Soon they were laughing and back slapping and without anyone really noticing he'd filled his five-gallon container in no time at all. As we pulled away Bill mentioned that he'd tried this a few times and never had any problems. Apart from a mouthful of fuel.

We then made good time and arrived at the Kodokan at 9:31 p.m. Just one minute after the unofficial lockdown. The old caretaker had already mounted his push bike and didn't look best pleased to see me. I waved to him and his eyes shifted towards the wall with the fire escape behind it. He also looked up and raised his eyebrows in a kind of gesture that said you've done it before so you can do it again. This time I raised both hands and pleaded with him in my best Japanese to let me in. He muttered something in

Japanese that I'd never heard before, climbed off his push bike, and opened the door. So much for me thinking my Ninja Warrior escapades had gone unnoticed. I guess, back then, safety first didn't apply and the old caretaker didn't care about me breaking curfew.

The following day, at noon, I arrived at our meeting point where quite a few people had also gathered. There were no signs of Nobuko which didn't surprise me really as I arrived half an hour early. I always liked to arrive early for meetings if I could. If I had a meeting at a place I'd never visited I wanted to make sure I arrived on time. Plus, as in this case, I wanted to learn something about my meeting point which I knew had become one of Tokyo's most popular landmarks.

Hachiko, pronounced Ha-chi-ko, is a meeting point close to Shibuya railway station in Tokyo and is named after a dog called Hachiko formerly owned by Hidesaburo Ueno. Ueno, born in 1872 at a place called Hisaishi, that later became known as Tsu, in Mie Prefecture, graduated from Japan's Imperial University of agriculture. He began teaching as an assistant professor and by 1902 he'd reached associate professor level. Eventually, he became a professor at Tokyo's

Agricultural University. Professor Ueno brought Hachiko, an Akita dog born in November 1923.

Each morning when Professor Ueno left home for work Hachiko would accompany him to Shibuya station. Later that day Hachiko would return to the station to meet his master's train and they went home together. They became a bit of a talking point with other commuters who couldn't help but notice the faithful Hachiko when he greeted his master every afternoon. But on the 21st of May 1923, as Hachiko waited in his usual place, his heart must have skipped a beat as the professor's familiar face failed to appear in amongst the throng of commuters. That day Professor Ueno never came home and he never would again. He died, whilst giving a lecture, of a cerebral hemorrhage at fifty-three years old. Hachiko returned the station the following day, at the same time, as his master's train pulled in. He waited and left disappointed. This continued even after Hachiko had been given away to another family. He escaped from his new owner and returned to Professor Ueno's house. In time he must have sensed his master wouldn't return but he never gave up his afternoon vigils at Shibuya station. Each day he waited. Each day he left disappointed. But in doing so he captured the attention of other commuters who'd remembered him meeting his master. They knew why

Hachiko waited. They knew Hachiko's dream of seeing his master again would never be fulfilled. Hachiko touched their hearts and to console him they brought him food to eat whilst he waited. On the 8th of March 1935, Hachiko stopped his afternoon visits as he passed away.

Prior to this one of Professor Ueno's former students noticed Hachiko at the station and became so interested that he studied his history and researched the Akita breed of dog. He discovered that at that time there were only thirty left and this included Hachiko. The former student often visited the station to see Hachiko and published several articles about his incredible loyalty. In 1932, a piece published in Tokyo's largest newspaper propelled Hachiko into the national spotlight. He became an overnight sensation but this didn't stop him paying his regular station afternoon visits which he kept up for ten years. Not only had he touched the hearts of the regular commuters at Shibuya he also became a symbol for loyalty and family spirit for Japan's people. Teachers and parents used Hachiko as an example for children to follow. Now, on the 1st of April 1962, I stood close to Hachiko's statue outside Shibuya station waiting for Nobuko. I watched as families, couples, and people on their own, approached and looked on in admiration for this remarkable dog. Pictures were taken and many handkerchiefs were out mopping up a few wayward tears.

My thoughts were soon disrupted by someone calling my name Bl-ian, Bl-ian. I turned and saw Nobuko with two of her friends about ten feet away from me. I loved the way she pronounced my name. She had a problem with her R pronunciation which came out like an L. I'd picked her up on this a few times and when she really concentrated she got quite close. But I actually found her natural attempt quite romantic and decided to just let her get on with it. She introduced me to her friends, one of whom spoke English quite well, and she explained the plan. I could spend two hours with Nobuko, whilst her friends did something else, and we would meet back in the same place. I looked at Hachiko who seemed to approve of this plan.

I knew Nobuko felt shy about spending time alone with me and I'd half expected to spend the day with all three girls when I first saw them. Which I didn't feel too bad about as I felt confident in my ability to entertain them. In fact, to be honest with you, I think I would have preferred all three as one represented different challenges. But the other two went their way and we went another. I didn't know if I should walk in front of her, behind, or by her side. I thought about holding her hand, quite a few times, but each time I bottled out at the last moment. Nobuko, despite my doubts, seemed quite confident and unconcerned that she just happened to be the only teenage girl in Tokyo, that Sunday afternoon, out for a stroll with a young teenager from London's East End. Well, there might have been others but we didn't pass any. We looked in a big department store which even when compared to today's standards amazed me. Nobuko took a special interest in china dolls which I noted as I knew she had a birthday coming up soon. We walked more, stopped for noodles in a small restaurant shack kind of place before we walked back to Shibuya station where the others were already waiting. We were half an hour late although it didn't seem that we'd been that long. Time just flew by. The girls went into a huddle, had a giggle before they looked at me and said goodbye. Nobuko gave me a nice smile, and a little wave, which I interpreted as thank you.

I looked at Hachiko who again seemed to be giving me his seal of approval. I smiled, waved to him, and walked in another direction. As teenage first dates go I think this must have been pretty much the norm for fifteen year olds in terms what we did and how we reacted to one another. We had a few awkward moments, communication problems as we struggled with each other's languages, and of course, we were a couple of innocent virgins. Outside the norm, we were from different countries and used to completely different cultures, although I seemed to be on a go-fast crash course to learn all about Japan. We didn't hold hands or enjoy a goodbye kiss. As we walked, there were moments when due to the crowds that our bodies touched, and I have to admit I found those quite exciting.

During my first six months in Japan, I'd always found weekends the toughest times to handle. When I had less to do and more time to think about my family and England. More than once I sat in my room, cried and wrote more letters to Mum and Dad which expressed my true feelings. I think putting my thoughts on paper helped me to deal with my situation. It helped me analyse and look at things from different angles. Most of these letters were torn into tiny pieces and thrown in my bin. But this weekend, at Meiji with Bill and Cory followed by Nobuko on Sunday, proved another breakpoint for me.

As for Hachiko, he's ingrained in Japanese culture and his story has been brought to the attention of the world in books and movies. Each year, on the 8th of April, there is a service of remembrance at Shibuya railway station that many dog lovers attend. Shibuya bus routes have even been named after him. In 1987 director, Seijiro Koyama, directed a blockbuster Japanese film called The Tale of Hachiko, all about Hachiko's life right up to his death. In 2009 American actor Richard Gere, who cried when he heard Hachiko's story, starred in an American version called Hachi A Dog's Tale, directed by Lasse Hallstrom and filmed in Rhode Island.

18

THE FOLLOWING MONDAY I dramatically transformed into nineteen year old Professor Jacks. Not a graduate of Japan's Imperial University of English. But, on a totally different level, a product of Mr. Best's esteemed Forest Hill Comprehensive English class. The back of the class rabble who graduated with the back of the class master's degrees in joking around! A few old friends from school and teachers, who I knew were following my progress, might have been staggered with my incredible rise to professorship status six months after leaving Forest Hill! But as I stood on a packed train, with an hour to go before my first lesson and with no idea what I would teach, this is what I'd become.

An hour later Professor Jacks stood in front of twenty kids all aged between six and twelve. A few sat in the front, a few in the middle and of course there were six at the back. My mind flashed back to Forest Hill and the hard times a few of us had given our teachers. People say what goes around comes around and it had for me. Or the real truth of the matter is that I should really have been sat back there and not stood out in front. I felt totally inadequate and right out of my comfort zone. How could I teach kids given my academic background that consisted of an A+ in woodwork followed by Ds and Es in all other subjects? But I had a blackboard and some white chalk so I winged it.

I drew a stick man picture of me on the board and wrote my name by the side of it. My name is Mr. Brian. I got each kid to repeat this and just change my name to theirs. They got that. I followed this up with pictures of a mum, dad, sister, and brother. I explained about my family and they did the same. We worked on numbers and I wrote fifteen on the board. I am fifteen years old which I quickly changed to nineteen. I did the same with London and explained the reason for this and capital cities. We had a little game to see who could name capital cities from other countries. Obviously, kids sat at the front, as you would expect, hung on my every word. The middle lot did their thing and those at the back fooled around. One, in particular, a chubby little eight year old called Ishy, seemed the worst of the bunch. Every time I turned round to write something he moved to another seat or just stood somewhere. I lost count of the times I told this cheeky little so-and-so to sit down. Yes, I know what you're thinking. He could have been me!

Family basics and capital cities managed to eat the first hour of my two hour class. For the second one, I had absolutely no idea until I looked at tubby little Ishy again and my mind flashed back to Meiji and burgers. Ishy had obviously eaten far too many but he saved my bacon. Although I just wished he'd sat in one place and stopped disrupting my lesson. At one point, when I turned back, I couldn't see him at all. Much to the amusement of the rest of the class, well those at the back and in the middle, he'd positioned himself on the floor under my desk. I'm sure my old geography teacher Mr. Ashby would have considered that a caning offence. But really it was so funny and I had a job to keep a straight face!

I drew a picture of another character, this one slightly more rotund, lived in Scotland. He owned a farm and I drew a picture of a farm to make sure they all understood. Once they got that I introduced this character's name. Uncle Jock MacDonald a distant relative of my Mother. Uncle Jock MacDonald had a farm and this proved E-I-E-I-O for the rest of the lesson as we belted out all kinds of renditions of the popular nursery rhyme Old MacDonald Had a Farm. We used pigs and the kids loved their oink, oink, oinks. The same applied to cows, moo, moo, moos, ducks and quack, quack, quacks, and lambs and chickens where baa, baa, baas and cluk, cluk, cluks reverberated around the classroom. We finished with one more version and were on the pigs again with me out the front acting like a pig.

'With an oink oink here

An oink oink there

Here an oink, there an oink

Everywhere an oink oink

Old MacDonald had a farm, E-I-E-I-O.'

I'm going for it big time and all the kids are on their feet going for it as well. This lesson had probably turned into a total back of the class affair but none of us realised that the head of human resources now stood in the doorway. He must have wondered what the flipping heck had happened here and why Professor Jacks had suddenly turned into old Jock MacDonald. But Ishy, of all people, came to my rescue as he explained to his dad, yes Ishy's dad ran human resources, exactly why we'd all just behaved like pigs. He seemed happy, as did the kids who all left with smiles on their faces; I'd winged it and had just made £16 in the process.

That's how April 1962 started for me and I felt fantastic. The kid, in the Kodokan chocolate factory without the chocolate, had now found the chocolate. Not literally. But

I'd found a girl and a way to make extra money. Could life get any better? Well, the answer to that is yes and no. No, as there were still a few students who would never forget that day I tried to throw Sato and they still took every opportunity they had to make my life hell. Also, I think a few had spotted that I had affections for Nobuko, and her for me, which upset them as well. This gave them two reasons to gang which they made the most of. The yes answer to this question came thanks to Bill, yet again, as he introduced me to a person called Yusef who ran a modelling agency. Yusef seemed keen for me to sign up and arranged a meeting with a photographer. Pretty soon he added my portfolio to his collection.

Now I mixed judo, teaching English, singing for my supper and modelling. I still had to sing for my supper as the English teaching money wouldn't start rolling in until the end of April and I had to wait for modelling work. Sundays were Nobuko days and we did a lot of things together. We went to the cinema where I sat through movies and tried to understand as much as I could. They were in Japanese with no subtitles as they didn't exist at that time. We looked around shops, ate together and generally had a very good time. Our chemistry, despite my foreign status, seemed to improve the more time we spent together. I had this thing for

Nobuko and I wanted her to be happy. I'd even met her parents, many times, after I'd walked her home. They were strict but I think I won them over with a few Japanese words that Nobuko helped me with. I'd even persuaded her to spend some time in my room although she never came alone. I tried but she wouldn't have any of that. We were at the holding hands' stage and a goodnight kiss on her cheek. Until her 16th birthday!

I used the Kodokan gym for a couple of hours most days where I pushed weights and ran the treadmill. With that, my judo, and running up and down seven flights of stairs a few times a day, this meant I must have been the fittest I'd ever been and the Japanese gangs couldn't throw me as easily as they had before. Plus I threw a few more of them and not just the tall, skinny and goofy looking ones. I felt completely on top of my game. You know the feeling you get sometimes when everything seems to be clicking into place and you feel invincible. But we're not unbeatable and sometimes, when you least expect it, something will happen to remind us that we are only human. For me, this came in the shape of a stomach throw. With my history, I'd always been a bit cautious and gone out of my way to protect my stomach. I practiced this with a Japanese student under the watchful eye of Watanabe who issued instructions in Japanese and

English. The Japanese student, standing, put his foot in my stomach and threw me over the top where I should have gone into a rolling break-fall. This totally winded me and I had severe stomach pains again. I worried that I might have sustained more damage and my judo career could be over. I laid low for a few days and never mentioned it to anybody because if those Japanese gangs had known I had a weak spot they would have gone for it big time. After three days my pains disappeared and I started to include more exercises to strengthen that part of my body. Sit-ups seemed one of the best ways and within a month I could do a hundred every day without any pain. I also made sure no one caught me with that throw again.

On the 20th of May 1962, Nobuko's birthday which conveniently fell on a Sunday that year, I decided that we should do something special and with Bill's help, I had a car, with a driver, to take us out. We had a nice lunch in the Ginza followed by a trip to the To-ji Temple to see the pagoda which Dad had suggested I visit. Unfortunately, they'd closed it for restoration work. Towards the end of the date, sat in the back of the car holding hands, I gave Nobuko her present. The china doll that she admired every time we went out. I hadn't budgeted for it but I felt she deserved it and it would be £3 well spent. Her eyes lit up when she opened her package and she squeezed my right hand tight as she rested her left hand on my thigh. This felt very nice and I could feel a bit of excitement stirring. Back at Nobuko's home, we had a blind spot where nobody could see us from the street or the house. Our secret spot where I usually kissed her cheek. But I'd worked hard today and I think she must have realised and felt I deserved a bit more than that. We had a big kiss and cuddle that must have lasted for about ten minutes. I felt fantastic but unfortunately, we were interrupted by Nobuko's mother calling her. I quickly made my exit without speaking to her parents.

19

AFTER EIGHT MONTHS in Japan I'd developed a good understanding of how things worked. I still faced challenges, almost on a daily basis, but now they were expected and I tried not to let them faze me. By this, I'm not especially referring to judo, which continued to be a huge test, as I strived for perfection. But I mean everyday life challenges which people face when they move to a new country and have to learn a completely different culture. Outside of judo I continued to teach English and some students even requested private, one to one lessons, which I found quite difficult as they required more planning and there were fewer opportunities to have fun in that kind of environment.

Meanwhile with Nobuko, after our 'intimate' moment we shared during her birthday, things had rapidly cooled down. We seemed to have reached some kind of impasse. Our moment in the blind spot had long passed and as much as I tried I could never recreate it. We were back to cheek kissing. Most Sundays we enjoyed ourselves with more movies, shopping, lunches, and visits to Tokyo's Ueno Zoo. But she always had to be home before 6:00 p.m. and there were times when I felt quite frustrated with the strict rules we had to follow. The barriers that I'd spent so much time breaking down during the early part of our relationship, especially on her birthday, were now very much back in force again. No doubt her parents played a big part in that. I mentioned this to Bill and said he would see what he could do. But he stressed that we were too young and that I should just forget about her. I'd grown up quickly, played in the big boys' playground, but I still remained fifteen.

At the beginning of August 1962, my thoughts were all about judo, my main reason for being in Japan, and I had a mission. It still annoyed me that I'd been demoted from a brown belt to the British equivalent of a blue belt when I'd arrived, and this had been recorded in my Kodokan assessment grade book for eternity. I couldn't erase it or make a remark that this could have been down to their concerns with Bobby and his performances on the mat. At the time it had shocked me but I sucked it up. Now, a little over nine months later, I had an opportunity that I knew I had to grab with both hands. In Japan, they have something that is known as a red and white contest where two groups of players get to together with one set wearing red belts and the other white belts. It's where a brown belt has an opportunity to move up to a first Dan or a first Dan has the chance to move up to a second Dan. You have to stay within your grade level which meant I lined up with brown belts. The players with white belts line up on one side with reds opposite them. Each pair facing each other then fight with the winners staying on to fight the next person in the line opposite. Any player winning six contests automatically received a recommendation for a promotion to the next level.

I felt so determined and excited as my turn neared. Nothing could stand in my way and for the first five fights, nothing did. I won them all very easily. For the all-important sixth, I had some problems. Nothing I tried worked and he had the same problem with me although at one point he had me down and he was kind of suffocating me. I felt trapped, my breathing became erratic, and I thought it might be curtains. I had to submit there was nothing else I could do. Right at the last moment, I had some kind of power surge that started in my toes and rushed through my entire body. An adrenalin rush from nowhere which enabled me to escape from the jaws of defeat. I couldn't snatch a victory but at least I hadn't lost. I felt proud as well as disappointed. So close yet so far. But my examiner had been impressed with my performance. He'd noticed that I'd won five fights, all with different techniques, and this convinced him to recommend me for a Kodokan upgrade which soon received the official seal of approval.

I'll never forget that day, 9th of August 1962, when at fifteen years and 308 days I became, at that time, the youngest person from Great Britain ever to be awarded a black belt. I'd made history. I felt elated and wanted to do a Kodokan lap of honour. I resisted that temptation. I didn't want to do anything to wind up the Kodokan gangs who still had some members who wanted to cause me some serious damage. All kinds of thoughts flashed through my mind. Sitting on the bank, Sydenham General Hospital, Dad throwing the huge policeman at the Chelsea show, Thriffwood, Forest Hill Comprehensive, the LJS, and even Mum's pie and mash. A plate of that would have been a perfect way end my fantastic day. I had to find a way to talk to her or Dad and Bill suggested trying the phone in the office. They agreed as long as I reversed the charges. With nine hour time difference, and Japan time now close to 6:00 p.m., I knew Mum and Dad would probably be at work and it didn't surprise me when no one answered. Later, Bill, Cory and I went down to the restaurant to celebrate my news with Nobuko who seemed happy and awarded me a kiss on the cheek.

That night I found sleep difficult. I couldn't come down from the high I'd just experienced and all kinds of thoughts buzzed through my mind. I kept thinking back to my sixth contest and that huge adrenalin surge which that enabled me to break that hold. Where did that come from? I thought about Mum and Dad and all their sacrifices that I knew had pushed me this far. I would never let them down. How could I? They wanted this as much as me. They were my parents, they were my friends and they were my fan club. Without them, none of this would be happening.

The following afternoon, about the time I knew Mum and Dad would be getting up, I called again and Dad answered. I felt so excited to hear his voice. I joked with him that I'd beaten him in our private race for a black belt. But I knew, from the sound of his voice, that he didn't care about that. He just felt ecstatic for me. A few days later the Kodokan presented me with my black belt and the official certificate to confirm my upgrade. As soon as I could I posted my certificate home. A couple of weeks later Nichidai University's director of judo, one of the biggest universities in Tokyo, invited me to train there and I immediately accepted.

I trained at Nichidai two hours in the morning and two hours in the afternoon. I followed this up with two hours in the evening at the Kodokan. Watanabe had once said to me, 'If you are a champion, and you trained for three hours a day, to stay a champion you must train for six hours a day.' At Nichidai and the Kodokan, I knew I had a long way to go to before I could be a champion at those places. The Japanese students were so good and they knew so much more than me. But I'd improved and if I kept working hard I had a chance.

I'd accepted Nichidai's offer without really thinking about it which really taught me a lesson. If you ever get invited into the lion's den think twice about it! Of course, these students knew me from the Kodokan where I'd walked into their space with all my cocky cockney bravado. They weren't impressed especially when I tried to throw Sato. Being awarded my black belt didn't help although many began to show me a bit more respect. But the hardcore lions would never forget and now I'd dared to enter their university space. I could see the looks of disapproval on the usual suspects' faces. They prowled their arena, with their chests puffed out, and snarled at me whenever I caught their eyes. They were pumped with their testosterone levels off the scale. Trapped in the lion's den turned out to be a horrific experience and very close to my worst time in Japan. In fact, it could well have been the most unpleasant.

The lions roared, licked their lips, and now they had me for their breakfast, lunch and as well as their usual

Kodokan dinner. They were relentless and now, when looking back, I don't know how I managed to keep taking the punishment. The more torture they dished out the more I went back for. But I kept going because I had it in my mind never to give up. It didn't matter what they did to me. I would always keep going. It hurt. I suffered niggling injury after niggling injury although I tried not to show it as they would have preyed on any weakness. Plus I already had a problem with the stomach throw. I had to make sure none of them got me in one of those. They wanted a piece of me and I'm sure they gained great satisfaction every time I crashed onto the mat. They hurt me but they would never break me. Many times I thought of Dad when he won his trophy at the Chelsea show, I felt so proud of him. Now I would do everything possible to make him proud of me even if it meant stepping on a few lions' toes. They could do what they wanted, I didn't care, I would win and soon they would know.

There is no doubt that the Japanese University students were amongst the hardest working individuals I'd come across at that time. Most trained for six hours a day on the mat and many spent more time in the gym working on other aspects of their fitness. But once a month they did like to blow off steam with a special get together. Bobby Boulton had mentioned this before when we were in a sake shop looking for presents for the old ladies. He'd attended one of these events and joined in with all the fun. He'd mentioned that they were formal, with all the students dressed in full student uniforms, and the coaches in jackets and ties. He also said they acted kind of silly, drank lots of sake, joked around, and sang songs that sounded like nursery rhymes to Bobby.

Bill, who'd attended a few of these, suggested it would be a good idea if I went so I could blow off steam. I joined a group of about fifty, all sat around tables placed together in a square shape. Head coaches were sat at both ends and all the students sat facing each other on the sides. For me, during the early part of the evening, they behaved like young kids and old farmer Jock MacDonald wouldn't have been out of place here. They sang their songs, played what I thought were quite childish jokes, and stood and toasted each other as they drank shots of sake. Bill, sat next to me, forced my shots down. As the evening progressed many of them seemed to get melancholy and as one stood up, and blasted out the Japanese version of what could have been God Save the Queen, a few burst into tears. I had a job to keep a straight face and Bill had to keep a firm grip on me. I'd never tried sake before or any other kind of alcohol. With the room, slightly spinning for me, everything ended quite quickly and Bill suggested we should visit the Ginza for a nice meal. He had a place in mind that served western food and where he knew there would be a good mix of locals and westerners.

We arrived, found a table, and were soon joined by two American women who knew Bill. Sharon and Carol, both from San Francisco, were in Japan teaching English. Carol seemed quite attached to Bill and they sat together. Sharon, who said she was thirty but I thought she seemed more like forty, sat next to me. She looked about five feet seven inches tall, quite slim, with long blonde hair and she appeared very friendly as she kept putting her hand on my knee. She wore a low cut top that provided me with a fantastic view of her amazing first bases. Sharon didn't know anything about judo which meant we didn't really have a lot in common apart from being English teachers. As the night wore on we joked about that and I discovered that old farmer Jock MacDonald actually came from America. During this time white wine flowed, Bill seemed quite concerned that my glass remained full, and the room spun more.

20

OH, MY HEAD hurt. A team of road mechanics could have been in there digging a tunnel. My body also ached like it never had before. Where was I? How did I get here? I staggered out of bed, wrapped a towel around my waist, quietly I opened the door and descended down some stairs in front of me. I heard noises which led me to a kitchen where I found Bill. The kitchen clock had just ticked past midday. Bill greeted me with and asked if I'd slept well. I had no idea. The last thing I remembered had been sitting in the restaurant staring at Sharon's cleavage. Bill filled in the blanks. He said when the waiter asked me if I would like a dessert I'd pointed at Sharon's breasts and said I'll have a couple of those with cherries on top. At that point, Bill thought it best we left and Carol and Sharon helped me to Bill's car. At Bill's apartment, he helped me into his spare room where I'd crashed out.

For the next few months I focused on judo, trying to make extra money with a few teaching and modelling jobs, and of course Nobuko. I still saw a lot of Bill who continued to amaze me with some of the things he got up to. At the Kodokan, there were still a few who absolutely hated me. I knew. They knew that I knew. And that would never change.

With eighteen months of my five year programme complete I found myself back at Tokyo's Haneda airport on a wet and miserable Wednesday morning at the beginning of April 1963. I waited and my heart pumped more than usual as crowds of people headed towards me. Single travelers, who paid no attention to the masses around them, hustled through. Couples, more relaxed, chatted and smiled when they saw family or friends who waited for them. More than once my excitement increased as I thought it was them but I'd been mistaken. The crowds thinned, I checked my watch, and for a moment I thought I might have the wrong day. I seemed alone in the terminal. Then I spotted them, weighed down with loads of luggage, and Shayne sat on a suitcase in the baggage trolley. My heart skipped a beat as I watched my family walk towards me. The taxi to Tokyo had arrived! I wanted to run and help but airport security wouldn't let me through. I could see Dad looking for me. I waved. He saw me. He waved. He spoke to Mum. She waved. Pretty soon we were all waving. For the next ten seconds, everything seemed to move in slow motion and all the other people in the airport seemed to disappear. We, well I did for sure, went into a private Jacks family world as we greeted each other. Mum started first, then me, followed by Barbara and Dad. I'd prepared myself for this moment but when you haven't seen your family for eighteen months emotions take over. I couldn't keep myself in check. Shayne, now four years old, although happy to see me didn't cry. He seemed happier playing with the baggage trolley.

Do you remember that day at Heathrow airport when Dad promised me he'd visit me in two years? Well, that day had arrived but I knew it hadn't been easy for Mum and Dad to make this happen. Dad who'd before I left and after had continued to try and find me some kind of sponsorship which included my interview with Trevor Leggett, had been unsuccessful with that mission but at least I got to eat a much-needed dinner. Another idea included Dad driving his taxi from London to Tokyo. He would have as well had Russia not refused him permission to drive across their country. Meanwhile, Mum, soon after I left England, had managed to find a position with BOAC. As I mentioned before Mum made the best pie and mash with liquor sauce in the East End and BOAC soon caught on to this and hired her in their kitchen. She became the first female chef to work for them. So whilst I accepted Japan's challenges Mum took on the challenges of BOAC kitchens. She didn't take a day off for eighteen months and worked every hour of overtime on offer. This provided her, and ultimately us, with triple benefits. This enabled Mum to save her holidays and take them all in one go. She banked the extra overtime cash. But probably most important BOAC provided hugely discounted tickets for all my family to fly to Japan. This is why we were having our tearful reunion. The taxi to Tokyo idea didn't take off but my family certainly did thanks to Mum's efforts. Not only that they had a return ticket for me so I could spend a two week holiday in England.

Back in England, Dad had some concerns about my judo. He believed my technique had greatly improved but I didn't seem as strong as before I left. For this reason, as my return flight to Japan neared, Dad had a decision to make. Should he let me go or should I stay?

Mum and Dad who supported me so much.

With Bobby Boulton in Japan just before my 15th birthday. The adventure begins.

With Bobby at Tokyo's Kodokan. I showed a red flag to
Kodokan's bulls and paid the consequences.

With Kyuzo Mifune one of the best known judo players the
world has ever known.

Stage 3

SAT ON THE COACH

21

SAT AT THE front of the team coach I looked down at a machine gun that pointed straight in my face. To say I found this moment unnerving would be a massive understatement. The holder of this weapon, despite a rather stern looking face, seemed quite young with possibly quite a good figure hidden behind her uniform. She didn't smile, blink or say anything. She just stood there rooted on the bottom step. Her two fully armed colleagues had already ventured further down the coach to check we weren't snuggling in any unwanted guests. They also offered no smiles. Still, she didn't move. Her job must have been to guard the exit in case anyone did a runner. I looked at her, she looked at me, but she didn't change the direction of her gun that still pointed straight in my face.

22

My return flight from London to Tokyo left without me and I could not believe what happened a few days later. After nearly two years of fighting, heartache, and pain I'd slipped down the ladder. Instead of beating my main opponents, with my usual consummate ease as I had before I'd left for Japan, some now had the upper hand on me. Rivals, I used to dispatch in no time at all, now presented me with much stiffer tests. But, much worse than that, some of them were even beating me. Hadn't they read the script? They shouldn't have been doing this let alone flipping beating me. I felt sick. Sick of the whole business. I hadn't dropped the ball and I'd remained totally focused. Yet somehow I'd lost ground and I could see some smug looks on a few faces. Since I'd returned from Japan people were talking about me. I'd created a buzz in the judo world. Every time I competed crowds gathered around the mat and I knew what they were thinking now. The golden boy had taken his eye off the ball and now a few others, possibly more deserving in their eyes, could step up to the plate and take some glory that I'd deprived them of before. I felt so bad for Dad. Something had gone wrong and needed to be fixed.

Dad and I were travelling back from Crystal Palace after I hadn't performed as expected in the Southern Area Championship. By that I mean I hadn't won the lightweight title which is how the script should have been written. I hadn't performed that badly but I'd gone out in a whimper and something needed to be done. Dad had already recognised this which is why, in June 1963, we were at Crystal Palace in London together rather than me being alone at the Kodokan in Tokyo. To be honest with you I wanted to go and I wanted to stay. I felt torn. I missed Japan. The food, trains, and the Kodokan even though all three had caused me nightmares in different ways. I missed Bill and of course, I missed Nobuko. At sixteen and a half years old Thriffwood's attractions, such as the park, the woods, and the railway lines, no longer appealed. It's very hard to explain and I think I felt in a kind of no man's land. Maybe I'd grown up too quickly. I'd been in the big boys' playground and I didn't want to go back with the kids. Don't get me wrong I loved being back with my parents but I also missed the independence that I'd had in Japan. I'd discovered a way to look after myself which I quite enjoyed.

After the Southern areas, Dad knew drastic measures were required to get me back on top of my game. He also understood that the LJS no longer represented the best club for me to be with. If you look at this in terms of football today the LJS standard had dropped to say something like a championship level. The second tier. To be noticed, and meet the best players around, I had to be in judos' premier league. The top tier. Although at that time in 1963 I didn't have to become an exclusive member of one club. I had options to move around and Dad took full advantage of this. This enabled me to still spend time at the LJS although I spent more time at the Budokwai and Renshuden clubs where Trevor Leggett coached. He'd impressed me and we knew that for me to progress I had to spend as much time in his classes as possible.

Dad also enjoyed visiting all kinds of different clubs and listening to ideas that other people discussed. He knew he had to keep taking ideas and trying them with me to see if they worked. Of course, he had his own as well but he had no qualms about using anything that he thought might be good for me and it didn't matter if ideas came from sports unrelated to judo. He would take an idea, analyse it, and if he thought it had value he would apply it to me. If I questioned him he would give me one of his looks and bring out his old chestnut, 'fail to prepare, prepare to fail.' At this stage, Dad ran had his own judo club, located at Dog Kennel Hill, where he coached every Tuesday and Thursday.

To help me improve Dad presented me with all kinds of challenges and even though he'd only spent a short time in Japan he must have picked up some of their brutal training methods which he now applied to me. We lived about eight miles from Dog Kennel Hill and Dad made me run there. Well, that's how we started until Dad thought I might have a problem making my weight, lightweight at that time, so he came up with an ingenious plan to control my weight. He made me wear a plastic wetsuit that went right up to my neck and down to my toes. On top of this, I wore my tracksuit. Not long after that, he came up with another idea. Instead of wearing running shoes he made me wear big boots that came up to my shins. Eight miles in bovver boots! I found that incredibly hard. But Dad hadn't finished. Wrist weights were added next. He found some bands, with gaps, which he filled with lead weights. He started with six pounds and soon increased this to ten for each wrist. Dad even made me practice judo still wearing those wristbands.

I'd had some horrific experiences in Japan and Dad certainly created something that wouldn't have been out of place there. I hated that run but Dad said I had to do it or I could go back to Japan and he would wash his hands with me. As much as hated it I stuck with Dad's strict training schedule that included creating handicaps for me when I came up against opponents who were obviously not as good as me. For the rest of 1963, my life totally revolved around judo. I ate, drank and slept it. A few of my old mates from school often asked me if I wanted to go to discos and stuff like that but I had no inclination to do that whatsoever. I lost myself in a training world that spun solely around judo, visiting different clubs and gyms. One day I would visit the Budokwai, another day I'd be at Renshuden followed by the Judokwai, and of course Tuesdays and Thursdays I'd be at Dog Kennel Hill. At the Budokwai, I think I mentioned before that Trevor Leggett had a special Sunday class which he only invited certain players to join. He invited me and I didn't need to think twice about accepting. This presented more opportunities and exposure.

As for Japan, I kept in touch with two people, Bill and Nobuko, by letter. They both said they fully expected to see me in October 1964 for the Olympics which provided me with extra focus. I didn't want to let them down or my family. I still missed Japan and in a way, I think this might have helped with my judo as it provided me with the focus that I needed to blot out Japan. Although I must admit I always felt excited when I received letters from Nobuko.

As we moved through 1964 the judo world buzzed as it never had before with everybody speaking about the historic event that would be taking place in October. Having spent time in Japan people asked me questions about the country which I sometimes struggled to answer. I didn't want to talk about it. I loved the country. I'd created my own history there. But I had to remain focused and try and blot out everything around me. I knew how hard those Japanese players were training and I used this memory as a motivation dynamic to work harder.

However, Dad and a few others expressed concerns about the organisational process for Great Britain's judo team. We had three different associations and Dad worried about the communication links between them as they hadn't had the best relationships in the past. In fact, I think they basically ignored each other. But with an event as important as the Olympic Games they had to find a way to put a united team together for the benefit of Great Britain. Egos, if there were any, needed to be kept out of this. The associations were the British Judo Association (BJA), the British Judo Council (BJC) and the Amateur Judo Association (AJA). They'd never spoken in the past and they had this 'them and us' attitude. As each month passed this continued and Dad said if they didn't sort something out quick Great Britain wouldn't have a judo team in the Tokyo Olympics. A few others must have expressed their concerns as word reached the government who stepped in and issued instructions related to how everything should work. Each association had to submit eighteen players for an Olympic trial. This meant six lightweights, six middleweights and six heavyweights.

23

DESPITE THE EXCITEMENT of the forthcoming Olympic trials, and obviously the games, the European judo world had to put the Olympics on the back burner for a few days to focus on the fourteenth European Championships to be held in East Berlin, East Germany during the weekend of the 24th to 26th of April 1964.

At the beginning of April that year the following people received letters from the BJA informing them they'd been selected to represent Great Britain in East Berlin. Heavyweights Tony Sweeney, Tony Macconnell and Doug Young. Middleweights George Kerr, Jimmy McWade, and John Bowen. Lightweights John Jenkins and Norman Hayes. George would be team captain with John Newman acting as team manager. Oh and I almost forgot one more lightweight. Brian Jacks. I remember being in my bedroom when Mum shouted out that a letter had arrived from BJA and did I want her to open it. Now I knew that the Europeans were on the horizon, but so were the Olympic trials, which meant quite a few letters were flying around at that time. Anyway, I ran downstairs, grabbed the letter out of Mum's hands, and opened it. The Olympics didn't get a mention, which didn't really bother me, as I'd been selected for Great Britain's team for East Berlin.

At sixteen years and 177 days, I think this might have made me the youngest person ever to be selected for Great Britain in a European championship. I looked at Mum, she looked at me, and I read the letter out loud before I passed it to her. She couldn't believe it although she'd known that I'd been working very hard under Dad's expert guidance. We were both so excited and we hugged. Dad had already left for work and I knew, with this being a Tuesday, I would have to share this news with him later at Dog Kennel Hill. That night, with my letter safely tucked in my tracksuit pocket on top of my plastic wetsuit, I made the usual run with a kind of spring in my step that I'd not noticed before if that's possible in bovver boots. In fact, the usual pain of the run didn't hit me and I could have been running on air. I think might have even set a world record that night for my run.

Later Dad found me in the changing room and he saw the letter, now a bit screwed up and stained with sweat, on the bench next to where I sat. He looked at me and I looked at him. I said go on Dad read it.' He didn't have to. He knew the European letters were due out and he could see in my face exactly what it said. I gave him a sweaty hug as he congratulated me and said that the hard work had only just begun. And indeed training for Tokyo remained in full swing for the rest of that week and the next two as Dad still had concerns about my weight and we needed to make sure I kept this under control. But the week beginning Monday the 20th of April Dad revised my schedule. He knew the Europeans were a massive step for me and he didn't want me leaving everything I had on the training ground. He wanted me to have plenty in my tank for the weekend as I would be taking part in the juniors and the seniors. I felt excited about this, as well as nervous, and also extremely fit. With my shackles off, by that I mean my wrist weights, heavy boots, and being allowed to use my favourite techniques, I knew I had a big chance in the juniors. For the seniors, I would be competing against people a lot older than me and much more experienced. Dad and I had one of our meetings about this, in our usual place, and he basically believed my raw talent could expose some seasoned players that I might come up against.

Thursday morning, after a fairly decent sleep, I met up with the rest of the squad and officials at Heathrow Airport for the first leg of our journey to Orly on the outskirts of Paris. Despite being the youngest I didn't feel out of place. I felt I belonged and everybody treated me that way.

During our flights, first to Orly and then on to East Germany, I sat next to Tony Macconnell, seven years my senior, and he kept me at ease with a few jokes. We also had a good chat about nerves and he mentioned that nerves were important and a good way to channel energy. I'm not sure if Tony had been assigned to sit with me, or if he did so of his own back, but I appreciated his support and we got on very well.

I found East Berlin's Tegel airport a stark contrast from London's Heathrow and Paris's Orly. Heathrow and Orly were full of people who moved about freely and seemingly with no cares in the world. But not too many people were around at Tegel and most of those that were dressed in uniforms with guns. Fierce looking barking dogs strained from leads as we walked across the airport to a coach waiting for us. I somehow ended up at the back of our party which meant I had to sit at the front of the coach as all other seats were taken. But before we left three armed guards boarded for their inspection. The first two walked up and down the coach whilst the third one stayed on the bottom step, with her gun that pointed right in my face. My mind flashed back to sat on the bank at school and sat on the plane to Japan. Unique life experiences for me and now I had a third to add to that list. When they were happy they left the coach and we were on our way.

From the airport to our hotel my first impressions of East Berlin were that everything looked grey. Our journey to the centre of East Berlin included a drive down Karl Marx Allee. A socialist boulevard built between 1952 and 1960. Although quite impressive it, like everything else, looked grey. We stayed at a hotel called the Berolina, at that time the finest hotel in the east, and which had only been open a few days. I shared a room with Welshman John Jenkins.

Despite my negative first impressions, East Berlin had everything organised with military precision. Thursday night we relaxed and enjoyed a very nice dinner at the hotel. Not just our squad. I think all the competitors from all the visiting countries must have been staying at the Berolina. To me, this felt like a who's who of European judo and it fascinated me as I kept spotting famous players. I even had a moment in the elevator that left me lost for words. I wanted to speak but my voice seemed to have stopped working. Me, lost for words, I know what you're thinking but that is exactly what happened as I travelled down, alone, and it stopped on the fourth floor to let someone else in. Well not just anyone, Anton Geesink of all people, joined me for the remainder of the journey. He looked down at me and said good evening. I looked up at him totally speechless. I wanted to ask for his autograph and I wanted to speak about judo.

But nothing happened. He just seemed to fill the elevator and I felt like a small boy.

Antonius Johannes 'Anton' Geesink, born in April 1934, came from Utrecht in Holland. At six feet six inches tall, and two hundred and sixty pounds, he almost completely filled the small elevator. Anton had also been the main man in European judo for about the last ten years. He'd totally dominated the heavyweight and open divisions taking golds at nearly every European championship he'd entered. Other heavyweights never stood a chance and neither did I as the elevator shuddered to a halt on the ground floor. I looked up at him as he looked down at me. I gestured for him to go first and he did. I kicked myself as he lumbered off in one direction and me in another. I'd met quite a few judo stars before, both in England and Japan, and I couldn't understand why I'd been so star struck by him. Later, when I thought about it I realised that our meeting place had completely thrown me. Had we met in normal judo surroundings I'm sure I could have handled the situation far better.

Friday all the players had to weigh-in. I made my weight but hung around to watch other junior middleweights, and senior lightweights, to see how they handled themselves on the scales. I had this idea, which I'd spoken about with

Dad, about the weigh-ins. I believed they could provide me with valuable information about my potential opposition. I hadn't nailed down this theory yet. It was just a kind of gut feeling but I made a few mental notes about how they looked. Were they nervous? Were they confident? Or did they seem relieved they'd made their weight? Later I knew I'd have to discuss this with Dad again to work out how we could process this information to my advantage.

Whilst the British team enjoyed a relatively a smooth journey and entry into East Germany, another team were also on their way to the championships, and they'd decided on a different kind of route that didn't include planes. Dressed in smart suits Uncle Bobby, Uncle Lenny and Uncle Harry all travelled with Dad in his London taxi. They took a ferry across to France and drove to Holland where they stayed the night. The following day their journey should have taken them through West Germany to the Berlin Wall. I say should as they didn't really have a clue where they were going and they took a few wrong turnings. Strange really as they were all taxi drivers!

Eventually, six hours later than anticipated, they reached Checkpoint Charlie where another problem soon became apparent. Uncle Bobby couldn't find his passport.

They all searched the car but had no luck. They realised that Uncle Bobby must have lost it in Holland which meant they were now stuck and they needed a plan. In the back of the car, Dad had a jacket with a union jack on which Uncle Bobby put on. Dad then spoke to the guards and explained that Uncle Bobby was part of the British Judo squad who had to compete in the competition. Somehow that worked and they were let into East Germany. Obviously, I knew they were on their way and Dad had called me to mention that they might be delayed.

During Friday's lunch, I mentioned this to John Bowen and Tony Macconnell and Mac picked up on it as he cut his meat. He said: 'Brian, look at my meat. It's got bullet holes in it,' and then he went on about how Dad and my uncles must have been having an argument at the border about who got the tip. This continued for a while and a few others joined in with a few more jokes at my expense. The typical kind of fun joking you get when a team of blokes is together for a game or competition.

24

SATURDAY MORNING OUR team coach, with our usual armed guards, ferried us to the Werner-Seelenbinder-Halle sporting arena located in the Prenzlauer Berg district of

East Berlin. This stadium, opened in 1950, had been named after West German's wrestling champion Werner Seelenbinder. Seelenbinder had a strong interest in Marxism which enabled him to compete in Moscow competitions in 1928 and 1929. Unlike over 200 other West Germans who were banned from these events. After his first trip to Moscow he became a member of the Communist Party of West Germany and in 1933 he refused to give the Nazi salute when receiving his medal at the West German Wrestling Championships. This upset the Nazis and he received a ban him for sixteen months. Obviously, this created a bit of a rift between Seelenbinder and the Nazis but he found a way to continue and train. He also carried his message across West Germany and as one of his country's top sportsmen people listened. This upset the Nazi's even more.

As the 'Nazi' 1936 summer Olympic Games approached two things came to a head. Seelenbinder wanted to boycott the games but his friends persuaded him to compete as they wanted him on the winners' rostrum without giving the required Nazi salute. In turn, the Nazis were concerned that he wouldn't give the required salute should he make the rostrum. The Nazis were torn as they needed him to compete as they wanted a West German medal in this event. He finished fourth, keeping him off the rostrum, which avoided a potentially embarrassing moment for Adolf Hitler. But the rumblings of discontent continued until the 4th of February 1942 when he was arrested and life then became pretty bleak for Seelenbinder. The Nazis tortured him for eight days and prison camps followed. During the next two and a half years he spent time in nine prison camps before receiving a death sentence death for treason. Below is the farewell letter that he wrote to his father.

'The time has now come for me to say goodbye. In the time of my imprisonment, I must have gone through every type of torture a man can possibly endure. Ill health and physical and mental agony, I have been spared nothing. I would have liked to have experienced the delights and comforts of life, which I now appreciate twice as much, with you all, with my friends and fellow sportsmen, after the war. The times I had with you were great, and I lived on them during my incarceration and wished back that wonderful time. Sadly fate has now decided differently after a long time of suffering. But I know that I have found a place in all your hearts and in the hearts of many sports followers. A place where I will always hold my ground. This knowledge makes me proud and strong and will not let me be weak in the last moments.'

Obviously, when I heard about this it put my own experiences in Japan more into perspective. I hadn't suffered anywhere near the same torture as Seelenbinder had. Yes, at that time as a young fifteen year old, I'd shed some tears and believed that I'd entered some kind of torture chamber. But torture is a big word and often misused. For real torture read the letter again. I knew, and Dad always told me, that there were always people far worse off than me.

We arrived at the stadium at around 10:00 a.m. and it felt great to finally be there. As our team coach pulled up to the players' entrance there were crowds waving and I saw a few British flags. I waved back, unsure if any of them had any idea who I was until I spotted a group of four men all immaculately dressed in hats, suits, and ties. My family who'd booked into a small bed and breakfast close to our hotel. As I stepped from the coach I stopped for a second to listen to the cheers and applause from the British supporters. I felt proud for them having made the journey to support our team. Very soon I knew I would be taking part in the sport I loved for my country. I suppose that's the pinnacle for any individual. But those fans were there because they loved judo and they'd given up their time, spent money and probably lost money they could have earned. This definitely applied to my family. I think fans who support their country, at home and overseas, are amazing individuals as long as they don't travel with intentions to cause trouble. We, as athletes, sometimes receive medals. Fans, as fans, receive nothing. So it's up to the individuals, or teams, taking part in any kind of competition to always give the fans their money's worth. For me, I hadn't really realised this until that moment I stepped off that coach. But I knew, right there and then, that I had to do my best for them.

Inside the stadium, we still had some time to kill before the opening ceremony so I walked around the arena with John and Tony. Close to seven thousand fans had already gathered and a cold chill went down my back as I saw them for the first time. I knew I would be performing soon and that a capacity crowd of ten thousand would be watching. Strangely I didn't feel any nerves or shy. Instead, I felt strong and confident. I'd survived Japan's lion's den experiences. Here I knew my opponents would be tough but I didn't expect them to be stronger than Japan's players. As I soaked up the electric stadium atmosphere I felt up for this. As we walked I heard a well-known voice shout. 'Hey, Brian. We're up here my son.' I knew the voice belonged to Uncle Harry and I soon traced my family in the tenth row of the tiers that rose to the roof of the building. All four stood and waved as did a few other British fans as they recognised

John, Tony and some other team members who followed us. I knew when I competed I would be alone on the mat but to have my family so close meant so much. They provided me with extra strength and belief in myself. I knew I couldn't let them down.

After all the waiting my time had arrived at last. We were down to the business end of the show. Well, my show at least and the beginning of the junior middleweight event. The first time Great Britain had ever had an entry in this championship. I suppose I had a lot weighing on my shoulders but I never gave it a moment's thought as the eliminations for the juniors commenced. All three weight categories, light, middle and heavy, started at the same time with the middleweights assigned to the centre mat. In the first round, I fought Gunter Dobrauz from Austria. I soon realised that I had the upper hand on this stocky little Austrian but I couldn't manage a score. I'm not sure why but it just didn't happen for me in this fight although I won with a decision.

Next up I had to fight Phillipe Baudin of France who'd decisively beaten his previous opponent from Holland with a clean throw. Baudin came at me, obviously looking for the same kind of throw that he used in the previous round, but I'd seen this and I knew he'd be looking for it. I soon found my rhythm and I felt confident at the halfway stage. Then I saw an opportunity and went in for an attack but somehow I ended up down on the mat and Baudin saw his chance. He followed me down for a hold. At one point I'm sure he thought he had me, as did a few of the crowd when the referee's hand went up to signal a full point. But everyone soon found out who'd been victorious as the referee rolled the unconscious Baudin off my body. I had strangled him from underneath. This put me in the final and I couldn't wait to get this on. I looked up at Dad and he gave me the thumbs up. He tried to come down to mat level but armed guards wouldn't have any of that which meant we had to communicate with hand signals, facial expressions and a few words that I could just about hear above all the other stadium noise.

In the final, I came up against Vanantko of Czechoslovakia who'd had a good day and beaten East Germany's well-fancied Hilmar Wolfe. I knew I had to be careful at the start as I didn't want to try anything stupid. We were both looking for our favourite holds and I tried an attack that took us both off the mat. I tried more and he defended. I knew, as contest go, this hadn't been the most exciting and might have left the crowd disappointed. But the referee raised his hand in my direction to confirm I'd won the gold medal. I punched the air as a few of my teammates rushed over to congratulate me. Most of the crowd politely applauded apart from one small section in tier ten. They didn't applaud instead they went slightly bonkers. It was a kind of bizarre spectacle in the middle of the slightly reserved and mostly East German crowd. The guards, who might not have been trained in the art of how to deal with spontaneous outbursts of excitement from East Enders, looked on curiously. But I didn't care and neither did my family. I'd become middleweight junior champion of Europe and I wanted to shout it from the rooftops.

The medal presentation followed thirty minutes later and I waited in anticipation with Tony, John, and George, for my name to be called. The whole stadium went quiet as the East German announcer said. 'And the European junior middleweight gold medal winner Brian Jacks of Great Britain.' Tony pushed me forward and a great cheer erupted from tier ten. Pumped up I made my way to the number one spot on the rostrum with a huge smile on my face. I felt so good up there, so at home, I'd found my place and I wanted more of this. An official approached, shook my hand, and I bowed my head as he placed the gold medal around my neck. I stood straight as the East German police band began to play God Save Our Gracious Queen. I held my head up and watched the union jack flag as it climbed up the flagpole. As it did a tear escaped from my left eye and slowly rolled down my cheek. I looked in the direction of tier ten where my family sang. A chill went down my spine, what a moment, I felt so incredibly proud. Coming down off the rostrum my teammates congratulated me. They even grabbed hold of me and threw me in the air. Team manager John Newman shook my hand and commented that I had made my country proud. I looked up again at tier ten again and eight thumbs up were pointed in my direction. I knew they were proud as were the rest of my family in England.

Despite my victory, which bought some joy to the British spectators, team GB didn't have a good day. Prior to me taking gold we'd gone out at the first stage in the team event. This kind of took the shine off my day although inside I felt absolutely elated.

25

AT THE END of the day one we had to follow the strict rules laid down by our East German hosts. This meant a quick shower and then on board our team coach for the journey back to our hotel. There we had a late dinner before we slept. I really wanted to see Dad and let him hold my medal but he couldn't get near me in the arena. We did, however, manage a couple of minutes outside where I'd seen him earlier that day. We had a quick chat and I gave Dad my medal to inspect. I even said he could take it with him but he placed it around my neck and told me to savour the moment.

Day two and my pursuit for a second gold medal this time in the senior lightweights. In front of a packed house, with Dad and my Uncles now in front row seats thanks to my gold medal winning performance, I faced Zdravko Barsnik of Yugoslavia. He'd been the most outstanding lightweight in his country for the past five years but I managed to win with a choke technique. Armand Bourreau of France came next. The brother of Andre the great French lightweight. I knew he didn't have his brother's class and I got the decision. This put me in the semi-final against Karl Reisinger the Austrian lightweight champion twice in the last five years and ten years my senior. I went at it big time, caused him a few problems, and he couldn't mount any kind of attack. I think he thought he'd caught me a couple of times but I mixed things up with different holds and techniques that upset him. I felt strong and on top. After four minutes we went to ground. I had him in a stranglehold with my legs around his throat. Another technique picked up from groundwork master Ted Mossom. I tried to apply more pressure. I knew I had him. I could feel him about to choke. Soon the contest would be over and I'd be in my second final. Then for some bizarre reason, the referee called a break. I had to let him go. But he couldn't get up and he just sat on the mat with his head buried in his hands. I thought I'd won. I thought I'd made it to another final and I wanted to punch the air. The referee went over to him and he complained that I'd struck him below the belt. I couldn't believe it. How could I have done that when I had my legs around his neck squeezing the life out of him? Unfortunately, the referee bought into it and gave him two minutes to recover his breath that I'd just squeezed out of him. We got going again and close to the end he knocked me down. Not for a score but it must have stuck in the judges' minds as he got the decision. I felt sick. I nearly had him but the referee saved him and the judges seemed to forget all my good early work.

This put Reisinger in the final where he met Russia's Aaron Bogolyubov. Reisinger didn't stand a chance and Bogolyubov won with a straight arm lock. So Bogolyubov, eight years my senior, took the gold with Reisinger taking the silver. I along with Lesturgeon of France had to be content with bronze. As much as it hurt, listening to Russia's national anthem and watching the Russian flag being raised, I knew I had time on my side. The other three were in the prime of their careers or past it. They knew especially Reisinger who had a taste of me close up, that a new kid had arrived on the European block and they would have to watch their backs. At the end of the medal ceremony, when I shook their hands, I looked deep into their eyes. I wanted to convey a message that I'd arrived. I'm pretty sure Reisinger and Lesturgeon got it. As for Bogolyubov I would have to wait and see.

That night we had a party at the hotel and this gave everybody a chance to let their hair down and have a few drinks. Dad and all my uncles were there as they managed to convince the East German guards they were Team GB officials. It felt great to have them around and at one point I even managed to have a sensible conversation with the great Anton Geesink. He congratulated me on my gold medal and complimented me on my performance against Reisinger. He also mentioned that I should have got the decision. The following morning, wearing my medals, I boarded our team coach to begin our journey home. Our guards, who'd been with us every step of the way, made sure we made it to our plane safely. As I left the coach, the pretty guard who'd had her gun in my face that first day, nodded and smiled for the first time.

Later I spoke with Dad about my medals and how I felt. Obviously, I felt proud about winning the juniors especially as this meant, at my age, I would have the chance to defend my title for a few years. For the bronze, it didn't feel the same. Yes, I'd entered the seniors as a complete European championship novice, competed with men who were a lot older than me, and who'd been around the block and back again. So strictly speaking I should have been happy but I didn't feel good about it. I wanted to win and I didn't care about ages or reputations. Deep down I also really felt I'd beaten Reisinger and that the judges may have been swayed to give it to him as he had ten years on me. So, for this reason, I didn't really want the bronze or advertise that I'd won it.

Dad listened and nodded. He said that the judo world revolved around a special group of people who were all extremely dedicated and proud of what they did. We were a club, with unique skills, which put us on a different level to many other people. We'd learned and mastered these mysterious talents which we knew would always help us if we needed to defend ourselves. At the same time, we'd also learned about self-discipline and control. For my medals, Dad believed they were important and something to share with the rest of my family. As for the rest of Great Britain, and even the world, Dad knew that I'd made the sports pages of a few newspapers but he said today's papers would be used the following day to wrap fish and chips. I'd been there. I'd done it. People had watched. Some people had written about it which meant more people would read about it. But it was history. The moment I stepped off those rostrums meant a job had been done or partially done in terms of the bronze, and what happened next had far more importance.

Dad also discussed how judo slotted into the Great British sporting ladder in relation to other sports. He explained, even though I had a good idea already, that judo hadn't even made the first rung and that it might take a long time before it did. Judo just hadn't yet captured the imagination of the Great British public although we both felt that being part of the Olympic Games in a few months' time might generate more interest. But judo, with all its technical and sometimes hard to understand techniques, didn't put bums on seats in the way that other sports did. We also discussed my position, which on paper meant I'd climbed to the dizzy heights of joint third in Europe, and as much as it felt good being there we knew I had a lot more work to do. There were a lot of very good British and European players out there who'd missed East Berlin for one reason or another. I knew in my weight category of a few British players who would never accept that they were inferior to me. My Olympic plan had to remain firmly on track as another round of BJA preliminary Olympic Trials were scheduled for the 5th of July at Aldershot.

After arriving back in England late Monday night Dad did give me Tuesday off! But by Thursday we were back in full swing and I felt in fine shape for Aldershot's trials and managed to make the final selection of six from the BJA for the full Olympic lightweight trial scheduled for the 25th of July. The other five were John Bowen, Tony Orton, Jimmy Rudden, John Trick, and Dennis Watson.

I think I feared John B and Tony most from those five and I'd trained with them many times at the Budokwai. John B had dropped down from middleweight and I knew he would be a major rival for me. He had more strength and he performed fluid and consistent judo. He'd been Team GB's

Mr. Reliable for many years, apart from the recent championships in East Berlin where he'd performed well below his usual standards. We called Tony the 'Wing Commander' and he must have had some military upbringing in his background as he spoke very well, some might say he sounded posh, and he always dressed immaculately. He performed his judo in the same manner. He always stood bolt upright which made it very difficult for anyone to get a grip on him. Although after the sessions we had together, I knew if I met him, I had to get him moving around the mat fast and pull him out of his comfort zone.

John Jenkins made first reserve and when you consider that he'd actually been part of the Team GB in East Berlin you get a better understanding about the lack of talent that we actually had available for that competition. In addition to those five, I had another twelve opponents to contend with from the other two associations. All the players in the BJA squad were older and more experienced than me and I expected the other associations to also select older and more experienced players as well. That meant seventeen players, all fighting for one slot, with me the youngest and possibly least experienced in competition judo. Dad said I'd done well to make the final trial but this didn't mean anything unless I won the blooming thing. With this in mind, we remained on full steam ahead until three days before the trial. Then, as we had before the Europeans, we eased off to make sure I had a full tank for the weekend.

26

CRYSTAL PALACE'S NATIONAL RECREATION Centre, 25TH OF July 1964, had a special and unique feel about it. For the first time in British judo history, a group of fifty-four British players gathered to contest four Olympic Games spots.

Weight segregation had actually caused quite a stir in the judo world and really went against judo traditions set up by founder Jigoro Kano. Kano had always envisaged that anyone could fight anyone no matter how big or small they were or how much they weighed. In one corner people wanted to stick with Kano's principals whilst in the other, an argument raged that this wouldn't work on the Olympic stage. This group believed that many contests would be drawn which wouldn't create a great spectacle for people watching judo for the first time. They wanted action-packed contests that would excite Olympic crowds and viewers watching on television all over the world. This meant good news as I knew I wouldn't have stood any kind of chance in an open competition at that time. There were those who believed the Japanese had caved in to favour weight classes for another reason in the shape of Anton Geesink. In 1961 he dominated the World Championships and put the fear of God into the Japanese. They knew, if they just went with an open class Olympic event, that the great Geesink would be a strong favourite to win it. With Japan, being the spiritual home of judo, it would be unthinkable for them in their country not to win a title. With this in mind, they went with the European standard weight categories. Lightweight sixty-eight kilos, middleweight eighty and heavyweight eighty plus. Britain, France, and Belgium pushed for an open class and this became the fourth category.

Another question needed to be addressed and this focused on professionalism as the Olympics were all about following the amateur code. Some players had made money teaching the sport and this went against the policy. Geesink found himself in a bit of bother as he'd taught judo in France. The Dutch Olympic committee even stopped him competing in the 1960 Olympics when he tried to be part of the Dutch wrestling team. Obviously, a few Japanese administrators picked up on this and tried to ban him from Tokyo. They were unsuccessful. However Britain's George Kerr had received money from training and Charles Palmer, Chairman of the selection committee and Kerr's mentor a few years before, made sure Kerr didn't have a chance of making the Tokyo plane. I believed Kerr should have been part of our team and he didn't take very kindly to Palmer robbing him of his opportunity to compete. Kerr had spent three years in Japan and would have been a huge asset to us. But in Japanese culture, they have this big thing about revenge and I'm sure Kerr would have had this on his mind from the moment he heard his bad news. Time would tell if Kerr received his full revenge quota.

Dad took us there in his taxi and it felt like a bit of a day out as Mum, Barbara and Shayne all came to watch. We arrived early and Crystal Palace had a real buzz about it with people running everywhere trying to make sure that they had everything in place for the start of the first contest. In fact, it looked a bit frantic at times as people carried in chairs, tables, blackboards, gongs and all the other paraphernalia required to run and manage an event like this.

I spent a good twenty minutes having a tactical chat with Dad about my opponents although we knew that John B had already pulled out due to illness. We'd heard a rumour that he'd been taken ill at work on Thursday and that this could have been related to his extreme dieting. He later confirmed this and that his blood values were all screwed up. He worked as a lab assistant at the Royal Marsden Hospital and he'd received diet advice from an American research doctor. Working there meant he was in the right place at the right time to receive treatment to sort him out but it came too late to enable him to compete. Bad news for him but good news for me as I think he stood at the top of the lightweight rankings after all the Olympic pre-trials. Good news as well for John Jenkins who replaced him. This just left me with 'Wing Commander' Tony to worry about although Dad did say to be wary of my opponents from the other associations as some of these I'd never met before. After East Berlin, I think all my opponents had now heard of me and they would have liked nothing better than to knock me off of my pedestal.

As temperatures soared outside the stadium inside the tension intensified as we neared the start of the first contests. By 10:00 a.m. with the weigh-in, conducted by Captain Lilley, completed we were getting closer. In the crowd, and it didn't look like we were getting a full house, I'd already spotted Mum and quite a few other members of my family. They'd even made a sign that said 'Come on Brian.' Despite the wrangling between the three associations they'd pulled together on the day and created a superb venue for this spectacle of British judo. The mat areas looked excellent and gave the spectators a superb opportunity to witness the best that British judo had to offer.

In the lightweights, I came up against Ben Reed. Ben had caused quite a stir by turning out for the AJA as he'd been a member of the BJA for many years. He only recently switched associations after he'd failed to make the BJA cut at the Aldershot trials. He, like me, had spent time in Japan and he had only just returned to take part in the trials. He'd failed and I'm not sure why, or how, he managed to weasel his way back into contention. The other association must have known about his history and there were a few rumours floating about related to under the table payments. He must have been ten years older than me with a lot of contest experience. But Dad gave me a full rundown on him and I managed to get in quick with a good attack. He came back at me and had me in a bit of trouble on the ground. I escaped with an adrenalin rush and be honest with you I knew in my heart I could take him. The longer the fight lasted the stronger I felt. I could also hear Dad's voice in the crowd telling me to keep going and stay in control. Amazing really as quite a few other people were shouting and cheering. But somehow I could hear Dad's voice on top of everything. I took the fight to him and I knew he was desperate as he dug his heels in as much as he could. We went the distance and I got the decision. His backdoor plan had failed although I think he'd suffered in the same way I had when I came back from Japan. He had good technique but he lacked the right amount of strength.

After my contest, I had another long tactical discussion with Dad, mostly about the 'Wing Commander,' who'd only been on the mat for about thirty seconds, as he'd won his contests so quickly, and he looked in tip-top form. We discussed his strengths and weaknesses that we knew about from training at the Budokwai. So far he hadn't shown any flaws at Crystal Palace. We also knew that he knew my style very well and Dad encouraged me to mix things up a bit and try different techniques should I meet him later which is how things panned out. We would contest the final but I had to win as he'd accumulated more points. A draw would have been enough for him.

Dad and I had another five minute chat and he urged me to dig deep inside myself and drag out every ounce of energy I had left. Then, when I'd dragged that out, I had to go back in and get more. He talked about my runs to Dog Kennel Hill and why I'd done them. He said the 'Wing Commander' had made me do this, not him, and when I looked in the 'Wing Commander's' eyes he urged me to think about those runs that he'd made me run and take out all my pain on him. Payback time had arrived and I needed to make the most of it.

Just before the start, I heard Mum shout out 'Come on Brian' and I knew I'd come to the fight of my life. Winning meant the ultimate prize and a place in Team GB for Tokyo. Defeat would be the end of the world for me. The crowd knew the importance of this contest and he had his fans and I had mine. Before the start, I looked into his eyes and thought about the pain he'd inflicted on me by making me make those runs. I felt focused and ready. He must have done as well as one minute I thought I had him and the next minute I'm sure he felt he had me. In amongst the noise of the crowd, I could still distinctly hear Dad's voice and I knew that after about ten minutes he had the upper hand. I had to find something from somewhere to put this one to bed. As the clock, ticked on past the eleventh minute, that time had arrived for me to draw on all the resources that I had within me. Somehow I found the strength that I needed to throw him with a body drop which resulted in a full point. I'd won my place on the plane to Tokyo. That was what I thought.

I went to greet my family and had a hug with everybody. Mum, in tears, found it hard to talk. I asked her what was wrong and she said her tears were for the joy of me winning and the sadness of Tony. I couldn't really work that one out but she managed to say that she felt sad for him as he'd fought so well. Dad just smiled as did a few other members of my family who'd heard the exchange. Even though I'd won, which meant I should be part of Team GB for Tokyo, there seemed to be some kind of doubt in the selectors' minds. We'd all expected an announcement that day but it didn't happen and think my winning performance had thrown them. They left Crystal Palace after an announcement that they'd be meeting on Monday to confirm the British team. This left me in a bit of a quandary although Dad told me not to worry as the rules were clear. Who wins goes and that meant me.

On Monday the selected players were announced. Open Weight Alan Petherbridge fourth Dan. Heavyweight Tony Sweeney fourth Dan. Middleweight Syd Hoare fourth Dan and lightweight Brain Jacks first Dan. Alan would be the team captain and tentative plans were that we would fly to Japan towards the end of September although the judo contests were not scheduled to start until the 20th of October.

27

WITH MY EXCEPTION I think the selectors were well pleased with the way everything turned out at Crystal Palace. Tony and Syd were probably the best in their respective weights and Alan had also done enough to warrant his place in the open. This pleased a lot of people as Peth, as everybody called him, had been around a long time and deserved to be part of this tremendous occasion. I hadn't known him long but I knew he had the respect of a lot of people. As for me, the selectors' hands were probably tied as the rules had been made although they might have spent Sunday looking for some kind of loophole which might have enabled them to exclude me. They might have wanted John B in as he'd been so reliable over the years. But I was in. That night I wrote two letters, one to Nobuko and one to Bill, where I explained my news and that I couldn't wait to get back to see them and Japan.

Peth, born in October 1927, came from Swansea in South Wales and this meant that by the time of his first contest in Tokyo he'd be thirty-eight and close to the end of his glittering judo career which had started in 1945. At that time he and a handful of friends were stationed at the British Army Spandau Barracks in West Berlin due to the end of

World War Two conditions that stipulated that allied forces had to be there for a period of time. They used Yukio Tani's book as a reference to learn about judo. In 1949, back in Great Britain, he joined the Swansea Judo Society and a year later the Budokwai in London. He became the first Welsh person ever to gain a first Dan and in 1955 he won the Goldberg-Vass Memorial Trophy at the Royal Albert Hall. The following year Great Britain selected Peth for the European Championships in Austria but unfortunately, the Hungarian revolution at that time meant that the Austrian event had to be cancelled. He did, however, create history by being part of three Great Britain sides that won three European Championships in a row between 1957 and 1959. In Rotterdam, in 1957, he took silver in the second Dan category and the following year in Barcelona he won bronze in the same class. In 1962, at the age of thirty-six, he won gold at the European Championships in Essen this time in the third Dan group. At that time this made him the oldest person ever to win a European gold.

I found Peth a great motivator and always ready to provide advice. Hardly surprising really when you consider he'd been doing that for many years with a succession of young and upcoming players in Wales. In 1957 he founded the Samurai Judo Club in Swansea and he'd played a big part in developing some fine judo talent in that area. People like John Jenkins, Johnny Trick, and Lyn Reece. Probably, with this in mind, we headed to South Wales for close to two months of intense training under Peth's supervision. I found seeing Peth, close up in his own backyard, quite an experience. Everybody seemed to know and respect him. It also soon became clear that quite a few people feared him. He, perhaps in the same manner as Trevor Leggett who Peth trained with, would never stand for any kind of nonsense. If you tried it, and he caught you, you would suffer from his iron right fist that he would use to dig into the side of a person's arm or leg. I often thought of him as 'Dead Leg Right Fist' as he knew exactly where to insert it to generate the most pain. And yes I personally experienced it.

Outside of judo, he managed Swansea's Townsman Night Club, which later became Baron's located on College Street. Again his iron right fist ruled the roost here and a few dead legs were occasionally seen limping into the Swansea night after being caught up to no good by Peth. I'm not sure if the BJA sanctioned our Swansea training camp or if Peth decided this himself with Syd and Tony. I think it might well have been the latter as Peth had witnessed the debacle in East Berlin. Dad knew Peth as well and I think he might have shared his ideas about team bonding even though in Tokyo there wouldn't be a team event. But Peth, just like Dad, must have believed in preparation and the old saying 'Fail to Prepare – Prepare to Fail.' I don't think any of us questioned the decision to train in Wales. I certainly didn't. Dad just said you're going to Wales to train with Peth and stay in his house. So I did. Tony and Syd seemed happy with this arrangement as well and we were joined by many of Peth's local boys to keep us on our toes.

South Wales, in common with Tokyo and Dog Kennel Hill, turned out to be a real nightmare again with some really tough sessions. If I hadn't experienced those other two I might not have been able to cope with this. Syd had also spent time in Japan so he knew what it was all about as well. But Peth was tough and he did everything we did and more. Outside we ran and we ran and we ran. We used to run from Swansea to Ammonford, about nine miles, every day. We also trained on Swansea's beach that stretched for five miles along Swansea Bay. We ran this as well and often in the soft sand that tested us even more. As did the sand dunes that Peth made us run up and down countless times. If he felt we were slacking he would make us do it again and again and again. But he did it as well. In the gym, we did a lot of fitness work and loads and loads of judo under the watchful eye of Peth. At that time Peth had the best squad of judo players in

Great Britain, in all weight categories, and for me being close up with him I fully understood why. He had a phenomenal work ethic and fantastic respect from all the people he coached. I felt privileged to be there

28

ON THE 6TH of August 1945 an atomic bomb dropped on the city of Hiroshima. That same day, in the same city, Yoshinori Sakai was born. Just over nineteen years later, on the 10th of October 1964, Sakai came running into the Tokyo Olympic stadium with the Olympic torch in his right hand. I stood in the centre of the sporting area with 5,151 athletes, 4,473 men, and 678 women. Plus each team had had a few officials. We'd already marched around the stadium following the flags of our countries. British swimmer Anita Lonsbrough, who won a gold medal in the two hundred metres breaststroke in the 1960 Rome Olympics, carried our flag. Just behind her came Kenneth Sandilands 'Sandy' Duncan MBE and General Secretary of the British Olympic Association. Then came our forty-four women followed by the 168 men competing for Team GB. I took my place in row six with the rest of the judo squad.

We arrived at the stadium about 10:00 a.m. and we had to wait around a long time before we entered. I think we marched in at around midday and the noise from the 80,000 spectators almost blew me away. We'd heard them cheering other teams but as we entered they seemed to turn it up a few notches. A chill went down my spine as I heard the thunderous roar. The biggest crowd I'd performed in front of before had been 10,000 so nothing in my life had really prepared me for this experience. The wall of noise knocked me sideways and we couldn't talk to each other as we couldn't hear ourselves speak. I felt so proud, like a gladiator, trapped in a bowl and surrounded by adoring fans. I felt prouder still as I knew Mum and Dad were in that crowd. I'd got them tickets so I knew roughly where they would be and it was great when I saw them standing and cheering. My thoughts went back to the bank. I'd come a long way since then, suffered some pain, but this made it all worthwhile. Even though I knew I wouldn't actually be performing in this stadium, with these fans, I savoured the moment and even felt a bit choked. I caught sight of Peth, the hard man from Swansea who'd been around the block a few times, and I could see the emotion in his eyes. Tokyo had gobsmacked me before and now it had done it again.

Olympic flags were raised followed by hundreds of balloons that slowly drifted up to the skyline. Then the huge crowd all rose as one as Sakai entered with his torch in his right hand. If the noise had been deafening before then you should have heard this racket. I think we all had shivers down our spines and the hairs on our arms stood right up. It was unbelievable. Totally unbelievable. Sakai completed one lap of the cinder track, with quite a few athletes breaking line to get close to urge him on before he jogged up the steps to the Olympic cauldron. I counted as he climbed each one with the torch still held high in his right hand. There must have been about seventy. He performed this task superbly without the slightest hint of a stutter. If he'd tripped, with all the eyes of the world on him, he might never have lived that down. At the top, he paused by the Olympic cauldron and smiled as he faced the crowd with his arms raised before he placed the torch inside and the magnificent Olympic flame came alive to signify the start of the eighteenth Olympiad. Hundreds of doves were released and up above us, in the clear blue sky, jets created vapor trails shaped like Olympic rings. Japan's Emperor Hirohito addressed the stadium and Japanese gymnast, Takashi Ono, who'd competed in the 1952, 1956 and 1960 Olympics, took the Olympic Oath.

Sakai, a four hundred metre runner who'd just failed to qualify for the Japanese team, had been selected for his role as Japan tried to signify a new era of peace and reconstruction in its history. These games, which Japan had spent more than £180 million on, marked Japan's re-entry into international society after two decades of shame and struggle caused by defeat in the war. They'd come in from the cold, spent a lot of money turning Tokyo into an A-list city, and in doing that Tokyo had now become the biggest city in the world with ten million people residing there. But for me personally, it marked the end of a Tokyo that I'd actually grown to love. The Tokyo I knew had a shyness, and maybe roughness about it, that I eventually fell in love with after overcoming a few hurdles that I've mentioned before. I'd even referred to Tokyo as a concrete jungle which might have been an unfair analogy as it was kind of wooden as well. But the place had changed. Japan had decided to come out of the shadows and rejoin the world stage in a big way. The roadside markets, with vendors shouting out 'yakitori,' had now been largely replaced by restaurants. Sure they sold the same thing but for me, it didn't have the right feel about it as it had before. Well, that's how it felt to me. Tokyo with the Olympic Games had become a different place. The infrastructure had changed. It had become more sophisticated, more upmarket, but I preferred the more 'rough and ready' model.

Another part of Tokyo, which had totally been transformed, turned out to be my old favourite the Meiji Army Base. The Americans had moved out and I moved in. Well not just me. Meiji had been converted into the Olympic Village so most of the participating athletes and officials were staying there. Plus an old friend dropped by whenever he felt like it.

The village had been split up into sectors for each country with a flag to show which country stayed where. We even had a village flag ceremony with Don Thompson, the British race walker and the only British man to win a gold medal in the 1960 Rome Olympics, doing the honours. As we arrived quite late we didn't really have time to do anything and we just went straight to bed. The following day, what with the opening ceremony, it meant we didn't have a lot of time to do anything apart from a quick trip to the Budokan Hall, the venue for the judo competition, located in the Chiyoda area of Tokyo, and inside the grounds of the Imperial Palace. A purpose built indoor martial arts arena for the 1964 Olympics that officially opened on the 3rd of October 1964. They'd splashed £2 million on it and it looked spectacular. But as I said we just had a quick look as we were quite exhausted by the ceremony and were suffering from jetlag.

Back at the Olympic Village, I felt eager to have a good look around and I left everyone in the house for an early evening walk. It felt quite nostalgic for me being back there and I just wanted to take some alone time to reminisce.

As I walked the memories came flooding back. I thought about the American soldiers, who used to be on parade, plus the PX store, the pawn shop, the casino and the places I used to eat with Bill. The Americans had now been replaced by athletes and the store and shops had given way to restaurants. It felt a bit sad but I knew things had to change sometimes to progress. I also felt totally amazed to see so many different people, from totally diverse backgrounds, all in one village. In some ways, it felt like a holiday camp for fit people. As I walked I noticed discotheques and restaurants that specialized in food from all corners of the world. Japanese, Chinese, Korean, English, French, Italian, Russian and the Middle East. Anything I wanted I could have and it didn't cost anything. I'd been very impressed with the East Berlin efficiency during the European Championships but this totally astounded me. They also had these giant chess games where you could sit outside and play. I selected a Japanese restaurant and enjoyed the local food for the first time in a long time.

The following day we had the competition draw and we all knew we had a chance of a medal as long as we avoided the Japanese. Peth, of course, had to avoid Geesink in the open.

Seventy-two players were in the draw, all men as women weren't allowed yet, from twenty-seven countries. The youngest, Park Cheong-Sam at seventeen years and 346 days, came from South Korea. The oldest, Orlando Madrigal at forty-three years and 223 days, came from Costa Rica. Preliminary rounds would last ten minutes with fifteen for the finals. A round-robin pool system had been approved with the winner from each pool moving into the knock out stages. I drew Nakatani, the Japanese favourite. Syd avoided Japan's Okano in the first round but if he won he would meet him in the second round. On paper, it looked as if Tony had the best chance of a medal as he wouldn't meet Japan's Inokuma until the final. For Peth to win a medal he just had to win a couple of contests as the open only attracted nine contestants. But he drew Geesink and Japan's Kaminaga in a group of death. We still had over a week to wait and we trained much as we could. Peth continued to lead us even though he knew, as did we, that his Olympic dream had probably ended before it had even started. But regardless of this, he continued to push himself very hard.

I mentioned before that an old friend seemed to have the run of the village. He came and went whenever he pleased in exactly the same way he had done a few years ago. Yes, of course, Bill Backhus joined the party even though his presence hadn't actually been officially requested. He invited himself and he made sure he had all the correct credentials. I think he passed himself off as America's official interpreter and the Japanese guards, who were very strict, let him in every time with no questions asked. We had dinner a few times and he updated me with his current business which had changed since we last met. With many of the American army bases now closed this put a serious dent in his income. To counter this he needed new ideas and he came up with a couple. He formed a new company called Orient Wide Investigators Incorporated. A private detective agency specialising in surveillance. Plus he also had another lucrative sideline as he acted as the go-between in the Japanese arranged marriage system. He again found the American army bases another gold mine. He preyed on raw homesick American country boys and promised them an end to their misery by finding them a nice respectable wife from a good Japanese family. I asked how he managed this and he winked. He said the girls were nice, but he'd found them on the streets, and that he had no idea about their families. They did, however, want to be a GI bride so they paid him as well which meant he took money from both sides. Bill being Bill thought nothing about double dipping He also mentioned that he found ways to smuggle money, watches, and jewellery.

Bill, as usual, seemed to be involved in all kinds of things that some might consider a shade of grey. Seeing Bill didn't present any problems but Nobuko would have to wait as I had to focus on the games. Mum and Dad also had to do their thing.

As we approached our big days we knew that the Japanese were firm favourites to win all the medals with the exception of the open. We did hear a few comments that they feared us more than anyone else. Michio Tagagati, a high ranking Japanese master, said that he considered Great Britain to be the biggest danger to Japan's hopes of winning medals. Tagagati, a ninth Dan, said we had some fine young black belts and many of us had trained in Japan. He also said we had a fine judo tradition that stretched back to 1920 and that out of all the Western countries competing he thought we posed the strongest threat with the exception of Geesink. This is what happened.

Middleweight, Wednesday the 21st of October. Syd Hoare. First up he met European champion Lionel Grossain from France and things were pretty even for four minutes before Grossain took control and won the contest. This meant to have a chance of staying in the competition he had to beat Jan Snijders of Holland. Syd began well and took an early advantage but he couldn't build on it. Snijders hit back and won the contest.

Heavyweight, Thursday the 22nd of October. Tony Sweeney. George Harris, from the United States, came first for Tony in a contest that lasted three minutes and twenty-five seconds. Tony tried a foot technique but Harris knocked him down with a body drop. As Tony raised himself Harris took him out with a dropping shoulder throw. He then met Parnaoz Chikviladze from Russia who took an advantage and got the decision.

Open weight, Friday the 23rd of October. Alan Petherbridge Against the great Dutchman Peth didn't last very long. Geesink scored with supporting foot lift-pull throw. Against Japan's formidable Akio Kaminaga he lasted a bit longer before Kaminaga scored with big inside sweep.

Syd, Tony, and Peth were all out at the first hurdle and they had to watch as their weight categories unfolded. In the middleweight, Japan's Isao Okano took gold when he beat Germany's Wolfgang Hofmann in the final. Germany, for these Olympics, had a unified team. In the heavyweight final Canadian Doug Rogers met Japan's Isao Inokuma. These two had trained together so they knew each other's styles which resulted in a fairly quiet contest. Inokuma won with a decision. In the open final, as expected, Geesink met Kaminaga and I watched this fight closely as did most of Japan. The older Japanese players looked on with pained expressions on their faces. They needed their man to win as this would have shown judo in its true form that Kano had envisaged. A much smaller man winning against a much bigger and heavier man. But Geesink had already beaten Kaminaga in the pool stages and the big Dutchman soon won again. He didn't really celebrate and he made sure his coaches didn't run on to the mat as well. He stepped back from Kaminaga, knelt down and adjusted his clothing. Kaminaga did the same before they approached each other and acknowledged each other in a true sportsmanlike way. At that time they were the best two players in the world and they showed great respect for each other. Geesink, who'd left me speechless in that elevator in East Germany, behaved like a real champion. By taking this medal he'd kind of upset our hosts as judo had been their game for many years. But he didn't rub it in and he behaved like a real gentleman. He took my respect for him to new levels.

As for me my big day actually came before the others as the lightweight event took place on Tuesday the 20th of October. The previous day, when I didn't train, I did manage to catch up with Mum and Dad for lunch. I think they were amazed again as I tucked into Japanese food. They hadn't yet acquired a taste for it. Obviously, I spoke with Dad about Nakatani who I knew from my time at the Kodokan. We'd even practiced together and he would have noticed me being thrown around the mats. I knew how strong he was but Dad told me not to worry about this as I'd gained a lot of strength since returning to England. He knew that I would be much more of a challenge for Nakatani and he mentioned that Nakatani saw me as his biggest threat. He left me with a thought about my runs to Dog Kennel Hill. At Crystal Palace, he'd said that Tony Orton made me do it. Now he said that I'd done it because of Nakatani and I had to make him pay. Dad's pep talk worked and I felt good although I knew there were many very good players in my category. Russia had two, Oleg Stepanov and Aron Bogolubov, France had Andre Bourreau and from Austria my old friend Karl Reisinger.

The night before I just wanted a quiet night at our house in the Olympic Village. I felt a bit tense and the other guys, who still had a few days to wait, tried to help me to relax. Peth mentioned that I'd be the first person ever from Great Britain to take part in an Olympic contest. I suppose I should have known this but I hadn't really given it that much thought. Now, with the countdown well and truly on, I did. Not only that Nakatani would be the first person from Japan as well. We would be making history for our countries and millions of people would be watching around the world. With this thought, I found it difficult to sleep and this could have been down to excitement and a touch of nerves. The next morning I didn't really take too much notice of what was happening. I opened some telegrams wishing me luck and tried to keep my focus. Peth and others there made a few comments as they continued to try and help me to relax. At about 11.30 a.m. we left on the team bus for the journey to the Budokan Hall. As we parked at the entrance a few people were milling around behind a security barrier and I searched for Dad. I found him and we had a quick Dad and son moment. I felt so proud and pleased for him. He'd put so much trust and faith in me for this moment. Of course, he'd made sacrifices as well. We both knew that. But at just eighteen years old I'd reached the top of my level and we, me and Dad, were about to take part in the Olympic Games. The ultimate competition that had decided to let judo in for the first time. I'd given my all for this moment and so had Dad. We'd started together, remember that drive to the LJS, and now we were about to compete at the very highest level. I say we because I never went on a mat without Dad, not literally of course, but I always felt his presence.

'Representing Great Britain Brian Jacks,' said the announcer and I made my way first to the mat. I received some polite applause and a few cheers from the crowd that must have totaled close to 15,000. I'd already spotted Mum and Dad and we'd waved. Nakatani soon joined me and the crowd went absolutely crazy. I'd never heard anything like this before at a judo competition. With Japan, being such a pro judo country, this must have been a moment they were waiting for and they loved it. I did as well. Of course, they all wanted him to win but I didn't care about that. I'd found a new stage, as I had at the Europeans, and I loved being on it. Some people might have bottled it but not me. The more they cheered the more I wanted to get moving and shut them up. After our formal greeting, we started and I felt so pumped up that I decided to go for it. I went straight for him although I couldn't really get a good hold. He did manage to get hold of my lapel and he knocked me down to the ground. He didn't score but he pinned me down to take the contest. Again the crowd went wild.

For my second contest, just under an hour later, I took on Thailand's Udom Rasmelungon. The same crowd who'd cheered Nakatani with frenzy now seemed to switch their allegiance to me. Perhaps they saw something in me that they liked although they were an intelligent crowd and might have known about my eighteen months spent in Japan. A few might have even met me when I played different characters during that stay. I felt quite sharp against the Thai boy and got him with a good throw.

Nakatani took gold when he beat Switzerland's Eric Haenni in the final.

Japan ended up three golds with only Geesink getting in their way of a clean sweep in the blue riband open class. Not really unexpected as Geesink had already destroyed the myth of Japanese invincibility. The crowds loved it and judo had made its mark on the Olympic stage although we knew that Mexico was against including judo in the 1968 Olympics. For us, the pools might well have played a part in our downfalls. Peth especially and a kinder draw might have meant him getting a medal which he deserved for the effort he'd put into judo. He really was the founder of Welsh judo.

Japan's Olympic Games were definitely a major success and celebrated the country's progress and return to the world stage. Japan had become a peaceful country, no longer a wartime enemy, and they'd achieved that in less than twenty years. They clearly demonstrated that they'd fully recovered from the war and how keen they were to promote sports. The Olympic Village had been a major success and many believed that the best food in Japan in 1964 had been served at the village. The village dining areas were all the rage and you could certainly sample the best cuisines from around the globe, all in one place.

Team GB ended with four golds. Mary Rand set a world record when she won the 800 metres. Ann Packer won the women's long jump and Lynn Davies did the same in the men's event. Ken Matthews took gold in the twenty kilometer walk. We came tenth in the medal table rankings with the USA at the top. The Russians came second and Japan managed third with sixteen golds. Their best performance ever in an Olympic Games. The USA, whose national anthem became so popular that many Japanese whistled it as they went about their work, finished up with thirty-six golds that included one for an unknown heavyweight boxer called Joe Frazier. Away from the games, when I'd been knocked out, I did manage to escape from the village a few times. I met Nobuko and we had a nice dinner one night in the Ginza. She'd now completed her education and had an office job. Sadly I think I might have been a bit premature in thinking that she might be the girl for me. We still had a good chemistry but we were more friends. The schoolboy crush I had on her hadn't stood the test of time or the miles that separated us. Although I would always be thankful to her for being there when I really needed someone. She helped me focus and provided comfort when I needed it most.

One night, outside the village with Bill, we had a discussion about souvenirs and memorabilia. At the time we were stood by one of the Olympic flag poles and I mentioned to him that an official Olympic flag might be a good souvenir to take home. He agreed and suggested I climb up the pole and helped myself. We were in a dark area, with no other people around, and he said he'd keep watch. I pulled myself up and started to unhook the flag. Bill, who'd talked me up the pole, had suddenly stopped speaking. I looked down and noticed that he'd been joined by two of Japan's finest. I immediately slid down and Bill quickly advised me not to speak any Japanese. I showed them my Olympic pass and I tried to explain that I belonged to the British team. They didn't believe me and they took me to the police station. For some reason they ignored Bill. At the station, they drilled me until I surprised them by speaking Japanese. This completely changed their attitude and they made a call to the Olympic Village. About twenty minutes later a rather shocked looking Sandy Duncan arrived and bailed me out. As I mentioned earlier Sandy had been around for a long time, participated in many Olympic Games, but I don't think he'd encountered a situation before where an athlete had tried to walk off with an Olympic flag. I explained that I just wanted a souvenir of the Olympics. Unfortunately, I didn't get it and he didn't seem too impressed. Back in the village, when word got out, I took a lot of stick. Especially from Peth.

For the games closing ceremony, the fanatical Japanese fans filled the stadium again and we had a party in a superb carnival atmosphere. Fencer Allan Jay carried our flag although this time we didn't have the same formalities of the opening ceremony. We linked arms, marched with other countries and basically had a good time with lots of dancing, waving of hats, flags, and arms. Some athletes, who'd probably won gold, were carried shoulder high by their teammates. We'd trained long and hard for this and now we had an opportunity to let our hair down. Highlights for me were the crowd all waving white hankies, the word 'SAYONARA' on the big screen, the Olympic flame slowly disappearing inside its cauldron and, 'WE MEET AGAIN IN MEXICO CITY 1968,' which also appeared on the big screen. But we still didn't know if Mexico City would include judo. Japan's friendship games were over.

That was it. All the years of pain and I think I managed about six minutes on the mat. For Peth, who'd trained a lot longer than I had, he'd managed about two minutes. Had it been worthwhile? Yes of course it had. We loved judo and we'd performed on the biggest stage in the world.

29

NOT ONLY DID 1964 prove a pivotal year for Japan it also proved a monumental year for me as I made the same kind of statement. Neither of us, that's Japan and me, had it easy. But Japan had made a supreme effort and spent a lot of money to lift itself out of the doldrums. As for me, I didn't have any money to spend and I didn't have any depression to climb out of. I'd just put in a major effort to reach the top four in Europe and possibly the top ten in the world. I'd found my place, I wanted to stay there, and I had a good chat with Dad about it which resulted in no changes to the programme in 1965. We had a formula and we decided not to tinker with it.

First up on the 13th of March, just after I'd achieved my second Dan, came the Junior European Championships at the Kurzaal. One of the main centres at the famous Scheveningen holiday resort on the Dutch coast adjoining The Hague. Previously the junior event had tagged onto the senior event. But this year the juniors became more official and at a different time. Our team often included heavyweight David Peake, light heavyweight Terrence Garrett, middleweights Anthony Sefton, Martin Peake, Robert Sullivan, and Brian Jacks. Light middle middleweights Lyn

Rees, Alan Green, and Alan Hunter and lightweight Alan Jones. We were managed by John Ryan.

In the first round I had a bye and then I beat Dutchman Arty Geurtsen who won the junior event in 1962. This took me through to the quarter-final where I met Krystyn Wojcik of Poland. I managed to get him in an arm lock and he submitted. In the semifinal, I beat Volker Ebener from West Germany. This meant that only Peter Grosser from Austria stood between me and my favourite position on the podium. Nothing, not even quite a bad cut on my head sustained when my head came into contact with Ebener's knee that needed to be clipped, would stop me. As we lined up I could see the fear in his eyes and I went straight at him. He, as I had been in Japan, became my rag doll. But fair play to him it took a while before he gave up and I got him with a one arm hip throw. Alan Green won gold in the light middleweights and David Peake did the same in the heavyweights.

Just over a month later we were on the road again for the European Senior Championships in Madrid, Spain which were held between the 22nd and 23rd of April. Alan Petherbridge managed us.

This time I'd been selected in the team event and we were up against France in the first round where I faced the great Andre Bourreau in the light middleweight category. In East Berlin, I'd beaten his brother, Armand, but I knew Dad had paid a lot of attention to Andre. As we faced up we didn't flinch. I knew he had a fantastic reputation but he'd seen me last year. He knew I'd beaten his brother and he might have seen this as a chance for some family revenge. Dad even mentioned this and our game plan meant going for it right from the start with no jousting. He must have had the same idea as he came straight in and he had me worried for about a minute. Then I tried a throw and he ended up in between my legs. He tried to get past this so he could use his great groundwork. But I didn't let him and I slid my right fingertips into the left lapel of his jacket. With my left hand, I gripped his jacket just under his right ear with my fingers on the outside of his lapel. Slowly he tried to get around to my legs, to his right side, a tactic Dad had warned me about and I knew he really had lethal groundwork so I couldn't let this happen. With this in mind, I only allowed him to go to his left side as I applied more pressure to his neck. As he tried to stand I pulled him down. He tried to break free from my hands. I wouldn't let him. I rolled him over, which put him underneath me, with my stranglehold now full on. He struggled but I knew I had him. I applied more pressure to his neck with my grip. He couldn't take anymore and he tapped the mat. He'd completely gone. I'd rendered him totally unconscious.

From an overall team point of view, this put us on level terms with the French. George Kerr won his contest which put us in a good position. Sadly Tony Macconnell and Harry Winn were unable to capitalise on this and we were out at the first hurdle again. A shame really as we had a big advantage going into the last contest which meant Harry only had to draw. Unfortunately, he lost. Russia went on to take the title for the third year running.

In the individual light middleweight, I started with quite an easy win over Olympic silver medallist Eric Haenni. My mind did a quick flashback to Tokyo and I had an 'if only I'd faced him in the opening rounds and not Nakatani moment.' In the next round, I took on Jan Okroj from Poland who I threw for a full point. Finnish boy Kyosti Korpiola came next and he didn't present too many problems. I faced Michal Vachun of Czechoslovakia in the semi-final. I beat him and went through to the final to face Vladmir Kuspish of Russia. Or that's what should have happened but, for the first time ever, the European Technical Commission introduced another scheme which meant I had to have another fight. I won it but felt absolutely shattered and lost the final. I thought coming third in East Berlin, and watching the Russian Flag being raised, had been bad enough. But this time, watching the Russian flag again felt ten times worse. Syd Hoare also took silver in the open weight and Ray Ross a bronze in the middleweight.

For the remainder of the year, I continued to train, flat out, with my sights set on the next European championships scheduled for Luxembourg in May 1966.

Now, at the age of nineteen, I started to worry about Mum and Dad. I trained. I ate. I slept. Now and again other judo events were held, domestically and internationally, and I entered whenever I could. I really didn't do anything else and I still declined all offers from friends to visit discos and pubs. It just didn't appeal to me at all although never having any money might have played a big part in this. I used to ride a push bike all the way from Sydenham to South Kensington to train at the Budokwai as I didn't have any money to pay for transport. I mentioned just now that I ate and thanks to Mum and Dad I ate very well. I needed to as this gave me what I needed to train. But I knew my needs were putting a huge strain on the family budget. Barbara and Shayne also needed to be fed and clothed as well. Plus Mum and Dad needed some kind of life that didn't revolve completely around me. Dad never said anything and I knew he loved travelling around Great Britain and the World to support me. But in my mind I worried. I knew I had to do something to bring extra money into the house.

For the last six months of 1965, I worked as a lifeguard at Eltham Swimming Baths outdoor pool. I worked four hours every morning from 5:00 a.m. until 9:00 a.m. This enabled me to stick to my regular training programme and use the baths for extra training. The income helped but I needed more. One night, after a training session, a few of us were having a coffee and I mentioned that I needed to find something that enabled me to earn extra cash and that didn't interfere with my judo. Chris Metas, a very accomplished player who I trained with many times, managed a nightclub in London called Lulu's owned by Louie Brown and Leonard Bloom. They were quite well known around the club scene at that time and they must have had around twelve discos and nightclubs. Chris explained that the hours would be from around 10:00 p.m. until 1:00 a.m. and that he'd put in a word for me with the owners. I asked about the money and he said I could expect to earn something like £20 per night.

Chris asked around and discovered that a club, located in the West End's Duke of York Street just behind Piccadilly Circus, called Birdland had an opening for a doorman. This sounded like the perfect opportunity for me and I went and spoke to the manager. He gave me a long coat, which came down almost to my ankles, and a kind of chauffeur's hat to wear. I stood outside Birdland and opened and closed doors for three hours. As I said this represented fantastic money for me and it allowed me to get home by 2:00 a.m. so I could still have a good sleep before training. Life, as it had in Japan when I had money, became a lot easier.

After about three weeks a big maroon Rolls-Royce turned up and out stepped my big boss. Multi-millionaire Mr. Louie Brown with one of the most stunning young ladies I'd ever seen. She looked about eighteen years old which made her fourteen younger than Louie. They entered and I forgot about them until I received a call to go downstairs to see Louie in his office out the back. He had a fantastic office. Teak desk, leather chairs, and a huge leather sofa, that might have doubled as a casting couch. She sat there filing her nails. Louie said he had a proposal for me and promptly promoted me to Assistant Manager. I negotiated a bit of extra money and a slight adjustment to my hours. I would now finish at 3:00 a.m.

As Assistant Manager my main functions were to take the cash from the door, check membership numbers and enroll new members. Louie turned up again, two weeks later in the same car but with a different stunning bird, and this time when he invited me into his office he offered me the Manager's position at Birdland as the current Manager had been promoted to manage Samantha's, one of Louie's bigger and better clubs. He offered me £350 a week which I accepted.

I really didn't want this to have a negative impact on my judo but I had to do it as I needed money. I couldn't keep going without it although I knew this meant that I would have to devote more time to the club. I had to find a way to balance the two things and in the end, I cut my training time down and pushed myself harder. As Manager one of my responsibilities included depositing the weekly takings every Thursday and Friday and we had two methods for this. On Thursday I would take to the bank a set amount of cash. This could have been something like £1,500 or £1,800 and I normally selected the amount based on what kind of week we'd had. Any cash left over, and we always had a big chunk that ranged from £3,000 to £5,000, I had to personally deliver to Louie's main West End office in a large brown envelope.

This went on for three weeks and then Louie dropped by Birdland again. This time he said he wanted a meeting with me the next morning, in his main office, at 11:00 a.m. I arrived on time, a little bit wary as I didn't know if I'd messed something up, and waited for him for a few minutes which enabled me to engage in conversation with his gorgeous secretary. When he arrived I soon got the message that she was off limits although he didn't appear upset and talked about promotion again. I couldn't believe it. In a little over two months, I'd gone from Doorman to Manager and he wanted to promote me again. It turned out that he wanted me to take over at Samantha's as he'd just fired the manager. He offered me another nice pay rise and the use of one of his vacant apartments, for free, which he had in Onslow Gardens in South Kensington. That made life much easier as it dramatically cut down my travel times to work and to the Budokwai to train. I found out later that my rapid rise to the top might have been because of the brown envelopes I delivered every Friday. Apparently, I handed over £400 to £500 more than any of my predecessors. I didn't see Louie that much but I always enjoyed it when he turned up at my club or he had time for a chat when I visited his office. He seemed quite a shy and introverted type of person who you would never imagine could be one of London's biggest playboys in the swinging sixties and a legendary nightclub entrepreneur. Many locals even referred to him as the 'King of Clubs.' He lived in a luxurious apartment, at the end of Curzon Street in Shepherds Market, which I visited a few times, and he had a big house in Surrey with a Go-Kart track. In addition to his roller, he also drove an E-type Jaguar.

With his business partner Lenny Bloom, who preferred bicycle clips around his ankles to babe magnet flash cars, they produced the London club template which others followed. They also attracted 'A' list celebrities. People like Mick Jagger, Jimi Hendrix, Keith Moon, Diana Dors, Alan Lake, Jess Conrad, and Princess Anne before her marriage to Captain Mark Phillips. Of course, with Louie into babes, quite a few page three type girls turned up with young starlets and escort girls. I met quite a few well-known people including Marlon Brando.

Lenny Bloom, another millionaire, rode his push bike around the clubs each night keeping his own check on how things were running. He, in much the same way as Louie, resembled more of a banker than a nightclub mogul. They did, however, differ in how they played the game. Louie kept it all up front with a succession of beauties always on his arms, whereas Lenny preferred to keep things low key and secret. He even tried to get a thing going with a very good friend of mine called Christine Wildman. Chris, from Colwich Road in Nottingham, became the youngest British woman ever to win a black belt at the age of sixteen.

I first met her at Nottingham University during a judo meeting and she seemed quite taken by me. At that time we were both single and we chatted for a long time. Later I saw her in London and she even came to the Budokwai to train. At that time, with not many British women involved in judo, she found it difficult to find women to train with so a lot of the time she trained with us. I must admit the establishment didn't really favour women at that time so she had to bang on a few doors to be heard. But I didn't mind helping. I quite liked her and I even went back to Nottingham to meet her parents. I got on very well with her Dad who had this broad Nottingham accent that I absolutely loved. He would say stuff like 'hello duck' and 'nout has happened' which I found very funny. Chris later moved to London which made it easier for her to train at the Budokwai. She even moved into Louis's apartment with me and I suppose we became a bit of an item.

As I said I got on very well with Chris. She had a nice energy about her and we had the same kind of outlook on life. We both liked excitement and we were sometimes outrageous. Of course, we loved judo, and sport in general, but we also liked the stability provided by a normal family routine. We both got on very well with our parents. Moving to London might have changed her life and of course, she accompanied me many times to Samantha's where she discovered a completely different world. Lenny turned up on his bike one night and she couldn't believe that this very simply dressed character could be a millionaire. I introduced them and he soon created a position for her in our nightclub team. She became a receptionist/cashier. Not that she had that in her background but she soon learned and floated around the different clubs doing whatever Lenny required her to do. One night she came home all excited having met Tom Jones and Engelbert Humperdink. She said her heart fluttered when she spoke with Tom. I don't think he tried anything on with her! On the other hand Lenny, in his own quiet way, had been trying to get something on with Chris ever since he hired her. In my office, he'd even put down foam cushioned exercise mats, just in front of the safe, on the pretext that he wanted her to show him judo moves. So Lenny, who especially liked young blondes, had a thing for Chris and it even reached a stage where he offered her an apartment of her own when he already had another girlfriend in one of his penthouses. I thought 'what a cheek!' but I knew she had a massive thing for me and not mega-rich men twice her age.

I continued to impress my bosses and they loved having me on their team. They liked my outgoing attitude, sense of humour, and at the same time my particular management style. I think they were also happy to have an Olympian on their books. They knew I could handle customers and that I wouldn't accept any nonsense. Of course, when you get a group of young people together and alcohol is involved, there are incidents and we're talking about the swinging sixties. Some people, who without a drink were perfectly normal human beings, suddenly changed once they'd had a few too many. Sometimes, fueled by alcoholic Dutch courage, they crossed the line and things got a bit ugly. Obviously, we had to bring them back into line.

I had an excellent team that included another very keen judo player called Marc Carroll who I trained at Dog Kennel Hill when he was fifteen. He also came to the Budokwai, reached second Dan status, and became a British junior champion. I knew him very well and hired him when I heard he wanted to make a bit of extra money. I trusted him and knew that any jobs I delegated to him would be taken care of with the minimum of fuss. He had a certain presence about him and being very tall and muscular must have helped. Most of the time he just had to look at potential troublemakers and they would back down with the minimum of fuss. He also had a sharp tongue that helped. I wanted to create a party atmosphere, every night, where people could have fun with the knowledge that we were looking after them. In fact, I think I had about three birthdays a year and I sent out invitations to all members, to celebrate with me at my fabulous club, which might have said something about everything being free. When they arrived, and I explained that the invitation should have said that they were cordially invited if they were free and we had a joke about printing errors.

We had a few girls who worked for us. Cashiers, receptionists, waitresses and we had a girl who took care of customers' overcoats which they used to wear during the winter. Obviously, we took very good care of our girls and protected them whenever they needed our help. One night a group of ten turned up and my doorman alerted me. I came out and noticed that they were about halfway back in a queue of about fifty. This put us on red alert as we never let in groups of six or more males. I had a quick word with Marc and hung around the entrance just in case he needed my help. They must have got wind of something and only one of the group actually entered. He seemed a bit flash and had obviously had a few. We watched him as he paid and then approached our cloakroom girl to give her his coat. We heard him being rude to her and I suppose, to get her own back, she gave him his change back in one penny coins instead of a shilling. He took umbrage to this and threw the coins back in her direction. One actually hit her in the face and she screamed. I looked at Marc, conveniently stood behind him, and nodded. Marc put him in a chokehold, pulled him off balance, and dragged him to the street where he laid him on the pavement. Marc rubbed his hands together, another job well done, and turned away. But the guy made a big mistake. He clambered up, poked Marc in the chest, and announced that he had Sicilian blood and he would kill him. Now I knew that Marc didn't like people poking him, or threatening to kill him, and this could only end in one way which it did. Marc knocked him out with a left hook that the great Henry Cooper would have been proud of. Unfortunately, just as he released his left, Dad arrived after he'd parked his taxi. Dad always wore a very nice white shirt to work and blood, which rushed out like a torrent from the Sicilian's nose, ended up all over his shirt. With Dad's shirt ruined and we had to relieve the

Sicilian of some cash to pay for a new one. Marc is still going strong to this day so the Sicilian never carried out his threat to bump him off.

As time went by I looked at Louie and Lenny and imagined myself in their shoes. They'd started the nightclub trend in London and I knew if I stayed with them, and learned everything I needed to know, I too could become a millionaire nightclub owner one day. I think I treated people correctly, staff and customers, and that this would have helped me to succeed in this business. Chris said the same thing as she certainly fully understood how important I'd become to Louie and Lenny. But as much as I enjoyed it there were not enough challenges for me in this business. I also had other judo targets that I needed to focus on. After eighteen months I moved on and so did Chris

30

ON THE JUDO front 1966 hadn't been a great year for me. In the main events, the European junior championships in Lyon and the seniors in Luxembourg, I'd failed to win a medal.

In March I lined up in the junior middleweight division as a strong favourite but went out in the first round with a very poor performance against West German Uwe Lichtenhofer. The twenty year old Dave Starbrook also took part in the middleweights and he lost in the first round as well. As our conquerors also lost their next contests this meant we didn't have a chance to get back in the competition through the back door repecharge. This system allowed players back into the competition if they lost in the first round, and the person who beat them won the group. For me, I'd had an off day although I knew a few people around were thinking I might be finished. At that time I think they might have expected too much of me although I knew I'd set myself high standards which is why people expected more. For me, I worried more about my left knee that had started to give me a lot of pain. Something inside didn't feel right.

Back on the road two months later for the seniors in Luxembourg and in the team event, we were drawn in the same pool as East Germany and Finland. Against East Germany, George Glass came on first in the lightweight division where he met Dieter Scholz. George did well and we thought he might get the decision. He didn't. In the light middleweight, I beat East Germany's, Gunter Wiesner. I hammered into him and he didn't know what hit him. Although I didn't get him down I got the decision. With scores, even George Kerr gave Otto Smirat a very good fight in the middleweight division which went to a decision. We thought George might get it. He didn't. With the East Germans, one up Ray Ross came up next in the light heavyweights against Wolfgang Micka. Ray won which put the scores even again. Going into the last contest David Peake came up against Herbert Niemann and with a big points advantage, David only had to draw for us to go through. Unfortunately, he lost. This meant for the sixth time in a row we'd failed to make it through the preliminaries. Russia beat France in the final to take the title for the fourth year running.

In the individual light middleweight category, I started with decision wins in the first two rounds against Michal Vachun of Czechoslovakia and Manfred Penz of Austria. In the third, I lost a decision to East Germany's Joachim Schroeder. The Russians and the Dutch dominated this event with Russia taking four golds and Holland three. We only managed a meager bronze from heavyweight David Peake. A very poor performance and more worries for me about my left knee which resulted in a visit to Mr. Krelin at London's Kings College Hospital. He soon had his knife out and removed a cartilage. I did have one bright spot in 1966. At the same time as the England football team made front-page headlines by winning the world cup, I managed a few lines in the sports pages when I gained my third Dan.

As we moved into 1967 I had three main targets. The European Junior Championships in Lisbon, the seniors in Rome and World Championships in Salt Lake City. We knew all the big guns of world judo would be in Salt Lake because Mexico City had ignored requests for judo to be included in the 1968 Olympic Games.

First up in March came the European juniors in Lisbon. I'd won this in 1964 and 1965. In 1966 I'd been poor and, with this my last crack at the juniors, I really wanted to go out in style with a third win. I started off against Matjza Smoinikar of Yugoslavia who gave me a tough battle. I got him with a big throw for half a point and kept the pressure on to the end of the contest to win the decision. I maintained this form with my next three opponents, Pouchkarev of Russia,

Zirz of Germany and Pierre Le Caer of France, to reach the semi-final where I met Adri Van Polanen of Holland. He'd actually won the event in 1966 but I knew his form had dropped off and he'd only made it this far by the back door. I expected a walk in the park as I felt strong and really confident about my ability to beat him. Nonchalantly I came in for a throw but he hadn't read the script. He countered my throw, with one of his own, and I ended up flat on my back. He'd won. I couldn't believe it. For the first time in my life, I'd been thrown in an international competition. I'd been beaten a few times, with a decision or a technical thing, but that was the first time I'd had a complete knockout. This totally shocked me and gave me a massive wake up call. I'd been overconfident, perhaps big headed, as I totally believed I'd make the final. From that point on I promised myself that I would never go on to the mat with that kind of attitude. Alexander Shuklin of Russia beat Van Polanen in the final, which meant I had to share the bronze with Le Caer, and watched that Russian flag raised again! I felt so sick. I should have been on the top spot. I knew I was better them.

Rome came next with the senior Europeans and with more countries involved we switched to a three day event for the first time from the 11th to the 13th of May. In the middleweights, I came up against Sorensen of Denmark who quite surprised me when he ran off the mat to avoid groundwork. Much to the disappointment of the home crowd, I got the decision against one of their favourites, Carmeni. For the next two rounds, I won with decisions against Snijders of Holland and Vladmir Pokataev of Russia. This put me in the semi-final against George Kerr who came through the back door. George got the better of me this day but not Pokataev, who'd also made it through the back door. This meant a bronze for me and another opportunity to watch the Russian flag raised towards the ceiling. As I've already explained, standing on the third tier podium with a bronze medal around my neck, never thrilled me with pleasure especially as I'd already beaten Pokataev a bit earlier. George Glass and Ray Ross also won bronzes.

As much as I'd trained hard for Lisbon and Rome the real focus for me had to be the World Championships in Salt Lake City which would take place between the 9th and 12th of August. With Dad, we'd worked out a programme much the same as we had for Tokyo. Stamina work and practice on the mat using my least favourite techniques. This meant being thrown by people well below my level which before had shocked people but not now. They knew Dad wanted me to work on my weak points to make me an all-around better player.

We flew into Utah a couple of days before the start and my first impressions were that it looked a very picturesque place surrounded by a backdrop of mountains. They had very good skiing facilities which made it a perfect location for the winter Olympics. They had however recently lost a bid to hold that event to Sapporo in Japan. Maybe these World Championships would give them a chance to showcase their hosting skills for future international sporting events.

The location, the Fieldhouse at the University of Utah, didn't really seem the most suitable building for this event. They'd converted volleyball courts that didn't feel right and the crowd had to sit on uncomfortable wooden benches that cost an arm and a leg. Fortunately Mum and Dad missed this tournament so they didn't have to pay. They also hadn't provided adequate facilities for the press and television. The Japanese were shocked when advised that their television crew couldn't film as all television rights had already been sold.

I took part in the middleweights with George Kerr and in the first round, I came up against Gordon Buttle from Canada. I got him straight away with an inner thigh throw. One of the big favourites to win came next, Heywood

Nishioka, an American with Japanese parents. I came at him with full force, got him on the ground, and strangled him out. Next, I came up Eiji Maruki who used to smash me around at the Kodokan in the early days. I suppose I had that at the forefront of my mind as I went for him right from the start. He had a job to keep me at bay and he didn't really offer any kind of attack. But at the end, I'd failed to score. I still thought I'd done enough to get the decision, as did the crowd, however, we'd all failed to consider the unwritten rule that referees seemed to have in place at that time. The rule that said when they were in doubt they had to give the decision to the Japanese. So Maruki got it but this time the back door system worked in my favour and I had another opportunity.

I met Patrick Clement from France next a very good player holder of the French title for the past three years. He didn't really seem up for this and I got the decision. Dutchman Martin Poglajen, nicknamed 'The Animal,' proved a tough contest as I knew it would. He'd taken gold at the Europeans in Madrid in 1965 and a bronze a year later. I also heard that he'd once been the army boxing champion of Holland. In the earlier rounds, he'd hurt his ankle and it was touch and go whether he would be fit for this one. I targeted his weak spot and spent time on his arms. I felt him wilting and I knew he wouldn't last much longer. Pretty soon he had blood coming from his nose and his ear which meant the referee stopped the contest and called for the doctor. Taking all his injuries into consideration the doctor advised him to retire. Poglajen refused and the break seemed to have done him some good. He came at me and I lost the advantage that I had earlier. At the end of the fight, he got the decision and I think he deserved it. This reminded me of my 1964 semifinal contest with the Austrian Karl Reisinger in Berlin. I'd had Reisinger on the ropes, in the same way, I'd just had Poglajen, but the referees called breaks and after the restart, I'd lost the initiatives. I needed to sort this out and planned a chat with Dad for when I arrived home.

In the final, a non-event really as Poglajen's body had been totally messed up in the early rounds and I think I'd broken both his arms; Maruki had no problems taking gold. I'm sure I'd have given him a better fight and that the crowd would have actually wanted to see that contest in preference to the one they watched. Poglajen should have taken the doctor's advice but I admired his doggedness in not taking the easy way out. I knew I'd tested Maruki and Poglajen and the result of both contests could have gone either way. The margins were so close but with my bronze medal, I became the first British player ever to win a medal of any sort in the

World Championships. I had some nice press and one quote went like this:

'It's no exaggeration to say that the best all-around judo of the entire week came from Brian Jacks. That he failed to make silver was a shame as on technique he really deserved it. He delighted everybody with his judo and had there been an award for exceptional style he would have been at the top of a lot of people's lists'.

Nice words but I knew I had some things to work on to reach number one in the world. At twenty I knew I had time on my side although being number three didn't cut it for me. I wanted to be number one. Japan took gold medals in every weight category except for the heavyweight where another fine Dutchman, Willem Ruska, followed on the tradition set by Geesink.

Away from the competition, I spent some time with someone who'd become a good friend. We'd met in a few competitions and I suppose we had a similar record against each other. He won a few and I won a few. We were around the same age and often referred to as the blue-eyed boys of our respective countries judo. I'm talking about Frenchman Jean-Paul Coche from St. Tropez on the French Riviera. We socialized away from judo and had some fun in Salt Lake

City. One day we were looking around and we noticed a gorgeous blonde girl in the crowd. In fact, I'd already spoken to her and let Jean-Paul know that I had first dibs on her. He couldn't believe it. 'Non, non, non she's mine' he said and that he already had a date with her arranged for the following day. I told him 'Non, non, non she's mine' and that he must be mistaken as she'd already agreed to a date with me. As we debated our predicament we looked across to where this girl sat and couldn't believe our eyes. Another girl had joined our girl and we were gobsmacked. They looked exactly the same. Same hair colour, same hair style, same complexion and they were wearing exactly the same clothes. They could have been twins and of course, they were. We'd pulled ourselves a couple of Mormon twins. The press might have had fun with that. The blue-eyed boys of judo and the Mormon twins of Salt Lake City!

After ten days living in a Mormon state, I didn't feel motivated to explore that religion further. Generally speaking, they looked like ordinary people but it felt so weird being in a place with no alcohol, smoking or swearing. Not that I did any of those three but I'd grown up around it so it seemed normal to me.

After Salt Lake, I spoke with Dad about my battle with Poglajen and he thought that I might have relaxed too much when the doctor came on. Maybe I believed I'd won already which caused me to lose some focus and in turn the contest. He even asked me if I felt sorry for Poglajen. I didn't but I had admired the way he wouldn't give up. We both agreed that I needed to be even more ruthless.

31

SO FAR IN this stage, I've tried to give you a good understanding of a British international judo players' life during the sixties and we've looked in detail at the European Juniors, European Seniors, The Olympic Games, and the World Championships. In between these, there were other events, both domestically and internationally, which I won't go into in full detail as it would take forever and sound repetitive. I will pick out a few more competitions later that will hopefully be of interest but at this point, I want to introduce two people who came into my life during the late sixties.

Dad, who'd continued to drive his taxi and coach at Dog Kennel Hill, also spent time visiting local schools to instruct whenever he could. I tried to accompany him but I found I had less time than before as I became more involved at the Budokwai where I coached as well as trained. One day, in mid-November 1967, he called me and said I had to go immediately to Battersea County School as he had a fifteen year old kid who he believed could hold me down. I said to him he must be joking as I'd just won the bronze medal in the world championships so there's no way a kid will hold me down. He said listen to me, Brian. You need to come now. Drop what you're doing and just come. I didn't want to argue so I went and Dad introduced me to this enormous fourteen stone kid with huge arms. He looked massive but there was no way he could hold me down. But Dad said it again. If he holds you down you won't get up. I told him again. I'm number one in Great Britain. He can't do it. This kid will never hold me down for thirty seconds. The kid listened and I reluctantly accepted the challenge to prove Dad wrong. I let him hold me down with the idea in my mind that I would push him off in five seconds. All right ten! Or maybe fifteen! As fifteen seconds passed I realised Dad might have a point. At twenty that point became clearer as it did even more after twenty-five seconds passed. This kid definitely had something. At twenty-eight seconds I just about managed to escape. The kid looked at me and I looked at him. Although now I no longer regarded him as a kid. He smiled. I smiled. We seemed to have some kind of bond. I shook his hand and said nice to meet you, Angelo. Angelo Parisi, born in Italy now living in London, had only had four judo lessons but Dad and I both knew he had something and together we were determined to help him make the most of it.

We saw Angelo as a kind of gentle giant who might need a bit of pushing to reach his full potential. So push him we did. One day I went to his house, as we'd planned an early morning run, and his Mum answered the door and said he was still asleep. She made me sit down in the kitchen and gave me food. This always happened when I went to his house and she was an excellent cook. Angelo had a tendency to be a bit lazy in the early days but he was so exceptionally strong for his age. Eventually, Mrs. Parisi let me go upstairs and I dragged him out of bed. I went to his wardrobe to look for his clothes and hundreds of Superman comics fell out. Apparently, he loved Superman but we knew he had the potential to be a real-life superhero. As I said his parents were Italian and they had one of the best ice cream shops in Battersea although I'm not sure how they could have made any profits as Angelo used to eat a gallon of the stuff every day. This must have been the reason why he'd developed such a huge size so quickly. He had twenty-three inch biceps. A few of us went to his shop and we watched him in action. They had these huge ice cream vats, where they mixed and stirred the ice cream until it went rock hard, and they used a big chrome spoon to scoop it out. We watched him as he scooped it out with no problems at all. Then he asked us if we'd like to try. We did and we couldn't do it. The ice cream was so solid but he had no problems and that must have been the secret of his strength.

He came with me to the Budokwai and still had sessions with Dad at his school. Even when he left he continued to seek out my Dad out for advice and coaching. I think he saw in him the same thing I had. He wanted to do well for him, and me, and he didn't let us down. We actually became very close during this period and I think he learned a lot from me. He certainly became fully focused and I never needed to drag him out of bed again. He'd bought into our philosophy and the benefits were amazing for him. He developed a great technique and between 1970 and 1973 he won three European junior golds. In 1972, the year he didn't take the junior gold, he took the European senior gold and the British open gold as well. Also in 1972, he won bronze at the Munich Olympic Game. Angelo had become a phenomenon in world judo and Dad and I knew he would be taking Olympic gold for Great Britain sooner rather than later. Possibly in Montreal in 1976. I travelled a lot with Angelo and many times we shared rooms. During these times we discussed our ambitions both personal and judo. Angelo had so much love in his heart and I knew he wanted to meet the right woman and settle down. I listened and joked with him about wild oats and all that sort of thing. But he really didn't seem a wild oats kind of person. He wanted love and, I suppose thanks to me, he found it.

We were in France, on a low budget training exercise, which John Lowe had organised. John, a member of the LJS and a second Dan, had become quite a distinguished character in the judo world. He always dressed impeccably in a suit with a waistcoat and he had a pencil moustache. At that time he must have been around seventy-four and he had this old bus which he'd modified so we could sleep on it as we travelled. It got us to France and I met this French girl called Caroline who spoke reasonable English. We were chatting and Angelo walked up and I introduced them. Well from that point on I didn't get a look in as those two only had eyes for each other. I thought that perhaps Angelo had found the love of his life and, as not long after they were married, he must have. As much as I felt pleased for him my introduction also changed the course of British judo history because Angelo went to live in France where he applied for French citizenship. This meant we could never be teammates again, which saddened me a bit, but I wanted my good friend to be happy so there were no sour grapes from me. Did Angelo take the gold medal in Montreal as Dad and I really believed he would? No, he didn't as red tape, related to his country change, hadn't been completed so he couldn't compete. But four years later in Moscow, he did. He won it for France but there were two English people who were so proud of him.

That's Angelo. Born in Italy, raised in England, and an Olympic gold medal for France. A real-life superhero!

He never forgot us and he even wrote a handwritten note to Dad that Dad kept in his jacket pocket from 1980 until 2008.

'Dear Albert If it was not for you teaching me and encouraging me from the start I would never have become an Olympic Gold Medalist. Lots of love Angelo Parisi (5th August 1980).'

Dad felt so proud. He valued that letter more than anything else in the world.

For the second person, we need to step back to 1968 when I enjoyed a rare night out with a good friend of mine called Geoff Bernard, another keen judo player. At that time Geoff was a bit of a lad and basically up for anything. One night, after a training session at Dog Kennel Hill, we decided to go to the Cats Whiskers disco in Catford. We had a bit of fun and on the way home, we decided to stop off at a Wimpey for a bite to eat. As we sat down I noticed two stunning girls sat at a table facing us. They were with a couple of blokes but they didn't look very happy. I tried to smile at the one liked but she had a long face and didn't respond. Despite that, she had something about her that I liked so I decided to go for it even though one of the blokes with her might have been her boyfriend. I wrote my telephone number down on a piece of paper, passed it to her as we were leaving, and told her to call me later and I would cheer her up. She just screwed it up and threw it back at me. I said what did you do that for? She said I'm not calling you. You have to call me. I said well give me your number then? She shouted out her number as the guy sat opposite, who could have been her boyfriend, looked on perplexed. I didn't have a pen and had to remember the number until I got home. I kept running it through my mind. I called her the following day and she refused to meet me. For the next four months I called her every day and on every occasion, she said no. Eventually, she said yes just to shut me up I think. Even though she thought this might be just one date Julie Wilkinson became my girlfriend that year and not long after Geoff met another girl and became a Jehovah Witness. Not exactly something I would have predicted for him as prior to this he'd done a lot of crazy stuff. He even tried to talk me into it but it just seemed weird to me. Like the Mormons in Salt Lake City.

Whilst most of the sporting world headed to Mexico for the 1968 Olympic Games we, in our unique little judo circle, had to continue with our usual annual events that included the Europeans, the British Open and a load of one-off events at home and abroad. One event that sticks in my mind turned out to be the LJS Goldberg-Vass Memorial Festival of Judo. My old friends, George Chew and Eric Dominy, certainly did a first class job of staging this event that attracted fine players in all categories.

Len Goldberg and Johnny Vass were members of the LJS who along with Bill Murray, from the Ryde Judo Club on the Isle of Wight, drowned whilst returning to a cabin cruiser called The Pelican in a dinghy from Ryde Harbour. This tragic event occurred on the 20th of September 1954. Goldberg, at five feet one inch tall and eight and a half stone, had a tremendous fighting spirit. He became very well known for his superb execution of single arm shoulder throws which he could perform equally as well on the left and right. He represented the LJS and if weight categories were around in his day he would probably have been one of the top lightweights. In 1953 at the Battersea Town Hall, he met Teizo Kawamura, one of Japan's judo greats who became a Kodokan eighth Dan, and they staged a demonstration where Goldberg showed outstanding techniques that impressed the crowd. He suffered a serious injury which threatened his career but he made a full recovery. However, not long after at the age of twenty-nine, he lost his life. Johnny Vass, a solicitor's clerk originally from Lancashire, also became well known in the judo world for his ability. He'd been a member of several clubs that included the Keidokwai in Blackpool, the Budokwai and eventually the LJS. He gained his first Dan ten days before his death. The LJS set up the Memorial Trophy, that later became trophies, soon after their deaths. Not too much is known about Bill Murray except that he founded the Ryde Judo Club in 1948 and later he became an associate member of the LJS.

For the 1968 competition the LJS, along with a few sponsors that included another old friend Mr. Ichro Hatta, had splashed out on some very nice oak shields faced with silver. In the open category, considered the ultimate event, the original Goldberg Vass trophy would be presented to the winner.

In the lightweights, George Glass took the trophy with a win over Japan's the UK trained, Kimura. Nelson took the light middleweight and Dave Starbrook the middleweight when he beat me in the final. Malloy and Paul Eales took the light heavyweight and heavyweight trophies. This just left the open weight where I beat Tug Wilson in the final. So even though I didn't receive one of the very nice new trophies I got the old one and I still have it. I wanted the opportunity to defend it but unfortunately the following year, and for the next 50, nothing happened. They came and asked for it back but I said no. I said I wanted to defend my title and that I would keep it until the day I lost. Even if they didn't have it again until I was 80! All they have to do is arrange another event and I will be there. At the time of writing this I'm 70 so maybe I will wait another 10 years. It's a nice trophy, must be worth a few pounds, but I just wish they'd hurry up and arrange the next competition!

I wanted a gold medal more than anything and, apart from the juniors, I seemed to be falling short in the international arena. When I say medal I think you know by now that I wanted to win. I wanted to stand on that number one spot on the rostrum and watch the British flag raised up the pole. Still being referred to as the golden boy of British judo meant nothing to me if I couldn't reach the top spot. Plus, at twenty-three years old now, the boy tag didn't fit anymore. Dad and I spoke about this many times as I prepared for the European Championships in 1970 which took us back to Berlin and the ultra-efficient East Germans.

In my first match, I came up against Kasovic of Yugoslavia and beat him in under five seconds. Egger of

West Germany followed and I managed to score against him. Horst Leupold of East Germany followed next. I got the decision and I also got the better of Laszlo Ipacs of Hungary. East German Otto Smirat had made it through the back door and we met in the semi-final. We started cautiously with both of us looking for our favourite holds. I knew he'd be looking for his shoulder throw. He had his right hand free and I knew he'd try and quickly insert it between my legs to try to score. But I wouldn't let him catch me like that as so many others had before me. Not today Otto. So it was all cat and mouse for the first half of the contest although as time ticked on I felt more confident. I rolled him with a shoulder throw, which put me in the lead, and towards the end, I knocked him down to clinch my place in the final. Memories of my first junior title in 1964 came flooding back. We were in the same city. This had to be my day.

On the other side of the draw Martin Poglajen, 'The Animal' from Holland had made it through to the final. This time I decided to bide my time. Previously I'd gone straight in and taken an early advantage but one way or another he'd soaked up the pressure and beaten me. This time he took an early lead with a knockdown which didn't really bother me. I turned him over and we both landed on the ground, where we did a bit of rough mauling. I managed to follow this up with three very good shoulder throws attacks which turned him over. Unfortunately, none scored as we'd gone off the mat. But it kept him at bay and I got the decision and put 'The Animal' back in his cage.

I'd won a senior gold at last and felt so proud. Plus I'd won with a broken right wrist. Poglajen knew I had a problem and with the help of team doctor Ken Kingsbury, we played a bit of kidology. Ken bandaged my left wrist instead of my right. I must admit I welled up a bit, stood on the top spot watching the British flag floating to the top of the pole, as the East German band played God Save Our Gracious Queen. Eddie Mullen took bronze in the light middleweight for the only other medal we won in this event.

At the end of September 1971 Julie, Angelo and I went out to Japan for a few months of pre-Olympic training for the Munich games the following year. For both of them, it was their first trips there and we stayed in a two bedroom apartment quite close to the Kodokan. My Mum, who still had airline connections, managed to secure us discounted tickets.

Julie and Angelo were, as I'd been before, totally stunned by Japan's crowded trains and stations. Even though Tokyo had upgraded itself, and that included trains which travelled a lot faster, they were still a nightmare. On one particular journey, the train driver must have touched his brakes, which caused a slight jerk, and all the people had to try and grip something to remain standing. As Angelo moved his right elbow he accidentally made contact with one of the windows which completely smashed. The train continued, with nobody injured, but two minutes later when it stopped at the next station they had a work crew on standby ready to fix it. Not only that they were stood in exactly the right place as the train stopped. A minute later they'd fixed it and we continued on our journey as if nothing had happened.

Angelo really wanted to use this opportunity to increase his judo techniques and try and have a close look at his potential Japanese opposition. Many teachers, especially the older ones, remembered me and they'd also heard of Angelo. They welcomed us and treated us very well. To keep Julie amused I thought it might be a good idea for her to try and earn some money in Japan so I introduced her to my old modelling agency boss Yusef. He seemed quite impressed, took loads of pictures, and checked all her details for her portfolio which he sent out to potential clients.

Whilst we were there we also wanted to try and upgrade our Dan status and our opportunity came on the 25th of November. I lined up with twenty Japanese third Dan's with ten stood on a line opposite each other. The least experienced were at the beginning of the line and more advanced at the other end. I'd had my third Dan since July 1966 and they placed me, more or less, in the middle. When my turn arrived I beat the first five, all with different techniques, and the sixth with a decision. They upgraded me instantly. Angelo completely cleaned up his opposition without breaking a sweat which meant promotion to third Dan. At that time I'm not sure if any other foreigners had completed this against the well trained Japanese.

Meanwhile, Julie's modelling career seemed to be taking off after she had an interview with the Hannah Morris Fashion House, one of Japan's top fashion houses, rather like Calvin Klein. They even sent her to modelling school to learn how to walk properly on the catwalk. When she'd mastered this they gave her a modelling assignment, a fashion show for Nancy Reagan, who'd flown into Japan with a large entourage. Ronald, her husband who became the American President from 1981 to 1989, didn't attend. Julie modeled clothes for Nancy and later Christian Dior and Yves Saint Laurent. Nestles chocolate also liked her and they used her pictures in supermarkets and on public transport. This provided a real bonus for us as the extra money meant we lived quite well. For Julie, it provided her with confidence as she'd always felt nervous about appearing in public and she felt great when she actually did it. Yusef, as he had with me, managed to get her work in movies as an extra and she even managed a speaking part in a bank robbery scene. She had to scream, 'That was Tani Hayato,' a local heartthrob at that time. In addition to acting and modelling, she also tried her hand at teaching English and ended up giving lessons to the Managing Director of Japan Airlines.

Angelo and I impressed our Japanese hosts and as the end of the year approached they asked us to perform a group of special throws at their New Year celebration. The fifteen formal throws of judo that we had to perform in the correct sequence. I looked at Angelo and Angelo looked at me. We kind of knew them but this represented a major challenge which I'm not sure if any other foreigners had ever taken on at that time in Japan. We were advised that all the high ranking Japanese teachers, eighth and ninth Dan's, would be attending with hundreds of university students. We couldn't refuse as we were guests in the Kodokan. We had to do it. Angelo and I trained solidly for three weeks to prepare as we knew we had to put on a perfect performance. We studied how to do it properly and we practiced again and again until we knew exactly what we had to do. On the day we demonstrated a textbook performance for our hosts and we knew we'd been given a massive honour to perform at the Kodokan.

In January 1972 Angelo had to return to England and I followed a few weeks later, which left Julie on her own in Japan. She had more time on her visa and we both decided that she should see it out and make more money. Yusef, who'd promised me he'd look after her in my absence, called her one day and asked her if she would like some irregular work. Julie, quite naive at that time, agreed. She said she would be available anytime thinking that Yusef meant irregular hours such as shooting at night. When she turned up at Yusef's office and learned the full meaning of his 'irregular work' expression, she did a runner. He wanted her to get her kit off and appear in blue movies. Obviously, when I heard this it didn't put Yusef in my good books!

Back in England, with my eyes were fully focused on Munich, I trained with more intensity that I had for Tokyo. Most days six hours per day.

Meanwhile, from a West German Olympics point of view, they were keen to banish the memory of the 1936 Olympics where the games became known as the Nazi games. Munich spent £300 million in an effort to try and erase that memory. David Broome, our Welsh show jumper who'd competed in the last three Olympics winning bronze in Rome and Mexico City, carried our Olympic flag for the opening ceremony. This, more or less, followed the same pattern as it had in Tokyo.

The Judo event took place at the Boxhalle Stadium and one thing soon became clear. Every competitor wanted gold. In Tokyo, not surprising really, the event had a kind of innocence about it and we all knew how tough Japan were going to be. But not now. The time had arrived for judo to enter the modern world of sport which meant more changes to Kano's original visions. The authorities, that included Charles Palmer, now President of the International Judo Federation, tried hard to retain some of the qualities and characteristics that made judo unique. But they had to balance judo in an ever-changing sporting world. Weight categories increased to six plus there were format changes and rule changes that meant greater penalties against passivity. The players had also developed and become more muscular to allow them to follow the Western style of strength moves as opposed to the more skillful Japanese techniques. Japan, for so long the world leader in judo, were not expected to whitewash these games.

Our heavyweight Keith Remfry came up against Canadian Doug Rogers in the first fight. Rogers had stopped competing for a few years but came back for this as he'd never seen Europe. Doug beat Keith but soon lost which meant Keith didn't get another opportunity, Dave Starbrook made it all the way to the final of the light heavyweights where he lost to Russia's Shota Chochishvili. In the lightweights, our entrant, Bobby Sullivan, went out early, and in the open Angelo Parisi won bronze.

I started in pool A in the middleweights and had some tough contests. Probably some of the hardest of my career. I beat West German Gerd Egger on a split decision that really upset the local crowd. I wound them up by shaking my fist at him. I then took a split decision to beat Jean-Paul Coche from France with a knockdown from a drop shoulder throw. In order to reach the semi-final, I had to beat Guram Gogalauri from Russia which I did. This put me against Japan's Shinobu Sekine. My pool contests had sucked a lot of energy out of me but I came at him in a confident way and nearly knocked him down. He came back at me with a body drop combination and I had to use all kinds of twists to avoid him getting a score. At the end of the day, he won the decision. Sekine beat Oh Sung Lip in the final and I shared bronze with Jean-Paul Coche. Japan won three golds, Russia one, and Holland two.

For Great Britain equestrian Richard Meade carried the closing flag and we'd also set a record with sixty-nine year old Lorna Johnstone. She became the oldest competitor ever to appear in the Olympics during the equestrian. Individual gold medals went to Mary Peters in the pentathlon and Richard Meade in the equestrian. We won five silvers that included distance runner David Hemery and David Wilkie in the two hundred metres breaststroke. American swimmer Mark Spitz, who'd won six gold medals in Mexico City, went gold crazy again. He broke records in the pool and took seven golds this time. Russia introduced a seventeen year old little pocket dynamo gymnast called Olga Korbut. At just four feet eleven inches she became a worldwide sensation with her superb performances. She took individual golds in the floor and balance beam exercises.

One old friend turned up in the village, who I'd kind of expected as I knew he now lived in Frankfurt. He seemed to have the run of the place, as he did in Tokyo, and he came and went as he pleased. I think the West German guards, just like the Japanese, believed he was America's official translator. Bill Backhus had left Japan a few years earlier as the country became more, as he put it, 'less Bill Backhus friendly.' I think he couldn't get away with some of his old stunts like bulldozing his way through traffic jams claiming to be a member of the Japanese police. Also, he might have fallen out with the local people with his Japanese wife scam business. But whatever had forced him to leave hadn't done him any harm. In Frankfurt, he now controlled a multi-million-pound multi-national company that had links in many parts of the world. He didn't mention the name but did say something about imports and exports. He also said he had a lot of current and former judo people involved as he believed people with judo backgrounds could be trusted. He said we all had a common secret bond. He knew I'd made nothing from judo but explained that I could earn big money with him if I came on board. Something like £50,000 a year plus bonuses and, with his business expanding in England, he would need a Director of UK Operations very soon. He also wanted me to keep him in the loop with all my judo competitions in the future. He said wherever I travelled people from his organization could be there and that they would take extra special care of me.

Overall the West Germans made a tremendous effort to put on a show and provide us with a great place to live. Munich's Olympic village had to be ten times better than

Tokyo's which you would expect really with the growth and development of the Olympic movement and the world in general. They must have had restaurants for every country in the world and they had discos and shows to keep everybody entertained. I'd marveled at the way all the world's athletes had come together in Japan and created a kind of carnival Olympic village. The same applied to Munich until that day arrived that completely changed everything. Many words have been written about the events of the 5th of September 1972 so I will not dwell on it too much. Except to say it was a very sad and tragic day in Olympic history that changed the shape of the Olympic Games forever. For me sport is sport and politics is politics. I, like many people in the world, loved sport. I wanted to take part, whenever I could, with the knowledge that people wanted to watch and enjoy without having to worry about if they were safe from any acts of terrorism. But when those eight Palestinian terrorists, members of 'Black September,' forced their way into the rooms of Israeli athletes inside the village, sport changed. They took Israeli athletes hostage and demanded the release of two hundred prisoners in Israeli jails. The events that followed led to the deaths of eleven Israeli wrestlers and weightlifters. The village went into lockdown and we were all devastated. For thirty-four hours we didn't know if the games would continue. It did. But the atmosphere, as you would expect, never recovered.

West Germany had made a very good effort to eliminate the bad taste from their 1936 Olympics. Unfortunately, this one would be remembered for totally different reasons.

32

JULIE AND I were married on the 4th of November 1972 at Caxton Hall registry office with Angelo as my best man. We couldn't afford a honeymoon so Julie went straight back to her work.

As for me, I'd spent the last ten years, and a bit more totally focused on judo. I'd travelled the world, competed in some fantastic competitions, met some wonderful people, and picked up some medals on the way. But as I reflected on this it dawned on me, as it had many times before, that I had nothing. Judo, apart from a small black and white television and some cutlery that I'd been presented within East Berlin, hadn't provided me with any kind of financial rewards. Don't get me wrong here I'd gone into this with my eyes wide open and I'd never expected anything from judo. I did it for love, not money. Now at the age of twenty-six, it hit me hard. I had a new wife to support and I had to think about the best way to do this. Especially as I knew Julie wanted to start a family. I thought it might be time for me to retire.

Before making any rash decisions I checked with Dad as he'd been with me every step of the way from the beginning. We found a quiet spot, no longer at the base of the apple tree as Mum and Dad had moved from Thriffwood some time ago, and I put Dad in the picture with my thinking. I talked about the opportunity that might be on the table with Bill and also about joining him in his taxi business. Dad looked at me in a quizzical way, which he'd had before when we'd discussed crossroad points in my life before he discussed each point. For judo, he still believed I had it in me to win a gold medal at the next Olympics scheduled for Montreal in 1976. This, for him, put retirement at this point completely out of the question. He said I'd come so close and that in four years' time I should still be at the peak of my career as long as I continued to train and prepare as I had before. For Bill, who he'd met a few times, he felt this sounded too good to be true but it could be something to consider later. As for becoming a London taxi driver, as much as he loved it, he didn't want me to consider that path. He had another idea. He'd watched my work at Dog Kennel Hill, and the Budokwai, and he'd seen how I'd helped students. He'd also noticed how they reacted to me. He said I had a gift as an educator and that I should follow this path. I asked him if he meant I should be a teacher and he said yes. I said to him this would be impossible as I couldn't write to save my life. He said this didn't matter because my actions, and words, as a PE teacher would be enough. Although he knew I would have to spend some time at college to get the right qualifications for this role. He believed I should start immediately with the aim of being qualified by the start of Montreal so I could begin teaching after the games. It sounded like a good plan. I just needed Julie to buy into it as she would have to be the breadwinner for the next four years. Thankfully she did although something unexpected cropped up.

One evening Julie, Dad and I arranged to meet at the Budokwai and upon our arrival, by chance, we found two smartly dressed men in suits waiting for us. It turned out they represented the Nigerian government and were looking for me. They asked if I could train the Nigerian team for the next All African Games. They said I'd have to go immediately as the games were only two months away. Dad asked how experienced the Nigerian judo team was. They looked blank. Dad asked if they had an experience at all and they said a couple had. Dad couldn't believe it. He said it would be impossible to train them to any kind of decent standard in such a short time. Plus he told them I'd only just got married. But they were on a mission and I think they'd been told that they couldn't return home without me. As much as I felt honoured to be asked I really didn't want to leave Julie so soon after we'd married. They solved this problem by inviting her as well. We worked out the expenses and despite Dad's reservations, we were on our way.

When we arrived in Lagos we were greeted by the same men who took us to a small house where we spent the first night. The following day they moved us to a very nice house on a golf course owned by a British guy called Stanley Burrows who worked for Standard Chartered Bank. We were however slightly unnerved by our neighbor, General Yakubu "Jack" Dan Yumma Gowon, who had his home and army barracks next door. We saw many armed guards and they had machine gun turrets on the wall. General Gowon, at the age of thirty, had taken power after a military coup and governed the country during the 1967 to 1970 civil war.

They gave us a car, a light blue Citroen, with a driver called Okoon. We also used Stanley's butler named Antthony, with two ts, and he cooked, washed and cleaned. Well, he cooked if Julie let him and he seemed amazed that Julie even knew how to cook. On the second day, I went to the judo club, a small hall inside an army camp, to meet my twenty-six potential players and I must say they looked a fit lot. They were probably between the ages of twenty and thirty-five and most were from the Police College in Ikeja with a few from the military. We didn't try anything on the first day. I introduced myself, with a few bits about my background, and they did the same. I kept it light and we had a few jokes as the day went on. We seemed to bond but only three of them had any kind of judo experience. Alain George, the only other white man in the group, had a grandfather that originally came from Lebanon. He'd started judo at Brighton College, where he became a blue belt, and the Nigerian authorities scooped him up as they needed someone with a least some experience in their squad. Police Inspector Giwa had actually spent some time in Japan and Seni Williams had studied judo at Millfield School in Somerset, England where he'd also gained his blue belt.

As much as I enjoyed my first meeting with the squad I learned, after a private chat with Alain, that most of them had been press-ganged into it. He also mentioned this would be the second All Africa Games which had originally been planned for Bamako in Mali in 1969. A military coup there cancelled that plan and the organisers switched to Nigeria who originally planned a date in 1971. But that had been pushed back to 1973 due to problems. Fresh worries surfaced after the Munich games which meant a big increase in Lagos security as Nigeria, after their brutal civil war, wanted to put on a good show for the watching world. I also wanted my team to do well as this would reflect on me. But I knew this would be a big challenge.

I had six weight categories to fill and my two blue belts were around the same weight. Plus I didn't have anyone big enough for the heavyweights although I had loads of potential lightweights. That night I had a chat about it with Julie and I asked her what the heck I should do. She said I should just find the best way to train them so that other people wouldn't laugh at them. I slept with that thought and woke up in the middle of the night with a plan. I decided there would be no point in teaching them judo from the beginning as obviously, we didn't have time for that. Instead, I would look at counter techniques, ways for them to defend themselves, and I wrote out a training schedule based on this. To make this work I had to rely on my three who'd practiced judo before. I used them as attackers and all the others as counter-attackers.

At the training camp, I pushed them hard and then hard again. I had to. We didn't stand much chance anyway but the fitter they were the more chance we had. Plus they had to learn counter techniques in days rather than years which is how long it normally takes. Sometimes I worried about the tasks I gave them as I knew nothing about Nigerian culture or how far they could go. I questioned Alain about this and he advised me not to worry as they were enjoying it and Alain himself said my sessions were absolutely fantastic. He'd never experienced anything like this before and genuinely believed my sessions were well advanced from anything he'd ever experienced before. He even said that he believed my techniques were revolutionary which I thought not bad for a boy from the East End. So I pushed them even harder at the crack of dawn and much longer into the evening. I'm sure I heard the word 'sadist' mentioned more than once!

Prior to the start date, as Lagos put the final touches in place, they filled the games swimming pool with water to test it. They had no problems with the pool but the whole of Lagos, us included, didn't have any water that night. After that, they tested the stadium lights, which worked fine, but the rest of Lagos totally blacked out.

By the big day, they'd ironed out all the issues as Lagos welcomed all the African countries taking part in the second All Africa Games at their brand new stadium. For me, in front of a packed stadium, it meant another opening ceremony on an absolutely sweltering day. They had an All African torch that had been lit in Brazzaville, the capital and largest city of the Republic of Congo and located on the Congo River, a week before where the first All Africa Games had taken place back in 1965. Sporting stars from around the world were invited. Ethiopian double Olympic champion, Abebe Bikila, who set a marathon world record at the 1960 Rome Olympics running barefoot. Edson Arantes do Nascimento, known as Pelé, the Brazilian football star and regarded by many as the best player in the world. Muhammad Ali the American boxing heavyweight champion and possibly the best the world had ever seen, and Jesse Owens the American track and field athlete and four-time Olympic gold medallist in the 1936 games. Of course, I'd been invited as well but I knew I had a long way to go to be on the same level as those four. My next door neighbour officially opened the games that would last twelve days.

As for my team, they held their own as they knew how to defend. They just couldn't attack. I did manage to get one guy to enter the heavyweight category although on the day of the weigh-in he didn't get anywhere near the minimum weight so we poured gallons of water down him. But Iffidon, his name, proved to be our secret weapon as he managed our one and only bronze medal. Iffidon, a short guy, somehow managed a rear sacrifice throw that helped him make it as far as the semi-final. I think we were relieved to come out of this experience unscathed and we found Nigeria quite primitive. There were no bulbs in the traffic lights as people had stolen them and taken them to their homes. Often we noticed red, amber and green lights through people's windows. Lagos overall seemed very poor with many beggars. They asked me back but I declined. In fact, there were other offers that I turned down and recommended other people for. I gave Hong Kong to Dave Starbrook and when the Shah of Oman called I made a big mistake and passed that one on as well. I think the rewards in Oman included a Mercedes Benz.

May 1973, a month after I received my fifth Dan, we were on the road again, this time headed for Madrid in Spain for the European championships, which took place at the Palacio de Los Deportes stadium. They had a massive raised mat area which looked good but raised a few safety concerns. On paper, I believed we had quite a strong team and Roy Inman, in the lightweights, started well with a couple of quick wins. Unfortunately, he lost just before the semi-final stage and blew his back door opportunity. Dave Starbrook made it through to the light heavyweight final where he lost to Jean-Luc Rouge of France. Dave, not the most agile of players, performed really well. He had the kind of determination in him that could have made him a heavyweight boxing champion. Keith Remfry, in the heavyweights, made the final where he lost to Spain's Santiago Ojeda. The home crowd gave their man huge support and this might have had a negative impact on Keith's performance. In the welterweights, Vass Morrison made it to the semi-finals where he lost to the East German Dietmar Hoetger. I managed to take gold in the middleweights with the help of the back door. I beat Marco Trippi of Switzerland, Adri Van Polanen of Holland and Jerzy Jatowtt of Poland. Guy Auffray of France beat me but I came back in and beat Fred Marhenke of West Germany and Guram Gogalauri of Russia in the semi-final. I met the unbeaten Guy Auffray, who'd beaten me earlier by a narrow decision, in the final. Whenever we met we had a close fight and he always seemed to get the decision. But this time I took it in what might have been considered a dull contest.

Back in England I took Dad's advice and applied to Avery College in Greenwich to begin my quest to qualify as a PE Teacher. I had to sit three, three hour papers, to stand a chance of qualifying. I sat them, somehow passed, and applied for PE and Sociology. I had one assignment where I had to write a thousand words comparing the hip and shoulder joint. I handed my paper into Joe Jagger, the father of the Rolling Stones' Mick, and head of PE at Avery

College. He reviewed it and when he spoke to me later I saw my paper with all kinds of red marks on it. I thought oh no. He said to me. Mr. Jacks your spelling is absolutely appalling but I've given you an A minus because you are speaking through experience and we need your experience here. One thing I learned quite quickly from Joe involved something about time and energy in any situation. He explained it like this: 'In every situation work out the best way to do something with the minimum outlay of time and energy.'

One quote, related to this which has always stuck with me, came from author Barbara Knapp in her book called Skill in Sport. She said.

'Skill is the learned ability to bring about a pre-determined action with the minimum outlay of time and energy.'

With my new quest for education, and no longer sat at the back of the class, I eased off on judo just a little bit. Although as an honorary instructor at the Budokwai I continued with that and I tried to help Dad as much as I could when he coached at different schools and clubs. Obviously, I still wanted to compete for Great Britain but I became more selective in the events I participated in. This didn't sit that well with the BJA but I had to do that for three reasons. I had to save some time for my education. I'd reached an age where my body couldn't take all the constant travel and competitions. Plus I wanted to take a back seat sometimes to study my rivals and new talent coming through. I knew if I studied my opponents it would help me in the big competitions such as the Olympic Games and World Championships. I still had my ambition to be number one in the world and many times I paid to watch competitions and took notes about my main rivals. I tried to get into their heads so that when we met on the mat I knew exactly what they would try. This would enable me to counter their moves in advance. I knew when someone grabbed me in a certain way, exactly what they would do next. I wanted to eliminate the mysteries which gave me a big advantage. The BJA continued to ask me to compete in the French open, the Dutch open, the German open and the world championships but I knew if I continued to do that everyone would know my style. I had to say no sometimes to avoid giving away my secrets.

Towards the end of 1974, now fully established at Avery College and more or less cherry picking the competitions I entered, I had a call from Bill Backhus. We chatted, in English and Japanese, and he mentioned the World University Championships that would be held in

Brussels and asked if I could compete. Apparently, he knew one of the organisers and he'd promised him that he could get me there. He also said he needed me to do something for him and that he would make it worth my while. I didn't know why we'd used two languages. But knowing Bill he probably just wanted to test me to make sure I still understood Japanese. I checked it out and discovered that a few big names from Japan would be attending so I decided to give it a go. In the middleweights, I managed a bronze with Japan's Yoshimi Hara taking gold. Overall Japan managed five golds with Russia taking one.

I met Bill several times during the event and again we spoke English and Japanese, I asked him why he did that. He just said that walls have ears and that he liked to speak Japanese with people he'd spent time there with such as me. I didn't think too much about it and played along. He still lived in Frankfurt and his business, which he discussed with me in 1972, had continued to expand with more judo people from the old days now involved. He asked about my plans for the future and I explained about Avery and that I had a minimum of two years left before I could get a good job with a pension. Bill laughed at that and said if I joined his team I wouldn't have to worry about a pension and that I could retire at forty. I told him that sounded interesting but I wanted to finish my education first and have one last crack at an Olympic gold medal in Montreal. Bill's ears pricked up when I mentioned Montreal and he asked about the Montreal pre-Olympics scheduled for July 1975. I had a good idea that I would be taking part. Bill spoke in two languages again and from what he said I gathered I could make extra money by helping him with some business that he'd planned at the same time. He said he would discuss it with me in more detail later. He also asked if I could help him with his car. He had a big American Pontiac and part of his long-term plan, over the next three years, involved him moving his head office to London. He said he wanted to slowly move his assets out of Frankfurt, starting with his car, and that he wanted me to drive it to London. He handed me the keys and an envelope with £5,000 inside. I had to use half the cash for expenses related to storing the car and the other half for a belated wedding present. On the 4th of November I travelled from Frankfurt and, as fireworks exploded in the moonlit clear sky the following night, I locked the car in a long stay garage not far from my home.

33

I BEGAN 1975 with a few goals that all needed my full attention. From an education point of view, I needed to continue to push myself at Avery College and try not to fall behind too much. The other main event, outside the normal pattern of annual judo competitions, meant travelling to Montreal for the pre-Olympics at the end of July. But before this, on the 19th of April, we had the British Open at Crystal Palace. It took me a while to win this event, in my own weight category, but I eventually won it in 1973.

This year I made it to the final again with a few spicy contests along the way that had the crowd on their toes. I enjoyed this and I seemed to have a talent for bringing out emotions in people. I had my followers, Mum, Dad, and the rest of the Jacks' fan club. By that, I mean all my uncles, aunties, cousins, nephews and nieces. But I also think a few other people liked me as well. Of course, there were those who wanted to see me taken down a peg or two and I played up to them at every opportunity. Some reporters even compared me with the great Muhammad Ali for the way I stirred things up although I don't think I ever said anything about being the greatest. Well not that often!

In the middleweights section, eighty-five players took part with twenty-one from abroad. Before I reached the final one guy from the Midlands, called Les Hudspith, gave me a real battle. He knew his judo and if I hadn't been around at the same time as him he might have done a lot better. The same applied to Roy Inman who turned up at the Budokwai on a Wednesday afternoon one day. Roy became my student and now we were in the final of the British Open.

Our names were called and Roy went out to the mat first. At this point, Dad, who'd been giving me a few pointers under the Crystal Palace stands, told me to hang on. He wanted Roy to wait. They called my name again. Dad said to hold on again and a buzz went around the crowd. They wanted to get this contest on as I did. I said Dad I've got to go. He said no wait. They called my name for the third time and I knew I must have been close to the disqualification time for being late. I said Dad you've got to let me go and he did. As I appeared some of the crowd cheered whilst others booed. I'd experienced this before and I just waved and shook my fist which provoked more reactions from both sides of the fence. I suppose it was a bit like a pantomime. I gave them a chance to vent their feelings as opposed to just sitting there and offering up some polite applause whenever something good happened. With them animated I took it a stage further by walking up to the number one spot on the rostrum. There I blew on the sleeve of my jacket, blew on the number one spot, and then gave it a quick imaginary polish with my jacket sleeve. A kind of gesture which said the top spot belonged to me. Looking back now I suppose it does sound big headed but I went with the energy of the crowd. Poor old Roy didn't look amused. Anyway, we got started and I went on the attack. Roy came in and tried something that didn't work, which meant he'd hurt his own ribs. He recovered and we got on with it but we had a problem. As we'd trained together it meant we knew each other's game inside out. When I tried something, he anticipated it, and when he tried I did the same. So we got into a battle of the grips mostly around the edges of the mat. It must have been a bit dull for the crowd that I'd whipped up a few minutes earlier. With three minutes to go, we picked up the pace with a bit of a flurry which ended up with Roy on the judge's chair. The judge had got out the way but just in time. With time running out, and our equal scores, I got a penalty for pushing Roy out. This didn't give me a lot of time to remedy the situation. With the animated crowd behind both of us, which created an electric atmosphere, I went for it big time. Jim Coote of the Sunday Telegraph reported:

'It was a textbook demonstration of how to get in the maximum number of techniques in the minimum of time.'

Does that sound similar to Barbara Knapp's quote?

Anyway, I got the decision which met with a bit of a mixed reaction from the crowd. Roy, in the same way as Les before him, had put on a brave performance that might have won him a few more fans. Maybe my antics at the beginning had wound him up.

Next on my agenda came the European Championships in Lyon scheduled from the 8th to the 11th of May. A week before Lyon we had a visitor turn up at the house, completely out of the blue, carrying an Adidas sports bag and an Adidas tennis racket case that I assumed contained a racket. I said to him that I didn't know he played. He laughed and said he didn't. It just seemed the best way for him to carry what he had. I said what's that then and he replied that I didn't need to know. I invited him in and he seemed a bit flustered, not his normal confident self, so I asked him if he had a problem. He said no and that he just needed a place to stay for a couple of nights. I agreed and Julie made up the spare bedroom for him. When we were alone he asked if I knew a man, who knew a man, who could introduce him to another man for a bit of business. He also said he had something that would make everything worthwhile for anyone involved. Obviously, I asked him what kind of deal he had in mind and he raised his index finger to his lips. In Japanese he said walls have ears, at least I think he said that, and he suggested a walk in the garden. Outside he said he had something hot in his possession that he wanted to move on quickly. At this point, I seriously considered showing him the door. I had my future to think about and I didn't want to get caught up in some kind of scandal. Maybe he could tell by the look in my eyes how I felt as he'd known me for a long time. He wouldn't even tell me what he had in the case although he said it had nothing to do with drugs. He knew my feelings on that subject and that I wouldn't have them in my house. The following morning he disappeared with his sports bag and racket case. When he returned he only had a black briefcase. He stayed one more night and left the following morning with a promise to call me in a month as he had a business proposition he wanted to discuss with me. Bill Backhus, who I'd known for a long time and had operated in grey areas with dodgy deals, might just have been involved with another one. I had no idea what it was, or who he eventually dealt with, I didn't want to know.

In Lyon, I met up with Jean-Paul Coche and we had a good chat about the old days. We were both now twenty-eight, a lot more mature than when we chased the Mormon twins, and we still remained at the top of our games. In Salt Lake City we were the golden boys of our countries' judo and now we remained idols in many people's eyes. For the last five years, we'd almost totally dominated the European middleweight event. I won it in 1970 in Berlin. He took it in Voorburg in 1972. It came back to me in Madrid the next year with him picking it up a year later in London. The year we missed out, 1971, Guy Auffray took the title. The last time we'd actually fought had been during the Munich Olympics in 1972 when we were in the same pool and I beat him. Here in Lyon, we were destined to meet in round two if we won our opening contests.

I came up against Gerold Jungwirth of Austria and I toyed with him really. I didn't want to give anything away but did just enough to get the decision. Jean-Paul threw Gilbert Gustin of Belgium in the first minute to take his contest. As he left the mat he eyeballed me and I smiled back at him. Game on.

Obviously, he had the home crowd behind him as we quickly took hold. I attacked him with a shoulder throw to his left which I thought should have at least scored a partial point. The Dutch referee didn't see it that way and gave no score. On our feet again and he came at me with a similar move that won him a partial point. I knew I had to get at him quickly. I came straight back in with a few attacks that shook him and he took two paces out of the area. Head bowed he walked back to the centre and knelt down. I milked this moment and swaggered around the mat with my arms in the air. The home crowd, not happy with me taunting them, went bananas. They wanted blood, mine, but I didn't care. This was my arena and I did all I could to let them know. For his actions, Jean-Paul ended up with a warning. I felt confident and let him make some of the running. He tried a throw which left him with his back to the safety area and his feet on the line. I immediately came in for an attack and he stepped out of the area for the second time which meant instant disqualification. For some reason, the referee and the judges needed a conference and they decided that I'd pushed him. Unbelievably they gave me a warning. That cheered the crowd up and meant that we were halfway through with him back in front. Even though I'd dominated the contest! I shook my head in disbelief as did a few others. I went at him again and surprised him with an attempt at a stomach throw that turned into a standing arm lock. Jean-Paul desperately tapped the mat as he crashed onto it. I let him go, ready to taunt the crowd again, but the referee hadn't seen it and he didn't even want another chinwag with the judges. We raised ourselves again and battled for grips. I spun in for a throw and landed on top of him. The judges were off their seats as they called the throw. The referee, in keeping with his general overall performance during this contest, ignored them. He called us back to fight on as mayhem broke out around the mat. I found it incredible that this contest went to time and he won on points I think he did as well. He lost his next contest, to Russia's Alexey Volosov who in turn lost to the eventual winner Antoni Reiter from Poland. We were both well and truly out.

About a week before flying to Montreal for the Pre Olympics I had another one of those multi-language calls from Frankfurt. First, we spoke some small talk in English before he switched to Japanese. I managed to work out that he wanted me to hand deliver a package for him to someone who would meet me at the airport in Montreal. He went on to explain that I wouldn't be doing anything illegal but it might be best if I kept the package out of sight from everybody. By that, he meant I would have to wear a special body pouch and conceal the package there. I didn't like the sound of that and replied that it would be impossible for me to do this no matter how much he paid me. He then asked the same question as he had during his visit to my house. Did I know a man, who might know a man, who could put him in touch with another man? I didn't like him putting me on the spot again but without really thinking I talked about a teacher we knew without actually naming him. Bill confirmed he understood who it was and he hung up.

34

BY THE START of 1976, at the age of twenty-nine, I knew two things. My judo days were numbered. My body had taken a real hammering during the last fifteen years and the aches and pains were starting to bite. All sportsmen, professional and amateur, suffer from injuries and I'd had quite a few. I'd even been carried out of some tournaments on a stretcher and wheeled out of others in a wheelchair. But injuries and sport go hand in hand and as much as I'd broken all kinds of bones and dislocated all kinds of joints, I'd recovered enough to enjoy a long and successful career. I'd been lucky as I knew many sportsmen whose careers were shattered by injury. The second thing related to my teacher training at Avery College. The way things were looking I knew I wouldn't be finishing in September of this year. But despite my creaking body, we were in another Olympic year and I still wanted the gold that I'd come so close to in 1972. In fact, I wanted it more. With this in mind, I suppose I switched more attention to Montreal.

Things didn't get off to the best of starts as I squashed a nerve in my back when demonstrating a throw at the Budokwai. This meant a trip to St Stephen's Hospital in Fulham Road, Chelsea for a couple of weeks. This proved a setback in more ways than one as I also missed some important exams that I should have taken.

By the 10th of April, they'd patched me up enough so I took my place at Crystal Palace for the British Open Championships. Quite a few fans had also turned up to support us and they hung around all day, not just for the finals, which was very nice. Ray Neenan took the lightweight title with a narrow win over Constantine 'Alex' Alexander.

One of my best ever students, eighteen year old Chris Bowles from Tunbridge Wells in Kent took part in the light middleweights. I first met Chris at Dog Kennel Hill and Dad and I were both impressed. We knew he had talent so I took him under my wing and introduced him to the Budokwai where he continued to improve. He won a few domestic events and most kids in and around his age couldn't get near him. We called him 'Tonker Toy' and he was a very strong boy. He would go out to the mat, quickly sum up his opponent, and then destroy them with one of his favourite techniques. He looked good. But as his coach, I wanted more. I explained to him that if he went out there, and he knew he could beat his opponent before the start, he didn't need to just flatten him straight away with his favourite technique, I wanted him to use the opportunity to try different things. To use techniques that he didn't enjoy or couldn't perform very well. I explained more to him about self-handicapping and how this could be advantageous to him in the long run. It didn't matter if the other person actually threw him and they got big headed about it. It didn't really matter as long as he knew the truth and he would be better for it. I wanted Chris to follow this tactic the Southern Area Championship which we knew he would win. I told him that he could only use a certain technique. Chris refused and told me I was being ridiculous and asked me how he could expect to get in the British team if he could only do one technique. I took umbrage to this. I never questioned any of my coaches and I told him if he didn't do as I said he'd never train at my club again. During that competition, he won every contest with the technique I asked him to use. In 1974 he took gold in the European Cadet Championships in Tel Aviv.

Unfortunately, at the British Open in 1976, he went out early although he went on to take the European Junior Championships in Berlin the following year and he won the British open in 1978. For 1976, Vass Morrison, another player I trained at the Budokwai, took the title in a very close final against seventeen year old Neil Adams, who'd also turned up at the Budokwai when he was fifteen. Below is what Neil had to say about our early meetings which I hope he won't mind me quoting here!

'The first time I went to the Budokwai was on a Wednesday and I just went to watch. Jacks was running the Monday and Wednesday sessions which were the hard ones. His aim was to work you until you felt physically sick. Anyway, I looked in through the door and as soon as he saw me, he came up and said, 'I've got a surprise for you.' I had no idea what he meant until, a few days later, we practised groundwork together for the first time and he strangled me unconscious. When I came round, he was smiling and I swore on my life that I would never let him do that again. I tried to thump him, really thump him, but he was just laughing which was typical Jacks. I know now that it was only his way to get me to fight harder because that was what had happened to him in Japan, but I thought it was going too far. And if he had tried to do it again, I would probably have injured him. I have seen it happen in Japan, where first-year students are dragged off the mat because they have been strangled out by third-year students and I hate it. I think it is unnecessary. It is important to encourage young fighters but I have other ways. I have never strangled anyone unconscious, except by accident, which does happen in judo.'

Neil had great talent and I hope I helped him during those early days even though we obviously didn't see things the same way. Neil is one hundred percent correct when he mentions my early days in Japan that really shaped the person I became. Anyone who came to my sessions at the Budokwai had to be motivated or there would be no need for them to turn up. In fact, if I knew they weren't I'd show them the door. Chris, Neil, and Vass will all tell you that I pushed them hard, maybe harder than anyone had ever pushed them before, but I never asked them to do anything that I'd never done. I'm sure one minute they loved me and the next minute they hated me. At times some of my students were actually sick as Neil mentioned.

As I watched Vass and Neil in the final I felt proud that I'd played a part in shaping their careers. For Vass being a Londoner meant I wanted him to win. Neil represented the Midlands. They had a ten minute battle of tactics that some people might have found boring. But not me. I saw the intense concentration in Vass which enabled him to scrape through. With Neil, I knew it would only be a matter of time.

For me, in my eleventh British Open, my back didn't let me down and I made it through to the final where I came up against Adalbert Missalla from West Germany, a new contender who'd just arrived on the European stage. They called our names and as I made way to the mat I walked passed all the dignitaries sat close by including Great Britain's National Coach Raymond Ross. Something about him didn't look right. I stopped and glared at him. He stared at me. The officials and silent crowd ogled us. Ray wore a beautiful tracksuit jacket with a big British flag on it. I slowly walked up to him and asked him what he was wearing. He said it was the jacket for the Montreal Olympics. I said as the British team captain surely I should have it first. He said that I could have one as soon as they arrived and that his was a prototype. I said no. I want that jacket. He said if you can beat that guy on the mat he'd definitely make sure I have the first one when they came in. I said I can do better than that Ray. I told him I'd go out there and beat that guy in ten seconds and if I did that, he had to give me his jacket right there and then. We shook hands on it in front of the dignitaries, the four thousand fans, and of course with Missalla waiting patiently on the mat. There were whispers around the crowd and I think everyone must have known. I walked on, we bowed, and I didn't beat him in ten seconds. I did it in eight and walked straight over to Ray and picked up my jacket.

I think Missalla must have been totally mind blown by what had just happened. He expected me to come out, fully focused on my contest with him, but he saw me deep in conversation with Ray about a fancy tracksuit jacket. I think he froze and my jacket deal cost him the contest.

The following month we were off to Kiev in Russia for the Senior European Championships. For those nervous about flying this proved a massive test. We landed in Moscow where we picked up another plane for the second leg of our journey to Kiev. At about 1,000 feet the passenger rear door flew open. A huge gust of air burst into the aircraft and I thought 'That's it. Game over.' As did Dave Starbrook! He screamed his head off and certainly thought it was curtains. As I bit my bottom lip everything seemed to move in slow motion and I imagined us all being sucked out one by one. A Russian soldier sat close by, bravely began to move towards the door. Constantine 'Alex' Alexander, a former paratrooper in the British Army, as you would expect didn't panic. He clambered over Paul Radburn, who sat next to him, and held on to the Russian's legs to stop him being sucked out. A few others held on to Alex until the Russian had secured the door. This had to be one of the most frightening experiences of my life and I can assure you we all thanked that Russian soldier and of course Alex.

At a press conference on the 21st of June, Ray Ross announced the British team for Montreal and Alex had been included. I think Dave and I were well pleased he'd had made the team as we felt so much better when we flew with him! We even joked that he'd received the nod over Ray Neenan due to his quick reactions during that flight to Kiev although Alex's current form had been very good. How did I feel about being selected for my third Olympics in the last sixteen years? Well, obviously I felt proud, as did my family, but it had been an extremely hard journey with a lot of sacrifices along the way. Judo, to reach the top and stay there for eighteen years, demanded superhuman levels of fitness that many people don't realise. If you didn't, and you've read this far, then you might have a better idea. You can't just turn up, perform, and then go home or to the pub. It takes dedication and the expression, 'no pain no gain,' might really sum up judo. I'd suffered a lot of pain and I'm not really sure if the gains balanced the pains. Pain is all part of judo. You get punished. Some, no matter how much pain they are in, will never submit. Remember Martin Poglajen. He would never give up no matter how much pain he suffered.

Doctor Ken Kingsbury once said. *It really is next to impossible to become an Olympic champion and do a normal job each day. Judo is the most exacting combat art of all. It is a life's work.*

A life's work and I knew exactly what he meant. But, unlike some of our counterparts in other sports, we seemed to have been ignored. In the early days, my parents made so many sacrifices which I've already written about. Now, in 1976, I had a lot to thank Julie for. She paid the bills and everything else. I never had any money but she backed me all the way with my ambition to win an Olympic gold medal. I'd been studying for nearly three years and I'd actually passed two exams. This meant I had one to go but there would have to be a delay in taking it as the date clashed with my Olympic training. This annoyed me as I believed someone somewhere could have made an allowance for my circumstances. I didn't miss it because my car broke down or I'd overslept. I never wanted any special favours but I thought to represent my country in the Olympic Games should have cut me some slack. It didn't which meant I had to earn a pittance as an unqualified teacher for a longer period. I might have been better off as a road sweeper. I felt annoyed at this time as I knew other countries, such as Japan, America, France, Russia and many more, would never treat their athletes in the way I had been treated. And of course many others like me. Despite this, I felt proud to be selected for the Team GB for

Montreal. I knew with the right kind of draw I had it in me to return home with that gold medal.

The Montreal Olympics ran from the 26th of July to the 31st of August with security much tighter due to what happened in Munich. There were no signs of Bill Backhus, walking around the Olympic Village as if he owned it this time. As with Tokyo and Munich, we went through all the standard Olympic procedures which I've described in detail before. Montreal wanted to put on a spectacle to show the world and they did very well. For judo, we had the pool system again which meant many good players meeting each other in the pool matches were knocked out. This allowed less talented players to go through to the final rounds. Many believed judo should have adopted a seeding system.

I started against Ibraheem Muzfer from Kuwait and threw him in under two minutes to take the contest. Against Carlos Santos Motta of Brazil, I got the decision. Yugoslavian Slavko Obadov waited for me in the next round and I knew this would be a much tougher test. He made a good start and took an early advantage but he had a penalty recorded against him which put me in the driver's seat. The contest had to be mine. Unfortunately, the recorder had made a mistake so the penalty didn't count. Obadov took the decision and it meant an early exit for me. We lodged a complaint but it didn't go anywhere. A bit of a disappointment as I knew this could be my last chance in the Olympic Games. Dave Starbrook did well and equaled my performance in Munich when he picked up a bronze. Keith Remfry won silver when he lost to Japan's Haruki Uemura, in the final of the open.

Vivien Fryer reported as follows:

'A sad end to a brilliant career. But we shall not remember Brian as defeated in Montreal, but as the European Champion, who won bronze in Munich and so many other medals that even he must have lost count. I'm sure as a talisman for success there can be no one better. Brian has done so much for judo in Britain, probably to the detriment of his own future. With the constant unfailing backing of his family from the word go aided by his own well-founded belief in himself and determination to win. Brian has won titles despite broken bones and in the face of hostile crowds. He has been an example to us all, and let's hope that his future as a coach, or whatever capacity, will be as successful as has been his overall competition record.'

John Goodbody said:

Jacks was unlucky. It was particularly sad that on an occasion when Starbrook and Remfry should have got medals to end their careers, Jacks should not have done so as well. He began brightly enough against Obadov a penalty point, mistakenly signalled by the recorder, and was cancelled by the referee at the end of the bout. Obadov should have got the penalty point in any case but the real point was that Jacks thought he was winning by the scores displayed on the boards and consequently paced his fighting accordingly. Thus the contest was awarded to Obadov in the most unsatisfactory manner. But despite this annoying defeat, nothing can tarnish his record. He has won more European Championship medals than anyone in the history of the sport except the Dutchman Anton Geesink. In addition, he took the World Championship bronze in 1967 and the Olympic bronze in 1972. He has pioneered Britain's recent eminence in judo. In twenty years time, we will recall his victories, not this unfortunate defeat.

And Tony Macconnell said this:

Brian Jacks is simply one of the greatest athletes in any sport that Britain has produced in the last twelve years. In judo he is unique. He seems capable of winning anything, absolutely anything.

35

BACK IN ENGLAND, I pondered my retirement questions. Everybody expected me to do it and I had more chats with Dad. He felt I should now be looking at a normal life. Julie understood and I think she wanted to begin a new life, with a nine to five husband or as close as I could get, and start a family. Dave and Keith, fresh from Olympic success, confirmed they wouldn't be competing anymore. It should have been an easy decision for me as my body had been telling me for some time it couldn't take any more.

In October of 1976, Bill Backhus turned up at my house again and stayed a few days. This time I don't think he had anything 'hot' that he needed to move on quickly and he had a few Americans with him who he trained. He said they were the American national team who wanted some experience in England. They stayed in a nearby hotel but I never met them. I questioned Bill about his car and I even took him to the garage so he could check on it. He seemed happy and said he expected to transfer all his operations to England very soon. He asked me to keep my eyes open for an office block in central London for his new headquarters. He also mentioned another venture he'd started which involved people who we knew in Eastern bloc countries who wanted to escape to the West. He even asked if I'd offer my house, as a kind of 'safe house,' for these people. I shook my head and he didn't mention it again. I'd been to those countries, seen how the people lived, but I couldn't be involved in anything like that.

Before the year finished Dad mentioned that Peter Coller, a keen judo fan who trained quite a bit but didn't quite have the ability to make it at the highest level, wanted to open a judo club with me. Dad and I had discussed this before and we thought that now would be a good time. We found a vacant building in Orpington and signed a twenty-five year lease for part of it. Obviously, we had to cover the expenses and we believed we could do this with a minimal cost to our members. We were not about making profits as we wanted to provide a service to the community. We called our club B and P Judo and Peter proved exactly my type of partner. He let me get on with it and agreed to most of my suggestions. We attracted some of the best junior talents in England and also received great support from top British players who provided their time for free.

On the 23rd of April 1977, with England rocked with strikes and go-slows that made it difficult to travel anywhere, I sat with a group of people as we listened to a short speech from Charles Palmer, still Chairman of the BJA and President of the IJF. He introduced, in public for the first time, the association's recently appointed joint full-time Team Managers, Dave Starbrook and Tony Macconnell. They took a bow to some huge applause as did Keith Remfry when introduced as the new part-time Development Officer. Palmer thanked them for all they'd done for British judo over the years before he made one other comment which Tony Reay reported like this:

'Mr. Palmer thoughtfully noted that the fourth member of the British 'greats' over the last decade, and quite a bit longer, was still competing and described him as the 'Evergreen Brian Jacks.' Brian stepped out of the ranks of competitors, paraded for the finals, to bow and wave to another round of thunderous applause from the crowd.'

I hadn't done it. I couldn't bring myself to hang my kit on a lonely peg, in an empty dressing room, and walk away. Not yet. Despite everything, I still wanted to compete and of course, win. Now at the British Open Championships in London, I made the final again and faced one of my students. Vass Morrison. As we were about to start I made a comment about some mats that had been forced apart during an earlier contest. As usual, this wound up a section of the crowd and they used this opportunity to let their feelings known. In this instance, I don't really think I intended this as showmanship as I only wanted everything to be right before the start. Showmanship would have been a quick polish of the number one spot on the rostrum which I didn't want to try with Vass. I knew he'd give me a real battle because whenever we trained together I found him a difficult opponent. He had great flexibility which meant he could bend his way out of most attacks. But despite my innocent request a few of my usual hecklers gave me stick. No doubt they'd have loved it if Vass had managed something unexpected and dumped me on the mat. I went in immediately and he, as I expected, bent out of the way. Obviously, we knew each other's styles, which made it difficult. I couldn't get a grip on him and he felt like a piece of rubber. He swayed one way and then another way. He came in low and deep with a shoulder throw which I didn't quite read and he managed to lift me in the air. He received a partial point and the stadium erupted. I think many of them couldn't believe it. This put me on the back foot and I knew I needed to get in quick with a reply. I tried a few things but he kept coming back at me. He seemed like a man possessed and I'd very rarely seen him handle pressure in the way he did at this moment. He surprised me with the way he stood up to me and the way he fought back. The crowd were on their feet. I tried everything I could but nothing worked. We kept the pace going right up until the last seconds as the crowd roared and raged. When the klaxon went he threw up his arms. He'd performed like a true warrior and thoroughly deserved his victory. Now he let me get hold of him. I gave him a hug and shook his hand.

Thursday the 12th of May, when I eventually arrived home, I thought it a bit strange that two official-looking black BMWs were parked outside my house. But then I remembered that the Nigerians had been trying to contact me again and I assumed they'd found me. I smiled to myself.

But five stern men in suits sat in my living room and they were definitely not Nigerian. Julie looked worried. Detective Chief Superintendent Dennis Greenslade introduced himself as he flashed his official-looking credentials. The other four were German detectives on a special mission to see me. I asked Julie what was going on and she said she didn't know. Apparently, they'd arrived about an hour ago, she'd let them in, made them coffee and given them biscuits as they waited for me. I asked Greenslade what he wanted and if he had a warrant to enter my house. He said he didn't but they just wanted to ask us both some questions to clear up a few issues they had. He also suggested we kept things cordial as he didn't want to upset his German colleagues. Part of me wanted to throw them out and another part of me wanted to hear what they had to say. I couldn't think of any reason why they would want to talk to me and even thought that maybe Julie had been up to something.

They wanted to speak to me first and Julie to left the living room. I asked if I needed a lawyer and they said no. They just wanted me to listen first and comment later. They began by talking about something called 'Operation Judo,' an international drug investigation that revolved around the world of LSD, also known as acid. A psychedelic drug known for its psychological effects. Of course, being part of the psychedelic swinging sixties and in the nightclub business, I'd heard of it but I'd never had anything to do with it. They believed otherwise and then his name came up. The person, who'd been like a second Dad to me in Japan, and who'd helped me through one of the toughest periods in my life.

Apparently, Bill Backhus had been arrested in West Germany and accused of being the big boss, of the European half of an international gang, smuggling drugs into the

United States. They said he'd been responsible for smuggling a total of nearly twenty-one kilos of Ergotamine Tartrate (ET) to California between December 1975 and April 1977. Apparently, ET is produced by a number of major drug companies for its legitimate use in the treatment of migraines. But, according to the guys sat on my sofa, it's also a vital component in the manufacture of LSD. At this point, I still didn't understand why they thought I might be involved until they stunned me with their next pieces of news. They knew I'd driven Bill's car back from Frankfurt and they'd even been to the garage and taken it apart looking for drugs. They knew Bill had stayed at my house twice during the last two years and, what totally gobsmacked me even more, they had a record of every telephone conversation we'd had over quite a long period of time. They'd bugged my telephone and they also wanted a name. In one particular call, Bill and I had talked about a person who might be able to help him with a special delivery. We were speaking in Japanese and English about a friend of a friend who lived in a place that Bill knew. I used the word teacher as well to make sure Bill had fully understood. He had, and it's important to note here, that Bill had assured me that he wanted to transport legal medicine to the states unofficially. I needed a bathroom break to collect my thoughts.

Bill's 'walls have ears' comments had certainly proved true although we had discussed many people from the old days even if we hadn't used their full names. We used nicknames and other ways to identify people. One person, who'd kind of gone off the radar recently, had been Ronald Cory the Las Vegas card shark who I'd met at the Kodokan in 1962. He'd actually died, which is a pretty good reason for going off the radar. But I didn't know if they knew. Plus I needed time to think. When I went back in there I threw Cory's name into the ring. Pleased with a name they soon left.

I discovered that 'Operation Judo' had been going on for some time and, for a long period, had been running in tandem with another LSD investigation known as 'Operation Julie.' Yes. 'Operation Julie.' Two operations, both with possible to links to me, as judo and Julie were all I lived for really. People might have been putting that connection together and making all kinds of assumptions!

International Investigations into the murky world of LSD had been going on for some time with police operations in the United States as well as Great Britain and Europe. There were, as 'Operation Judo' suggests, strong links with people in the judo world. Many had been around in the sixties when Bill first surfaced in Japan. During 1974 the American Drug Enforcement Administration (DEA) began an enquiry into Theodore Ted Crowton, a six feet five inch tall Hells Angel in the amphetamine business. He acted as a courier and at the time of his arrest, he had six pounds of chemicals. This led them to a small island on the Sacramento River where they found a sophisticated pill press, half a million amphetamine tablets, and over seven thousand grammes of powdered amphetamines. From there they moved on to a drug laboratory run by a West Point failure called Nicholas Andrade, in the California state capital of Sacramento opposite the City's fire station. During the last five months, $5 million of wholesale speed had been manufactured. Most of the equipment, including chemical vats used by large pharmaceutical firms, had disappeared along with Andrade. At his father's funeral police arrested Andrade. A couple of days before his trial a federal informant in California received a telephone call from a judo expert, Lee Frickstad Hassler, who'd appointed an attorney to monitor the trial for him. Andrade had decided to plead not guilty which badly frightened Crowton who'd been called to give evidence. This concerned Hassler and he wanted to know what evidence the police had. He felt afraid that parts of his network might be blown apart under cross-examination. Days before the trial Hassler was murdered and Andrade changed his plea to guilty. Police searched his room and soon discovered he'd been a leading dealer in amphetamines and LSD. Detectives found two cars he owned with a cache of weapons inside that included a submachine gun. They also found a small black book with notes and dozens of names and telephone numbers. It also included addresses of people throughout the world and alerted them to an apartment Hassler owned in Hanover, West Germany, plus two safety deposit boxes where they later found fifteen litres of ET and $6,000 in cash.

Bill's name figured prominently in Hassler's black book which soon came to the attention of drug enforcement forces in London, Frankfurt, Amsterdam, Tokyo, Montreal, Helsinki, Hong Kong, Paris, Seoul and other parts of America where other special task forces were trying to track down the source of the ET. They checked Hassler's movements and discovered he'd spent time in West Germany and that he'd been in constant touch with Bill. They even had evidence that Hassler believed Bill had ripped him off to the tune of $100,000. This threw up questions about his murder. Had it happened as a result of this money or because of Andrade's trial? The West German special task force tried to put Bill under a twenty-four hour watch which proved complicated due to his inside knowledge of surveillance techniques. He also had a habit of using public telephones for important calls. Remember he set up a company in Tokyo called Orient Wide Investigators Incorporated the private detective agency which specialised in surveillance detection of bugging devices. But now and again he let his guard down and used his house phone which provided detectives with more leads. He made two calls to me and from those calls, they determined that he'd asked me to take medical supplies to the states and that I'd said no. We did speak about other people who might be interested such as a mutual friend called Cyril Carter, although we never mentioned his actual name. This report found its way back to England where 'Operation Julie,' still searching for the source of ET being processed by Richard Kemp, the chemist at the heart of the LSD manufacturing, became very interested. A section of the team, under the operational control of Inspector Richard Lee, the former head of the Thames Valley Drug Squad, were dispatched to keep an eye on Bill when he visited London on his way to California for a skiing holiday. But due to the shoestring nature of 'Operation Julie,' this plan had to be abandoned.

Back in West Germany, when shipments were being traced, the special task force witnessed an extraordinary attempt by Bill to get his hands on Hassler's assets and contacts. He even acquired the uniform and credentials of an American Major in the Military Police and went to the house in Hanover which Hassler had shared with two teachers. Hadley Caesar Watson twenty-five years old, from Portsmouth, Virginia, accompanied him posing as an interpreter. Bill announced that he intended to remove Hassler's belongings which included $200,000 in cash and paperwork. His search for Hassler's safety deposit box keys proved unsuccessful. 'Operation Julie' detectives were convinced that one delivery had been channeled through England by a professional couple, probably in teaching, in February or March of 1976. Detective Superintendent Greenslade's attempts to track down this couple had so far proved unsuccessful. No doubt Mr. and Mrs. Carter were relieved about that.

In West Germany during June of 1976, at an Interpol meeting, police decided to check companies who'd made strange pharmaceutical purchases and in doing so they discovered a blunder made by the network. A Dutch national named Johannes Cornelius Bluming had purchased ten point five kilos of ET, up to December 1975, and exported the substance back to Holland. But he hadn't bothered to claim back the eleven percent tax due to him which meant a $5,000 refund. At the same time, the DEA in Frankfurt were given information about a drug smuggling network in Germany and provided with Bill's name which almost immediately identified the judo pattern.

After Bill left Japan he went to Holland where he renewed his links in the LSD world. He had a huge number of judo contacts and he hooked up with Bluming, One of Holland's former judo stars who he'd met ten years ago in Tokyo. From there he soon moved to West Germany. Eventually, Dutch police traced the ET purchases back to Bluming and this opened up a whole new ball game. The Dutch police handed things over to another special task force from Wiesbaden, in West Germany, specifically set up to deal with terrorism and drug trafficking.

Judo clubs with ET connections were discovered in Oakland, California and another in Reno Nevada run by a judo expert named Garry Friedrichs. The drug teams made a critical breakthrough when they arrested Friedrichs after an informant had persuaded Bill to let him fly across with a delivery of one kilo strapped to his body belt. Bill had instructed the informant to remove it in a restroom and put it in a briefcase the moment the plane had taken off so his body heat wouldn't spoil the ET. In Chicago, detectives followed the informant as he made his way to Reno where he completed his delivery. He called Bill in West Germany to advise him the delivery had been successful. Detectives arrested Friedrichs, who received a suspended sentence for smuggling. Bill and Watson were arrested in West Germany where police found Bill's house full of strange martial arts instruments and a huge collection of detective and spy thrillers. They didn't find any ET immediately but four kilos were later discovered in a locked trunk. He and Watson were both charged with being members of a conspiracy and dealing in drugs, offences carrying a maximum sentence of ten years.

The night of the 12th of May 1977 obviously turned into quite a traumatic one for us and we didn't sleep well. In the morning I phoned a solicitor friend in London called John Wood. He listened to everything and suggested Julie and I went away for a long weekend whilst he checked a few things. We took his advice. When we arrived home the following Monday morning I found an official-looking letter addressed to me and soon discovered I'd been summoned to West Germany. I called John who advised me to meet him in his office at 2:00 p.m. I felt absolutely shattered as if someone had taken my life and flushed it down the toilet. In John's office, he didn't seem too worried. He quickly read the letter and more or less discarded it. He said I had the law on my side and didn't have to go. He just said ignore it and don't worry. I felt so much better and the more he talked the better I felt. John explained that he'd had lunch with a friend who knew about 'Operation Julie' and he shared the story with me.

'Operation Julie' started towards the end of 1975 and involved eleven police forces that resulted in the breakup of one of the largest LSD manufacturing operations in the world. A group of officers were trained to go undercover as hippies in Wales and they moved into a farmhouse, near Tregaron, which overlooked a cottage owned by the chemist Richard Kemp who first successfully synthesized LSD in 1969. Police knew him as a possible suspect in the drugs trade. His red Range Rover had been involved in an accident with another car near Machynlleth which resulted in the death of a passenger in the other car. This enabled officers to search Kemp's car where they discovered six pieces of paper which, after being reconstructed, spelled hydrazine hydrate, a key ingredient in the manufacture of LSD. This crucial lead gave police their first vital clue into a drug ring operating in West Wales and led to the launch of 'Operation Julie.'

The officers in the farmhouse watching Kemp were regarded by locals as 'Gay Hippie Birdwatchers' which didn't sit well with the squad. In an effort to change this they needed a female hippy to join them. Up stepped Sergeant Julie Taylor and the reason for the name of the operation. During a hot summer's day in 1976, as the under-cover hippies mingled with real hippies at a festival, they were forced to strip naked to avoid being rumbled by real hippies who'd stripped off. Surveillance of Kemp noted his regular fifty mile commutes between his home in Ceredigion and Plas Llysin, to an old mansion owned by an American, Paul Joseph Arnaboldi, in Carno near Llanidloes. Undercover police monitored the mansion from an old caravan before they broke in. In the cellar, they took water samples which chemically matched LSD samples they already held. Listening devices were also installed in Kemp's property. On the 26th of March 1977 'Operation Julie' officers swooped on eighty-seven homes in England and Wales. Gang leaders were caught and a total of 120 suspects were arrested. At Kemp's home police found a package containing £11,000 as well as LSD crystals and other equipment.

John had reassured me and that night I took Julie out for a nice meal. I explained to her that I'd done nothing wrong and that the West German police couldn't do anything about making me go. I think she believed me. I didn't tell her that ten percent of me still felt they might try and pull some heavyweight strings and force me to go.

More questions were asked about my retirement after I lost in the final Vass and I kind of answered them depending on how I felt. If I felt down I might have said yes. But if I felt good I might get bullish and speak about going for gold at the Moscow Olympics. So nobody really knew, except me, and I didn't know either. The BJA, who might have heard me on a down day when I could have mentioned that I'd retired, acted on that. They wrote to me advising that they would promote me to sixth Dan. No British fighter had ever fought at this level and I suppose that should have been that. At the age of thirty-one, I should have taken that as a signal to retire and walked away. On the 7th of August 1977, all the formalities were completed and I became Great Britain's youngest ever sixth Dan. Did I quietly walk away or did I become the first ever British player to perform as at that level?

At Avery, I'd passed my final exams and became a real-life teacher, the real Professor Jacks, and taken a position at Woolwich College in London. They gave me a job on one condition. During term time I would not be allowed to take any time off for judo competitions. I could still practice and coach. But they wouldn't allow me to take time off to travel to competitions. I knew this meant I would have to give up competing internationally unless an event took place during holidays. With thoughts about my long-term future, I agreed and accepted the very nice package they offered which meant I only had to work three days a week. With my new career I had to cut back on judo, which I didn't mind, and in fact, a few things happened which lead to me handing in my resignation as a senior instructor at the Budokwai. For me sport is sport and politics is politics. They should never be mixed. But things were happening which meant politics were taking over sport and I didn't want any part of that. I'd always tried to promote kids, to bring them on, and I didn't approve of the politics being followed by the new committee.

On the 1st of October 1977, the Phillips All-England Championship took place at Harrow's Leisure Centre. BBC's television cameras were even there to record the event with a plan to show highlights during Grandstand at 2:00 p.m. on the 15th of October. They'd also covered the event the previous year. At last, judo had begun to receive more exposure although it's a shame they didn't show it live or at least the week after. But they were there. And guess what? I'd had made the trip as well.

To be officially recognised, throughout the World especially Japan, as a professor of judo felt fantastic. I can't begin to describe how proud I felt. Should I have competed? Well as I mentioned earlier I'd got a bit fed up with the way politics kept creeping into sport. Maybe, if I'd been politically correct, I wouldn't have. But that didn't sit well with me. They, the BJA, didn't think I'd do it. So maybe to spite them I did. In the final of the under 86 kilos I beat Nicholas Kokotaylo.

Things at Woolwich were going well. I had a great relationship with my students and I enjoyed the occasional jokes with the other lecturers in the staff common room. Academically there were a few in there on a much higher level than me but it didn't seem to matter. I think they, even though they would have never admitted to it, felt quite excited rubbing shoulders with an Olympic medalist.

36

FOR THE REST of 1977 there were no further alarm bells from West Germany. At least none related to me going there. One night we had a shifty looking character turn up with an envelope for me. I thought oh no, not again, but shifty soon disappeared and inside the envelope, I found a brief handwritten letter which said:

This is for you and thanks for the favour from a friend in another country. You've done exactly the right thing so stay on the same track.

That was it. The usual, cloak and dagger mysterious kind of thing, which I'd learned to expect from Bill Backhus. I knew that after the detectives had interviewed me they checked all the people they could find who had judo connections in Japan during the 1960s, who weren't Japanese. They certainly believed someone with a judo connection had to be involved in the shipment that went through London and not another kind of teacher, up to his armpits in debts, who desperately needed money.

My retirement question lingered on and on and I still couldn't answer it. My body, despite a few usual twinges that I'd learned to live with, overall still felt capable of mixing it with the big boys in the world. But I knew, with my job at Woolwich College, this would be out of the question as I'd agreed never to take time off for competitions or to train for them. Part of me resented this. For more than sixteen years I'd done my thing, more or less my way, and I didn't enjoy the constraints that a full-time job placed on me. At times I felt shackled. But another part of me knew that Woolwich provided me with stability, which perhaps Dad didn't have with his taxi business, so this had to be the way forward whether I liked it or not. I taught I trained, I coached, and I won the British Open in April beating another one of my students, Peter Donnelly.

The European Championships were held in Helsinki during May and of course, I couldn't compete. Did I miss it? Yes. I wanted to be there. The thing about being a PE teacher meant I spent most of my time in a tracksuit out in the field. The same applied to my free time. I felt fitter than ever and with still a few months to go before my thirty-second birthday. I didn't feel ready to stop. I wanted to compete at the highest level. Peth had taken part in his one and only Olympics at the ripe old age of thirty-eight. I studied the judo event calendar for the next two years.

April 1979 – British Open.

May 1979 – European Championships in Brussels.

December 1979 – World Championships in Paris.

April 1980 – British Open.

May 1980 – European Championships in Vienna.

July 1980 – Olympic Games in Moscow.

I wanted to take part in those tournaments and end, on a real high, by taking the gold in Moscow. That would be closure for me. The perfect way to end my competitive career and I would still only be thirty-three. Woolwich College could also share my glory as I really believed it would be a huge kudos for them to have an Olympic gold medalist on their staff. They'd already seen the impact I made with the kids who responded in a very positive way. I'd accepted the position with a promise to virtually give up my international judo career. Now, having proved myself, I believed they would change their stance. To me, it sounded like one of the biggest no-brainers of the century and I decided to run it by my superiors.

We also followed 'Operations Julie and Judo' during 1978 with many reports written in newspapers and on the television. For 'Julie' fifteen defendants appeared at Bristol

Crown Court and in total, they received combined sentences of 120 years in jail. As a result of the dawn raids over a million tablets, and enough crystal to make a further six point five million tablets were discovered and destroyed. The price of LSD tablets also rose from £1 to £5 each. There were other amusing stories about the under-cover hippies, apart from them being naked on duty at a festival, which would later give the operation a comic connection as well as the obvious more serious elements. This comic angle helped 'Operation Julie' to live on in the memory through numerous books, films, and television. The undercover hippies even staged fights with local police who were largely unaware of the hippies' real identities and English rock band The Clash released a song called 'Julie's Been Working for the Drug Squad.'

Meanwhile in Germany, on the 26th of September, Bill defended himself in court. One thing about Bill, wherever in the world he operated, he learned the local language. Possibly because of the way he worked he knew that one day he might spend some time in court. At forty-one that time had arrived and he'd been accused of being half of an international gang smuggling drugs to the United States. He pleaded not guilty and spent most of the first day providing a detailed account of his life and background.

As the trial advanced my name came up and the fact that I'd been asked to arrange a special shipment of legal medicine to America. The court also heard that I had no idea that this had anything to do with the huge LSD operation. Bill made a four hour statement in court and explained how ET had been purchased. Bill said that, although he'd been involved in smuggling the drug, he'd no idea what it would be used for. He'd been advised it would be sold to private clinics, used by movie stars, and that it would only be used for legitimate medical purposes. Bill explained he'd been introduced to ET by American judo expert Lee Hassler, who advised him that he wanted to start an import-export business. After Hassler's murder, Bill decided to try and continue the runs across to America and deliver to other friends. With his limited funds he relied on his own judo contacts from his days in Japan. Bill advised the court that he'd asked me and that I'd declined. He also mentioned that we'd discussed a mutual acquaintance. Bill went on to say that this person later changed his mind. As for the tapes, made by the police of my telephone conversations with Bill, he said they'd been misinterpreted. He said these conversations were about Eastern bloc athletes who wanted to escape to the west.

Bill submitted a copy of the Guardian newspaper to assert his claim that his smuggling had in no way been connected with the LSD ring broken by 'Operation Julie.' He waved the article headed 'The Judo Connection' which first revealed the story about his involvement with an LSD ring. He said that the fact that 'Operation Julie,' had been going on at the same time as his smuggling operation was a horrible coincidence. Bill claimed he'd only shipped one kilo of ET, the one taken by the informant, which had led to his arrest. He also claimed that the police theory, that the majority of the rest had been shipped to the US by Hassler, to be just that. A theory. He said he believed that large amounts of the drugs were still in controlled temperature storage somewhere in Southern Germany. He even said in a fur company's premises and recommended newspaper publicity to try and find them. Bill said the chemical was one hundred percent legal and not a narcotic substance. He'd purchased it legally and the tax had been paid. Then he played the blame game. He said that governments and the chemical industry should share the blame for not establishing proper controls if they felt the chemical could be misused. In his final statement, Bill said:

'I feel it's a clear case of negligence.'

Had Bill's smooth tongue talked his way out of this one?

In a meeting with my superiors, I put my case forward that I'd carefully thought through during the last couple of days. As well as six events in 1979 and 1980 I had another one that I felt I really needed to take part in. The Kano Cup to be held in Tokyo on the 23rd of November 1978. I believed I had answers to all the questions they would throw at me. They listened, smiled and nodded. They understood my position and also felt that Woolwich College would come out this smelling of roses the day I walked in with a gold medal around my neck. We arranged a meeting with the principal who didn't seem best pleased with my request. The no-brainer for me turned into a major headache. Unbelievably he said no. He said he'd given me the position on the understanding that I wouldn't compete anymore. That was it. End of story. It was his way or the highway. I didn't even consider it. Or discuss it with Julie and my family. I walked that same day. I emptied the contents of my desk into a box and I walked out. I didn't speak to anyone. I'd been shackled and now the shackles were off.

I went to Japan and competed in the Kano Cup and for reasons which I will explain later it was a first class trip with all the trimmings. I competed well and made it through to the semi-final. Sadly, because of an arm injury, I couldn't make it to the final. This turned out to be a bit of a fun trip where I played a few pranks with some of my younger team members on their first visit to Tokyo. One went wrong which turned out to be quite amusing. With my experience on the trains, they relied on me in the same way as I had with Bobby Boulton back in 1962. I, unlike Bobby, decided to give them a first-hand appreciation of what I'd been through, by jumping off the train at the last minute. Everyone else just about managed to follow apart from heavyweight Arthur Map. He pushed his nose into the window of the train as it pulled out with the rest of us in stitches on the platform. I think he spent the day going round in circles.

Had Bill managed to talk himself out of a ten year prison sentence? Yes. Of course he had.

Great British squad for European Championships East
Berlin 1964

European Junior Champion 1964 East Berlin.

Training for the Tokyo 1964 Olympic Games in South
Wales. The fantastic Alan Petherbridge, on my right, took the
sessions and they were hard. Very hard!

Olympic Game Munich 1972 Medal Ceremony.

With Angelo Parisi. I landed on my feet.

Deep in thought sat on the mat.

Stage 4

SAT IN MCDONALD'S

37

ON THE 26TH of January 1979, whilst sat in McDonald's, I pinched myself just to check the reality of my situation. What had I done? In 1973 I'd mapped out my career path. Teacher training at Avery College followed by finding a good position, with a reputable college, and of course a decent pension. And I'd done exactly that. I'd qualified, found a really great position at Woolwich College, and begun the next phase of my life although something just didn't feel right. I should have been happy with the knowledge that I could now take care of my wife in a more traditional manner. I could be the breadwinner for a change in the same way Dad had been with Mum. Even though Mum, never flinched, about taking on part-time jobs to bring in extra cash. But Julie, who'd worked like a Trojan to take care of me since before we were married in 1972, could have eased off a bit and taken a break from work.

Julie went very quiet that night when I explained about my exit from Woolwich and my plans for the future.

She'd backed me so much before and I think she felt, oh no not again, but she didn't say it. Dad understood and I think he felt the same way as me. He still believed I had it in me to compete at the highest level. But now, sat in McDonald's in Orpington High Street, I didn't know how I felt. My actions towards the end of 1978 had opened up a whole new ball game and I needed to work out how to play it. In addition to this Julie had confirmed that the maybe we should start a family question no longer applied. We'd spoken about starting one but we'd never actually made a firm decision. It just happened.

38

TOWARDS THE END of 1978 three things happened which had a huge connection with my actions that resulted in me taking my way. Although some of my family may have believed I'd made a rash decision and privately thought that I'd lost complete control of my senses. But I'd decided to take a chance on three things. A huge gamble if you like. Although if everything went pear-shaped I still felt I could get back into mainstream education. The aces up my sleeve were:

1. Peter Brewis. From the Alexander Howden Insurance Company.

2. Malcolm Stanley. Fads DIY.

3. A telephone call from the BBC.

Ace One. - Peter Coller and I had done extremely well with B and P Judo. We attracted some of the best young talents in England and at one point we had seventy-five percent of the British Junior team with us. We also had a young lad called Harvey Brewis whose father Peter showed great interest and came to watch his son whenever he could. I got on very well with Peter who had a passion for life and his job. He worked for the Alexander Howden Insurance Group in Devonshire Square, London, established in 1964. He would often comment about how his company started in the same year as judo first entered the Olympic Games and even said we should do something to commemorate it. I humoured him and didn't really think too much about it until a few days later he came back with a big smile on his face and said we'd done it. I asked him what we'd done and he said he found a way to tie in his company, with me, to celebrate 1964. He said Alexander Howden wanted me to be their Ambassador and that they would pay me. I asked him what this meant and he said it involved meeting people, mainly in the evening, and giving a few speeches. He said I didn't have to quit my day job and that sounded very good to me. Shake a few hands, make a few speeches, and bank some cash for my club. I agreed. He also said that if I competed outside of London, and I needed help with transportation and hotel expenses, his company would cover everything. Of course, I accepted and I didn't even mention anything to anyone at Woolwich as this wouldn't impact my work there.

Ace two. - Malcolm Stanley, the founder and chairman of the Fads do it yourself chain, arrived on the scene not long after Alexander Howden. Malcolm's passions included rally driving, sailing, travelling, and luckily for me judo which led him to me. He impressed me with his thirst for knowledge about my sport although I never actually saw him on the mat. I think I impressed him as well with my coaching methods and he recognised a lot of young talent on my mats. Malcolm's father Alex had started the 'do it yourself' ball rolling back in 1945 when he opened his first do it yourself shop called Bargain Wall Papers in Bromley, Kent. People had returned to their run-down homes, after the Second World War, and realised they needed to fix them up quickly. Alex made the most of this opportunity and Malcolm joined him in 1946. Together they opened another shop. In the 1950s they embraced the idea of 'pile them high and sell them low' and they became the first do it yourself shop owners to sell paint by the gallon. In the sixties, Malcolm rebadged some of his stores as Fads –Fine Arts Discount Stores. He went public in 1974 with two hundred stores. Also, as a lifetime supporter of Charlton Athletic Football Club, he later sponsored his team for a year with his logo on their shirts. However, prior to this, he sponsored my judo club. He helped with equipment for the dojo, training kits for my students and something that proved a massive boost. A £7,500 minibus. I'll never forget that Saturday afternoon, back in 1979, when Malcolm sent Mr. Mazcoll with the keys.

Ace Three. - Completely out of the blue, ten days before my thirty-second birthday in 1978, I took a call from the BBC during a lunch break at Woolwich College. They asked me if I'd heard of a show called Superstars and if I'd like to take part. I said I'd watched it a few times and that I'd always fancied having a go but I never thought I'd get the opportunity. Well, he said it's your lucky day. We're asking now and I'll sign you up for this week. I said hold on a minute. If I'm going to sign up for something I need time to train. I knew the show included a number of events that I'd never tried before such as shooting and canoeing. Plus I'd never competed competitively before in swimming and cycling. For this reason, I had to say no and I carried on working.

Dick Button, the American figure skating champion, developed and pitched Superstars to three US television networks. The ABC group liked it and purchased it as a special for the winter of 1973. Button's original idea revolved around a multi-sports competition where elite athletes, from different sports, competed against each other. These were the top sportsmen, instantly recognisable household names, who regularly appeared on US television and in newspaper sports columns. They were awarded points for each discipline, depending on how well they performed, and obviously, the person with the most points won the competition. Pole vaulter Bob Seagran won the first Superstars event which took place in Rotonda, West Florida, in March 1973.

In Great Britain BBC One aired their first Superstars programme on the 31st of December 1973 and featured seven of Britain's top sportsmen.

1. Barry John. Rugby Union.

2. Bobby Moore. Football.

3. David Hemery. Athletics.

4. Jackie Stewart. Formula One Racing Driver.

5. Joe Bugner. Boxer.

6. Roger Taylor. Tennis.

7. Tony Jacklin. Golf.

They were billed as 'The Magnificent Seven' which they were at that particular time and you would be hard pushed to find another sportsman, in their particular sport, bigger than them. They were all British household names.

David Vine and Ron Pickering hosted the show which took place in and around the Crystal Palace stadium. Each contestant had to select eight events from a list of ten. The events were:

1. One hundred metres sprint.

2. Shooting.

3. Fifty metres swim.

4. Golf - Three holes.

5. Gym Tests - Shuttle runs, standing long jump, squat thrusts and parallel bar dips.

6. Tennis.

7. Soccer penalties - With Northern Ireland's Pat Jennings in goal.

8. Cycling – Eight hundred metres time trial.

9. Weightlifting - Adjusted to body weight.

10. Six hundred metres steeplechase.

Later other events were added, such as canoeing, rowing, archery, and basketball. A few of the original ten were dropped.

Seven points were awarded to the winners of events, four for second place, two for third and one for fourth. This competition actually took place between 21st and 22nd of August 1973 but didn't get screened until New Year's Eve. BBC's producers must have seen this as a big chance to win the New Year rating war.

David Hemery won three events, swimming, gym tests and cycling, with a second place in the weightlifting and third places in shooting and soccer. This helped him amass thirty-six points. Barry John, with wins in the one hundred metres, soccer and tennis came second with thirty points. Joe Bugner managed two wins, shooting, and weightlifting, which gave him twenty-five points and joint third place with Jackie Stewart who won the golf. Roger Taylor came fifth, Bobby Moore sixth and Tony Jacklin, with three points, came last.

One other important point related to the rules. If an event coincided with a person's particular sport that person had to skip that event. For example, Tony Jacklin had to skip the golf.

In 1974 there were seven superstars again but only one remained from the previous year, defending champion David Hemery, who'd been joined by:

1. Chay Blyth. Yachting.

2. Colin Bell. Football.

3. John Conteh. Boxing.

4. John H. Stracey. Boxing.

5. Mick Channon. Football.

6. Tony Greig. Cricket.

John Conteh, in excellent condition, took the title with a very good score of fifty-seven points. He took maximum points, now ten, in weightlifting, cricket, and cycling. David Hemery, suffering from a touch of flu, came in second with forty. This year David didn't win any events outright but he managed joint first in the gym tests. For this season shuttle runs and the standing long jump had been dropped and a standing vertical jump had been introduced. The parallel bar dips remained along with squat thrusts. Colin Bell finished third with forty-one points and Tony Greig fourth with thirty. Mick Channon came last with twenty although he did manage to outrun everyone to take the one hundred metres.

British Superstars took a year out in 1975 to allow for the first European Superstars for which there were five qualifying rounds. These took place in Great Britain, Sweden, Holland, Belgium, and Spain. However, Spain failed to find a suitable venue so their competition took place in Costa Del Aldershot.

During the British heat, which also took place in Aldershot, Dutch field hockey player Ties Kruize took first prize with fifty-six points. British boys David Hemery and Colin Bell came second and third with fifty-one and thirty-seven points respectively. John Conteh should have taken part but he injured his right hand in a fight with American Willie Taylor in August 1975. This allowed Colin in. With one event left David led Ties by two points but as this was the steeplechase, classified as David's specialty sport, he had to take a penalty. David started the race one hundred metres behind the rest of the field. He soon caught most of them with the exception of Ties and Colin who were in his sights. But at the final water jump, his foot slipped and he fell. This meant he finished sixth and out of the points. Colin won the race and Ties the competition. With only one winner qualifying for the final it meant David had to wait and see if his points score allowed him into the final as a wild card.

Over to Malmo in Sweden for heat two where Newcastle United's British football player Malcolm

'Supermac' Macdonald took first place with a total of forty-eight points. Malcolm won the one hundred metres in a new Superstars record time of ten point nine seconds. He also took maximum in the shooting and weightlifting. Dutch speed skater Harm Kepler and French F1 racing driver Jochen Mass shared second place with forty-nine points.

For heat three the European Superstars bandwagon rolled up in Holland for the Dutch competition won by local speed skater Ard Schenk with forty-seven points. Ard had been around the Superstars world for a while and participated in four American events. In 1974 he even won a preliminary round. He took ten points in the cycling, soccer, and steeplechase. Swedish ice hockey play Borje Salming came second with forty-five points and British F1 racing driver James Hunt followed behind in third with thirty-eight.

Over to Bruges in Belgium for heat four where French one hundred and ten metres hurdler Guy Drut took the top spot with forty-five points. Guy actually only won two events, rowing, and soccer, but he finished second in three so he was pretty consistent. Belgium soccer player Paul Van Himst came second with forty-one points. Great Britain's four hundred metres hurdler Alan Pascoe, who helped Britain's four by four hundred metre relay team to a silver medal at the Munich Olympics in 1972, came in third.

In Spain's 'Aldershot' heat Great Britain's fortunes didn't improve as the only British entrant, squash player Jonah Barrington walked out after the gym test squats. Jonah, known as Great Britain's 'Mr. Squash' after winning the British title six times in a row between 1967 and 1973, thought he'd completed seventy-five squats but his counter only credited him with twenty-five. With still a few events to go the shocked Jonah stormed off never to be seen again. The judge explained that Jonah's knees were not coming up to his elbows and replays seemed to prove the judge correct. Britain's last hope for another finalist had started so well when he came second in the weightlifting and he won the tennis. This put him on seventeen points after three events. Sadly this is where he remained as his disappearance meant he missed four events. Swedish pole vaulter Kjell Isaksson came in first with a very impressive sixty-nine points, a Superstars record, which included six wins.

The strongly fancied Kjell Isaksson arrived at the Ahoy Stadium in Rotterdam for the first European Superstars final as the strong favourite after his impressive heat win. David Hemery joined Malcolm Macdonald as Ties Kruize, who may have pushed Kjell, had withdrawn due to injury. He'd been involved in a car accident and ended up being thrown through his windscreen. He broke his leg which also ruled him out of the 1976 Olympic Games. Malcolm got Britain off to a fine start by winning the one hundred metres. He actually only ran ninety-six as athletes, such as David, were allowed to enter with a handicap. Malcolm would have won without the handicap although he didn't perform well from then on and ended up in seventh place. David, despite not winning any events, performed consistently with three second places and four thirds to finish with thirty-nine points. David, who'd won the first British event in 1973 and finished second in 1974 despite suffering from a bout of flu, came into the steeplechase with a chance of finishing second overall, his only rival for this position Ard Schenk. Again David fell into the water pit during the last lap and things looked bleak. But somehow he managed to scramble to his feet and race to the line where he finished third behind Holland's Harm Kuipers. Kjell won this event with Ard the last to finish, in seventh place. This gave David second spot but by the time the ceremony started he'd already been taken to hospital where medical staff confirmed he'd badly torn his ligaments. Kjell, as expected, took first place with fifty-six points.

In 1976 David Hemery, flu-less and with fully working ligaments, took the British title in the final held at Aldershot. David actually trounced his opposition to finish with fifty-five points. He won four events outright, kayaking, shooting, swimming, and cycling and shared top spot in the gym tests with my old friend Dave Starbrook. Kayaking made its Superstars debut and caused big problems for John Conteh, Malcolm Macdonald, and Stan Bowles. They all capsized.

Dave Starbrook created his own of Superstars magic moment in the gym tests arm dips. David Hemery managed thirty-eight and John Conteh, completed thirty. Dave followed those two and he soon moved past John's total. As Dave's count approached the mid-thirties he seemed to struggle. He really gritted his teeth as he pushed out thirty-five, thirty-six and thirty-seven. Approaching thirty-eight he straightened his arms and looked around at the crowd, his other competitors, and his eyes soon met David's. David stared back at Dave. Dave then winked at David before he quite easily pushed out a few more to finish with forty-nine. John believed Dave should have won an Oscar for his performance. David won the squats so they shared first place in the gym tests. Dave later mentioned that there might be a few other judo players out there who could do better but he didn't mention any names. John came second with twenty-nine points and James finished third with twenty-eight. Also, Jonah Barrington magically reappeared for this event and took all the jokes about his previous disappearance in good spirit. He finished seventh with eighteen points and managed a very good sixty, legal, squat thrusts this time! Dave Starbrook finished sixth with twenty-one points.

Also in 1976 the European heat and final format continued with the same five countries involved except for Spain. They dropped out and Belgium stepped in. The British heat took place in St. Ives with John Conteh taking first prize with forty-two points. Stoke City's England goalkeeper Peter Shilton, finished back in sixth place with twenty-seven. Austrian ski jumper Karl Schnabl took the Dutch heat with forty-seven points. British swimmer David Wilkie, fresh from winning an Olympic gold medal in the two hundred metres breaststroke in Montreal, which he still carried with him everywhere he went, finished back in sixth with twenty-eight points. Heat three should have taken place in Belgium but, like Spain, they couldn't find an appropriate venue so Bracknell Leisure Centre in Berkshire, England, stepped in. And this is the competition that produced one of the most memorable and talked about moments in Superstars history. The cycling head to head clash between one of Britain's top football stars Kevin Keegan and Belgium's soccer captain Gilbert Van Binst. They rode on a normal circular track and Kevin had the inside lane just behind Gilbert. Kevin had a few wobbly moments which made him question later if his wheels were fixed properly. Anyway as they went around the first bend, with Kevin pumping hard, Gilbert moved inside and Kevin's front wheel touched Gilbert's back one and Kevin went flying across the cinder track. He ended up with lots of grazes on his back, arms, and legs. He did however recover and they competed again. This time Kevin stayed upright and won. He actually won this heat with fifty-four points and commented that he'd finished the competition, rather than crying off early with injuries which he could have done, as a lot of people had turned up especially to watch him. I admired him for that. He seemed the type of character who once he made up his mind to do something he would give everything he had. In that respect, I think we had a lot in common.

Heat four took place in Sweden with local favourite Kjell Isaksson in fine form again. He won six events to win with sixty-six points. David Hemery, with his ligaments repaired, finished back in third with thirty-six. Over to Vichy in France for heat five and the great Swedish tennis player, Bjorn Borg took the top spot with fifty-three points. He won the soccer, kayaking, table tennis, and steeplechase. For Great Britain Welsh rugby union player, Gareth Edwards came in fourth with forty-two points.

After five heats Great Britain should have had two entrants in the final, John Conteh and Kevin Keegan. Unfortunately, Kevin had to withdraw due to football commitments. Bjorn Borg also dropped out. A shame really as those two would have been very interesting to watch in competition at the Ahoy Stadium in Rotterdam where Gareth Edwards stepped in to replace Kevin but flu meant he could only complete four events and finished back in sixth place with twenty points. Still, he did better than John Conteh who completed all eight of his but finished back in ninth place with thirteen points. In the gym tests, now down to two events, the parallel bar dips, and squat thrusts, Austria's ski jumper Karl Schnabl set a parallel bar dips Superstars record with fifty-three. However, he didn't win the overall gym tests as Kjell Isaksson managed more squat trusts which enabled him to take the ten points. He also scored maximum in kayaking, weightlifting, table tennis and swimming to finish with sixty-eight points.

On the 27th of March 1977, the first World Superstars event came to British television screens with John Conteh and Gareth Edwards representing Great Britain. However, they didn't cover themselves in glory. John finished fifteenth with fifteen points and Gareth managed thirteenth with one more point than John. At the other end of the table American pole vaulter, Bob Seagren came first with forty points. He beat fellow pole vaulter Sweden's Kjell Isaksson who finished with thirty-two.

In Great Britain, the British women finally got in on the act when they had their first competition. Badminton's Gillian Gilks took the top spot.

For the British men, 1977 saw the end of the David Hemery and John Conteh dominance as rower Tim Crooks took first place with forty-seven points. Shot putter Geoff Capes finished second with forty-five with boxer Dave 'Boy' Green third with thirty-three. Judo's Keith Remfry came seventh with nineteen points.

The European event followed this, with Spain re-entering the fray as Holland dropped out. In Switzerland, for Great Britain, James Hunt could only manage seventh place with eighteen points. A fit-again Ties Kruize took the top spot with fifty-six. Great British rugby league player Keith Fielding made certain at least one British player would be in the final by winning the second heat in France with fifty-four points. Heat three in Great Britain saw British entrants Peter Collins, motorcycling, and Geoff Capes finishing second and third with thirty-nine point five points and thirty-nine respectively. They trailed Holland's speed skater Hans van Helden who finished in front with fifty-three. My old judo friend, Jean-Paul Coche, won heat four in Belgium with forty-two points to become the first person from judo to win a Superstars event. In Spain's heat, Tim Crooks pushed French pole vaulter Francois Tracanelli all the way to the finish only to lose by one point. The Frenchman finished on forty-nine points.

Once again everybody gathered at the Ahoy Stadium in Rotterdam for the final with all heat winners available to compete. Keith Fielding got British hopes off to a fine start by taking the one hundred metres. Ties Kruize took the canoeing and Jean-Paul Coche the weightlifting. It looked like it might be a shoot-out between those three as Ties took the swimming and Jean-Paul the gym tests, in which he completed forty arm dips. Keith had now slipped down the field but he came storming back when he took the cycling. Going into the six hundred metres steeplechase Keith had to win and hope that Ties finished third or lower. Jean-Paul sat this one out. Keith won easily without being challenged. In the home stretch Ties got the better of his Dutch companion speed skater Hans van Helden, to grab second place and take the title. The Dutch connection could well have cost Keith first place. At the end, still out of breath from the race, a very disappointed Keith came out with one of Superstars' most famous quotes:

'It's a damn bloody shame that is.'

Ties finished with forty-eight points with Keith only two back on forty-six.

In 1978 World Superstars returned with a final in Freeport, Lucaya, in the Bahamas. Bob Seagren, defending his title, managed thirty-four points which put him in second place to Canadian soccer player Brian Budd who finished with forty-eight. Keith Fielding came fifth with twenty and Ties Kruize sixth with sixteen. This time, with Ties the only Dutchman in this final, he didn't have any connections to help him.

That's a kind of summary of how Superstars began and how the competitions gained momentum between 1973 and 1977.

Of course, I wanted to compete in Superstars and I found it very hard to say no when the BBC called. I'd watched judo's Dave Starbrook, Keith Remfry, and Jean-

Paul Coche and I thought I could do at least as well as them. I felt fit but I needed time to prepare. Everything I'd done in judo revolved around work, work, and more work. Plus I'd watched experts, such as Kisaburo Watanabe, and soaked up every word they said. That's how I'd reached the top. I didn't have any other secret. Everything I tried revolved around hard work. Natural ability? Talent? I'm not sure about that. I trained and trained and trained some more.

39

JULIE AND I NOW lived in a semi-detached bungalow in Cockmannings Road. We'd renovated it and were very pleased. Julie even became so proud that she developed a bit of an obsessive cleaning disorder. Maybe that's a bit of a strong statement. Perhaps obsessively house-proud might be more accurate. Everything had to be in the right place, one hundred percent of the time, and of course, nothing could be out of place. If I picked something up, an ornament or something like that, and I didn't put it back in exactly the same way she would move it and get the annoyed with me. Julie wanted the place absolutely spotless with all the carpets neatly vacuumed. Sometimes, after she'd just given them a good going over and they looked pristine, I felt afraid to walk on them. Not just me. I think Tito, our giant black Alsatian pet dog, felt the same way. Sometimes, if Julie left us on our own, we'd lounge around the house together. But as soon as we heard her key in the door we'd be up and trying to clean the place.

Julie and I were now in a very happy zone. We loved our home, obviously Julie more than me, and we knew that our first baby would arrive in June. But we had an opportunity to move, which we took, and soon we'd settled in at 48 Oxenden Wood Road where we became very friendly with Derek and Jackie Charlton who lived opposite. They'd just had their first son, and later, when we'd had our first and the kids got a bit older, it became quite comical. Derek practiced karate and had reached quite a high level. I think he'd reached fifth Dan status at that stage. Anyway, the kids played together and if they fell out, as kids sometimes did, one would say my Dad's a black belt in karate and the other would say my Dad's a black belt in judo. Stuff like that. I had some good laughs with Derek and we liked to play a few practical jokes with Julie sometimes on the wrong end.

On my thirty-second birthday I had another call from the BBC and this time they asked about my availability for the weekend of the 10th of November 1978. They wanted me to compete in the Superstars elimination rounds. A stepping stone to the final and this provided me with nearly six weeks of preparation time. I didn't need to think twice about it. I told them that they were on and I would be there one hundred percent. I signed up without even asking about money although I knew I had personal sponsorship from Alexander Howden in my back pocket and club sponsorship from Fads. Neither offered a nice safe pension and I had no idea where Superstars would lead but something inside me told me I had to do it. A gut feeling that I had to follow. This meant that during my final meeting with Woolwich I had all kinds of ideas floating around my mind which I hoped would lead to other opportunities.

I went straight to Dad and spoke with him about what had happened. He'd backed me in everything I'd done, up to this point, and I knew I needed his support again. I couldn't do this without him and he more or less told me that. He looked at me and I could see that old twinkle in his eyes that I'd noticed many times before. He didn't really want me in a classroom, gym or on a sports field. Not yet. Not when he knew I still had enough left in my tank to mix it with judo's big boys. But the good thing about Superstars, which appealed to both of us, was that I would have the chance to compete with stars from other sports. This meant Dad, a total sports nut, should get to meet some of Great Britain's sporting legends. I needed Dad in my corner. We'd watched Superstars together, many times, sat on his sofa. He loved the programme and just needed some time to think about it.

On Saturday the 7th of October 1978 Dad turned up at my house with my training plan all written down. I felt excited and so did he. We had a good chat about Superstars. He said he didn't want me to turn up, go through the motions, and return home without making an impression. He wanted me to approach this in the same way I had the Olympic Games. He also spoke about the first Superstars programme that we'd watched together, on his sofa at his house, and about the household names taking part. Dad expanded more on the household name theme. He said those guys were at the top of their sport and if we met them on the street we would know them and so would most of the British public. They were legends in their sports and people tuned into the programme just to get a glimpse of them. They knew Bobby Moore wouldn't be making a World Cup-saving tackle and that Joe Bugner wouldn't be delivering a knock-out punch. Tony Jacklin certainly wouldn't be sinking a twenty-foot putt. But the British public switched on their televisions to see their heroes because they were heroes.

Dad continued and said that in some quarters Superstars had picked up a kind of 'junk sport' label as viewers just wanted to see their heroes, make a fool of themselves, to put them in a light-hearted mood before they hit the pub for a Friday night pint. Dad wanted to continue but I said Dad wait. What are you trying to say? Do you want me to do this or not? He said yes Brian. I want you to do this. But I want you to do this as no other sportsman has ever done before. You have to do it that way Brian because no one knows you. Despite appearing in three Olympic Games no one outside judo knows you. Then he looked at me and I looked at him and he said. This is the time for you to change that. This is my challenge to you. You will be on television during peak viewing time and I challenge you to become a household name. I challenge you to totally change the public's perception of Superstars. I want you in this to win it and I will help you every step of the way. I said. Dad, I'm in it to win and he said great. Now let's get to work.

Dad passed me my training programme which he'd spent the last couple of days working on. He knew my strengths and weaknesses better than anybody else. He knew which events I should focus on and which ones I should skip. But we knew I had a unique position compared to many other competitors who had to skip an event that clashed with their own personal sport. With no judo on the list, I had a complete choice of all the events. He knew straight away that I should give running a miss which meant we crossed out the sprint and the steeplechase. Dad's programme focused on six other events that included the gym tests. Squat thrusts and arm dips. Dad had written down that I should complete four hundred arm dips every day. He'd actually written that on the first line. I looked at him and he looked at me. I said Dad I've never done an arm dip in my life. How do you expect me to manage four hundred every day? He asked if I wanted his help or not. I said of course I did but how can I do that? He said if you want me to help you have to. If you don't want to do it you can get someone else. Then he came up with one of his favourites. 'Fail to prepare Brian then prepare to fail.' I'd heard that so many times so I got a bit bolshie, maybe a bit big headed, and said, of course, I could do it and I gave him the look which I hope he interpreted as anything to stop you using that old prepare cliché again. On the second line, he'd written four hundred squat thrusts every day. I nodded. I just thought balls I'm doing whatever he writes. For the events, I would take part in I needed to spend some money. I bought a racing bike that I thought looked similar to the bikes they used in the show plus a couple of canoes, a crossbow and all other kinds of stuff that I believed would be needed for the next six weeks. I think we guessed a bit which events would be in the show from the programmes we'd watched before.

On Monday the 9th of October 1978 we began Superstars training in earnest and I managed four hundred arm dips. I didn't have bars. I just used a couple of park benches in Lullingstone Park Golf Course. I pushed them together and managed twenty the first time, took a rest for a couple of minutes, and managed another fifteen before I took another rest. I then followed that up with another twelve. That's how I completed my first four hundred in one day.

Banging out a few, short rests, and then managing a few more all the way up to four hundred. I kept track of each set in a small notebook. I followed the same pattern with the squat thrusts. Easy? Absolutely not! The next day I struggled to get out bed. My whole body ached. I couldn't do it again. I knew I couldn't. My body wouldn't let me. I got up, went over to those park benches on the golf course, and did it again. But it hurt. It hurt like mad. Never had I experienced such excruciating pain before from exercise. For the whole of the next week, my body ached like it never had before and that was with just those two events. My brother Shayne helped me as did my good friend Errol Field and another friend David Wilkinson. Errol and David were both from the judo world and sometimes other faces turned up to help as well.

For canoeing, we used Crystal Palace's lake and we mapped out a course of about one hundred and twenty-five metres. I canoed as fast as I could against each of them one at a time. By that I mean I stayed in the canoe and raced one of them. For example Shayne. I raced him and when he'd finished he jumped out and Errol jumped in and I raced him. When Errol finished I raced David and so on and so forth. This meant I had a little rest each time as they got in and out of their canoes. I just kept going backward and forwards as my training partners rested between their shifts. We did this for an hour. We then used the same routine for the racing bikes before we stopped at a cafe near Crystal Palace for breakfast. After breakfast, we went back to Crystal Palace for an hour practicing the crossbow. Next, we were in the swimming pool for an hour and I swam the fifty metres, almost nonstop, except for the short break to change partners. We finished in the gym with weightlifting, arm dips, and squats. I have to admit I ate, drank and slept, Superstars. Even at home, as I relaxed in bed, I would ask myself questions like what was I doing in bed when I should be exercising and I would get up and exercise some more with things like push-ups and sit-ups. But after those the first three days I felt in absolute agony. At the end of the first week, I felt totally shattered. The same applied to the second week. By the end of the third week, things started to get a little bit better. My body, which had complained so much during the first two weeks, had now have accepted the situation and bought into Superstars. The fourth and fifth weeks were much easier for me and by the beginning of the sixth, I could manage fifty dips straight off with no problems although it pushed me to the end of my limits.

A typical Superstars training day could last as long as five hours. We had our early bird morning session from 7:00

a.m. to 9:00 a.m., followed by ninety minutes for breakfast. Then we had our mid-morning session from 10:30 a.m. to 12.30 p.m. In the afternoon, after a rest, we would do 3:00 p.m. to 4:00 p.m. Most evenings I would be at my judo club for another ninety minutes of training.

As I said we used Crystal Palace. They knew me and they were happy to let me use their facilities. They even provided me with a key to open the gym so I could come and go as I pleased. On many occasions, I remember people standing in the doorways or looking through the windows and they were amazed as we worked on the arm dips, squat thrusts, and weightlifting.

Obviously, things didn't always go as straightforward as we wanted them to and we had to make a few changes. The canoeing proved a fine example. We started with slalom canoes and this turned into a real nightmare. The slalom is like a banana and spins around very easily when you pull too hard to one side. I couldn't get it to go straight at all. Every time I pulled the canoe forward it shot left and all sorts of strange things would happen. Later I found out that the Superstars canoes were kayaks which I found easier to control.

During stage three I mentioned the Kano cup in Japan and how this had been a first class event. By that I mean I travelled business class and stayed in a five-star hotel in Tokyo all thanks to Alexander Howden Insurance. They took care of everything and even the rest of the British team enjoyed the luxury of my hotel before and during the Kano cup. Peter Dupere, Howden Group's Tokyo Liaison officer, even held a reception for me at my hotel attended by many dignitaries from the insurance world and other industries. The British Ambassador and his wife were also present along with senior representatives from Japan Airlines. Of course, I made sure all the lads from the British team were invited and we had a great time.

I think Superstars training played a big part in helping me to take bronze in Japan. I didn't feel finished, far from it, in fact, I felt stronger than I'd ever been before and ready to take on the big boys from the judo world again in 1979.

40

BACK TO THE 26th of January 1979 when, at 8:00 p.m., BBC One screened heat two of the British National Superstars Championships for the Brylcreem Trophy from the Cwmbran Stadium Sports Centre, in South Wales. My opponents were:

1. Chris Baillieu. Rowing.

2. Phil Bennett. Rugby Union.

3. Mike Hazelwood. Water Sking.

4. Maurice Hope. Boxing.

5. Andy Irvine. Rugby Union.

6. Ian Neale. Gymnastics.

7. Duncan McKenzie. Football.

David Vine introduced me as the 'Hard Man of Judo' which I didn't really think too much about at the time but as I look back now I'm not sure if that's a correct tag. There were so many hard men in judo.

Not that many people in Cwmbran's stadium, outside my circle, had a clue about who the chunky bloke with the blond curly perm was! They didn't know me from Adam and most of them probably thought. Oh, a judo bloke, what's he doing here! But before I describe the events of the day I have to reveal a little secret. Superstars is about television. It's a show and the BBC needed to keep the viewers in suspense, for as long possible, before they knew who won. A bit of a tease really and not like a real live sport such as a football, rugby or judo match. This meant that the order in which the events were actually screened, were not in exactly the same order as they'd taken place.

Andy took ten points in the one hundred meters followed home by Phil with Duncan in third. I won the weightlifting with my first lift of one hundred kilos. Ian came second with Maurice in third. Phil, who failed to register a lift, picked up two points as the rest skipped this event. Over to the water for the rowing where I finished second in my heat and third in the final. This didn't please me at all. Mike, who looked very good, won and Ian finished second again. In the pool, I managed to win my heat but finished third in the final. Ian won and Mike came second to put Ian in the lead after four events. I sat in third place seven points behind him. Crossbow came next and I came on last which meant I knew exactly what I had to do. With two shots left I needed eighteen to draw level with Andy in first place. I tried to focus, even stopped to munch on an orange, but I had a bit of a shake and missed. I ended up joint second with Maurice.

For gym tests, one minute for arm dips and one for squat thrusts, I think I might have started as favourite. Mike completed thirty-four arm dips, Andy twenty-two and I managed sixty-four which broke the record. For squats, I completed eighty and used a method that we'd practiced with my knuckles down and my thumbs spread. Everyone else went with the palms of their hands flat on the floor. I seemed to be going okay and I heard Mum shout keep it up. Chris did well with eighty-one and Maurice with seventy-six. My overall gym test total of one hundred and forty-eight meant gave me a fifty-two point lead over Chris in second place. I felt good about this event and I knew my upper body strength played a big part. I also felt I could do better. But my scores, as Ron Pickering said, were two of the most remarkable scores ever seen in Superstars. Of course, judo helped me with this because judo is a tough sport and gym tests are a hard event. I now led the table thirty-three point five points.

Next, we were on the cycle track for my last event which I knew I had to win. In my first race I came up against Maurice and I soon left him behind which more or less meant a race against the clock. With my fans, clustered around the track, I came home in forty-two point twenty-four seconds for the fastest time of the season so far. Later Maurice mentioned that he hadn't been on a bike since he left school. I found it strange that he hadn't practiced. In the final against Mike, I went straight in front and stayed there to win in forty-one point thirteen seconds

Still, out of breath David Vine came over and congratulated me on winning this heat of Superstars as with only one event remaining no one could catch me. With my legs feeling a bit like jelly I explained to David that I felt happy. Very happy. And that I hoped more people might now start taking notice of judo. David then mentioned that I would have to do the same thing all over again in the British final. I replied:

'I'M GOING TO DO IT.'

'I'M GOING TO WIN IT.'

Mike finished second with Andy back third. I would have worried about meeting Mike in the final. He'd set a new record in the rowing and had youth on his side. I say would have because water ski commitments ruled in out.

In the final I would be meeting:

1. Tim Crooks. Rowing.

2. Lynn Davies. Athletics.

3. Brian Phelps. Diving.

4. Dave 'Boy' Green. Boxing.

5. Gordon Hill. Football.

6. Ian Neale. Gymnastics.

7. Andy Irvine. Rugby Union.

So what really happened to me on Friday the 26th of January 1979 the day I made my BBC TV Superstars debut? Well, I woke up early and drove up to Birmingham for some coaching with a couple of students from my club. I remember the day went well and we left a bit later than expected which meant we didn't arrive back to Orpington until about 9:45 p.m. I felt a bit hungry, as did Kevin Crickmar who always did, so we decided to have a quick snack in McDonald's. I wanted to be in and out in ten minutes. Kevin entered first and I followed. I suppose the place could have been half full. At first, nothing untoward happened as we approached the counter to order our food. Then suddenly someone said. It's that judo bloke from Superstars! McDonald's went quiet. Everyone stopped talking and eating. Slowly I turned my head as all eyes focused on me that judo bloke from Superstars. I couldn't believe it and what happened next left me absolutely flabbergasted as my quick ten minutes turned out to be about two hours and ten minutes. Everyone in there seemed to want to shake my hand and get my autograph. Other people, with no interest in eating, arrived to meet and speak with me. For the first time outside of judo, I seemed to have become famous and I had no idea if this would be for fifteen minutes or longer.

When I eventually arrived home Julie asked me what I'd been up to and I explained. She didn't seem too surprised and we sat talking in the kitchen until about 1:00 a.m. before we decided to watch the show. Julie, as we'd agreed in advance, had taped it so we could watch it together. I felt good about my performance in the gym tests and the weightlifting. I knew I had to make big improvements in the water with swimming and canoeing. With the way the shows were recorded and shown later, I'd already put corrective action plans in place which I will expand upon later. Julie slept as soon as the show finished but I just lay in bed unable to sleep. Several times my mind flashed back to McDonald's and the unbelievable reaction from all the people there. I had Olympic, World Championship, European and domestic judo medals in my locker and they hadn't created one iota of general public interest outside of judo. Now I had a Superstars Brylcreem heat trophy, not even a final, but people had sat up and noticed! With the adrenalin flowing, I suppose I only slept about three hours that night.

Julie woke me at 7:30 a.m. and said I should look out the bedroom window. A quick peep through a gap in the curtains shocked me again as twenty members of the paparazzi were camped outside my gate. I hadn't prepared for this and had no idea what to do. Julie said I should go down and speak with them but I couldn't. I had no idea what I should say. I'd said a few things during the show that had made me nervous, such as my prediction that I would win the final, and I didn't want to say anything right now that might drop me in it. Plus the final would be screened the following Friday so obviously it had been filmed sometime before. With that in mind, I decided to do a runner. I crept out the back of my house, ran across my back garden and climbed over the fence into the back garden of the house behind us. From there I ran across their back garden and out of their front gate where I'd arranged for a car to pick me up. I'm not sure if any of my neighbours saw me.

Saturday had started in a strange way and kept getting weirder and weirder with each passing hour. At my club, more people turned up than ever before and I had to wade through them just to get in. People wanted my autograph and I signed for everyone who asked. Inside everyone applauded as I entered and I had to tell them to behave. They knew me from before and they had to understand that I hadn't changed even though the world seemed to have. Well, maybe not the world. Just my bit. Someone mentioned that fifteen million people had watched the show which shocked me. I began to wonder if my fifteen minutes might actually stretch to thirty. That afternoon I went to collect an order for wood and in the shop the bloke next to me said. You're Brian Jacks. I saw you on television last night. Then all of a sudden there were forty people in the shop which only had room for about twenty. Later that afternoon my house turned into a kind of open house, not for the press who'd gone when I arrived home, but for my family and friends who turned up to congratulate me. Julie seemed to be taking everything in her stride although I could sense that she didn't feel happy about having our home invaded in such a way. Her well-manicured carpets were taking a bit of a pounding. With this in mind I called a halt to everything and Julie and I went to a Chinese restaurant where I'd booked a table for dinner. As soon as we walked in the other diners were whispering and looking in our direction. A few were brave enough to come and speak to me and ask for my autograph whilst we were trying to eat.

The whole day, which started with the paparazzi wanting a piece of me and ended with dinners staring and whispering, had been amazing. In fact, I think everything must have changed the minute the programme finished Friday night. For me, it was another total culture shock that I needed time to try and understand. As for the press I decided to give them a piece of me but not all of them. On Monday I met with Neil Allen after keeping a low profile on Sunday. Neil worked for the London Evening Standard and I'd seen him around at a few judo competitions. We met in a restaurant and as soon as we entered it all started again. A waiter remarked. You're that bloke who won that Superstars thing on television and a school kid shouted. Hey, aren't you that Brian Jacks bloke?

I just smiled and followed Neil to a kind of cubicle where we could get some peace. Neil asked me what it felt like to be suddenly famous after being one of Britain's top fighting machines for sixteen years. I had to admit that after all that time without being recognised the whole thing felt quite strange and that I hadn't quite got used to it yet. Neil mentioned that things could only get worse as he believed the

British public might be ready for Brian Jacks. We couldn't speak too much about Superstars, due to more shows already recorded and about to be shown, but Neil said my appearance must have been a major boost for David Vine and Ron Pickering. Plus the show, which might have at times been regarded as kind of gimmicky, had now entered into a new world, the Brian Jacks world, and the bar had been raised. I explained that nothing fulfilled and satisfied me more than judo. First and foremost I loved judo. But training in other sports such as cycling, swimming, canoeing, and the crossbow had excited me. I'd found it stimulating to learn something new and understand how statistically I could improve. For the gym tests, and I'd spent a lot of time in gyms throughout my life, I enjoyed the new challenge of the arm dips and squat thrusts. Neil also asked about my Olympic bronze medal in Munich and about my teaching career. I explained that I felt proud of Munich and proud that I'd re-entered education and qualified as a PE teacher. We also discussed my body and how I'd managed to remain in such good shape. He knew I'd suffered along the way with injuries. A broken leg, six cartilage operations, a broken wrist, six broken ribs, two broken shoulders, four dislocated shoulders, three broken fingers and a string of strains and other knocks. But in the tough world of judo, after sixteen years and more than three thousand contests, I'd come out of it okay. I didn't feel punched out and I'd even started thinking about the 1980 Olympics in Moscow. I explained to Neil that I had to think about it as I loved judo so much. But there would be no way that I would consider going if it was just for the ride. If I targeted Moscow and found myself lucky enough to be selected, then I would be going totally committed to winning the gold medal. Otherwise, there would be no point.

41

STRAIGHT AFTER MY Cwmbran Superstars victory, I went full on with my training for the final and due to the recordings and transmissions of the programmes, we do have to step back again to Monday the 13th of November 1978. I met Dad two days after I'd won my heat. I felt good about the events I'd won but I still wanted to improve them and do a lot better in the events I'd lost. Other people had seen me so I imagined them going flat out to knock me off my perch. I'd made a brash statement that I'd win the final and now I needed to prove I could walk the walk and not just talk the talk. I suppose this was down to the confident cockney in me that everybody in the judo world knew about already. But now, at least for the time being, I had a new audience who'd just had a small taste of me. I needed to do all I could to prove myself and possibly to become a household name like so many of the other competitors who'd appeared on Superstars. I'd just be doing it in reverse order! By that, I mean Superstars could make me a superstar to the entire British public, which judo hadn't done. Although at this stage, just about to begin training for the British final, I still had no idea what would happen. Remember we've stepped back in time again.

Superstars had given me a new motivation, plus a great opportunity to learn different sports and to compete against great sportsmen from other sports. I wanted to prove I could mix it with the big boys from British sport and by that, I don't mean stature. I'm talking about British sporting icons although I never felt in awe of them. I'd been and done it for my country on the highest stages possible. Just like they had. But I always felt honoured to meet them, to watch them, and to interact with them. I'd accepted an invitation on a journey and I had no idea where it might lead. It was like a challenge, a dare, and I felt confident in my ability to compete with the best.

Dad came up with an idea about bringing specialists into my group who were experts in the events in which I needed to improve, as well as for events that I'd won but still wanted to improve. He knew I had it in me to keep training and pushing myself as we didn't know how much time my competitors were putting in. Even though I didn't think they'd be training as much as me. But I kept pushing. I kept practicing. I had to stay sharp and now, thanks to Dad again, we added a new element. I had to learn new techniques which meant bringing in the experts. It all made so much sense. I always tried to approach things professionally and where possible learn from the experts.

For pistol shooting, I went to the local police station where I knew an inspector who took me to the firing range to learn the basics. From there I went to see a lady called Rosemary Edgar, British women's champion, and she coached me from then on. Rosemary was the twenty-five metre British women's champion from 1976 to 1983 before going on to become a national pistol shooting coach. At the World Pistol Shooting Championships, in Seoul in 1979, she helped the British team to a bronze medal in the ten metre air pistol event.

From the world of cycling Ron Keeble, an Olympic bronze medallist in the team pursuit event in Munich agreed to help. Ron came from Orpington and we were about the same age. He rode for one of South London's best known cycling clubs called 34 Nomads, formed in 1934. They had to add 34 to their name as the Nomads Cycling Club already existed. Ron taught me about the importance of setting up a bike correctly. How to make sure I had the seat in the right position and how to adjust the pedals. Many people just get on a bike and pedal away. I saw this with some of my Superstars competitors who just got on and rode with no preparation. Obviously, Ron passed on loads of other tips as well. We cycled together on London's roads and he used to ride close behind buses travelling at forty-five miles an hour.

When the bus braked he would actually knock against it but he never seemed in any danger.

Ron explained about banked tracks and said that most featured steeply banked oval tracks that consisted of two 180 degree circular bends connected by two straights. The straights transition to the circular turn through a moderate easement curve. Banking in the turns, called superelevation, allows riders to keep their bikes relatively upright to the surface while riding at speed. From the straight, the curve of the track increases gradually into the circular turn. This section of decreasing radius is called the easement spiral or transition. It allows bikes to follow the track around the corner at a constant radial position which allows riders to concentrate on tactics rather than steering. Banked track bikes don't have brakes instead they have a single fixed rear gear or cog, that doesn't freewheel. This helps to maximise speed, reduces weight, and avoids sudden braking. But riders can slow down by pushing back against the pedals. These tracks can be surfaced with different materials that include, timber, synthetics, and concrete. The first time I tried one of these my right pedal brushed against the wall, which felt pretty scary, but I completed the course with a very good time.

I found swimming tricky. I could swim but it was my hardest event and I couldn't swim that fast. You have to be light to be a good swimmer and I think my upper body muscle proved a negative factor for me in this event. At my best, I could swim fifty metres in thirty-two seconds.

With my reliable team, we trained for five weeks before the final although we were briefly interrupted by the Kano cup. Despite this, I still trained with Superstars in mind during my time in Japan. Back in England, we continued full steam ahead as we had before. Well, not exactly, as I now had professional experts to rely on such as Rosemary and Ron. Dad, my bother Shayne, Dave Wilkinson, and Errol Field continued to be a great help. They all pushed me in their different ways. At the Lullingstone Park Golf Course, we tackled that big hill and Dad, stood at the top, would go mad if I didn't run all the way to the top. He used his, It's not me making you run up this hill it's Lynn Davies or Andy Irvine, the same tactic he applied when I trained for judo to get me to work harder.

The final took place at Bracknell and a few of my competitors had concerns about the cycling. Kevin's accident had created a kind of fear factor about Bracknell and I could read this in the eyes of a few of my competitors. They even spoke about coasting the bends. They eased off and didn't pedal. But not me! When I got on the bike I switched off and went for it. You can ease off a bit if you get in front but as soon as you sense someone is catching you, you have to get going again. I never had a fear factor in anything I did. I just went for it.

During the final Lynn Davies, as expected, pushed me as I knew he would. He had to be one of the strongest British competitors I came up against. I knew him from Tokyo's Olympics in 1964 when he took gold for Great Britain in the long jump which made him the first British athlete to win an Olympic field event since 1908. He had great personal discipline and self-motivation and I knew that he rarely let a day go by in his life when he didn't put himself to some kind of physical test. I knew he would be the man for me to beat in this final and that's how it turned out. I won the weightlifting, gym tests and finished second in the canoeing. In the crossbow, I finished joint second and for the cycling and swimming, I managed third. Football proved my worst event and I finished sixth. This gave me a total of forty-one point five points. Lynn came second with thirty-three with Andy Irvine back in third.

Winning felt absolutely fantastic and I loved every minute of it. Did I think I could win the final? Well, not at the very beginning. Not really. But I knew I'd done enough training. It's just on the day you never know how you are going to perform or how the others are. One slip in any event, especially early on, could set the tone for the whole two days. So getting off to a good start was vitally important for me. This situation also existed in boxing and judo. In boxing, one lucky punch could finish a much-fancied champion. With judo one wrong move and you could be flattened in two seconds. I'd grown up never to underestimate my opponents and the same applied to Superstars although I felt quite confident after winning my first competition in Cwmbran. I think this is when it dawned on me that I could win without competing in two events where I knew I would never be competitive. I understood my limitations. I also realised that the same set of circumstances applied to all the others. They would have to take part in something that they knew they didn't stand a chance of winning. With my selected events I knew I had a chance of winning, or finishing second or third, in every event I entered.

I loved the way Superstars seemed to be heading and, quite quickly in Great Britain during the first quarter of 1979, I seemed to have become a bit of a hero to many people. I've already mentioned how people would recognise me nearly everywhere I went and this continued after the final. In fact, it seemed to get worse. Despite this judo remained my greatest passion and I felt I could beat anyone in Great Britain and many others in Europe. Plus I still had my heart set on winning an Olympic gold medal. Being part of the Alexander Howden Group helped immensely during this period. At the end of January 1979, my sporting ambitions remained very firm. I wanted to win an Olympic gold in Moscow the following year and I wanted to win the European Superstars competition which would take place early in February.

But during the second quarter of 1980, I started to have doubts about my participation in Moscow. I still wanted that gold but things had changed. We had the mortgage on the house and very soon we would have our first child. I had to think seriously about money. I'd also heard the British Government had serious doubts about Britain competing in Moscow's Olympics. I'd weighed up all these factors and decided not to make my fourth attempt for a gold medal.

On Friday the 16th of February 1979 at 7:55 p.m. BBC 1 screened the European final of Superstars. The competition took place at the fantastic indoor Ahoy Stadium in Rotterdam Holland. My competitors were:

Three from Holland: Hockey player Ties Kruize, karate champion Otti Roethof and motor cycling's Will Hartog. Irish showjumper Paul Darragh. Belgian cyclist Walter Godefroot. French long jumper Jacques Rousseau. And Lynn Davies joined me to represent Great Britain. Right from the start, it seemed that Lynn and I were up against a Dutch connection that included the partisan home crowd and the three Dutch competitors. At times they appeared as if they might be using 'team tactics' to ensure one of them won.

The stadium had this incredible banked track. Halfway up it felt like my shoulder would touch the ground. All the way up and I felt sure my head would touch it as well. It didn't and I pedalled up as far as I could go. My right pedal even touched the wall and Lynn said later he thought I would end up in the crowd. But I just went for it and thought if I come off I come off. I heard Dad shouting now, now, now, which meant I had to come off the bank and down. I did and I think I came close to breaking the world record. The Dutch, a nation of very keen cyclists, created a fantastic atmosphere during the cycling and nearly lifted the roof off the stadium. As well as the cycling I also won the canoeing. I finished second in the swimming and the weightlifting. In my other two events, the archery and the soccer I finished nowhere and third. The archery turned out to be a big disappointment as they introduced a bow that I'd never practiced with before.

I finished, as I always did, as I never took part in the steeplechase, before most of my competitors on forty-five points and had to wait and see how things panned out in that race. Now I mentioned before the Dutch connection and I think we have to go back to the soccer penalties to see how this worked. My main rival, Ties, hit five out of five. So did his fellow countryman Will Hartog. I managed three which put me in third place. Lynn, formerly on Cardiff City's football teams books as a youngster and normally very good at this, missed all five. Ties and Will had to have a shoot-out to see who won. Ties went first and fired his shot just over the bar. Will followed and his shot went so high over the bar it would have missed three goals, on top of one another, and the ball disappeared out of the stadium. An unbelievable attempt and a few people were scratching their heads. Up they stepped again. Ties rolled his into the corner. Unless Will scored Ties would take ten points. To me, Will's final effort looked more like a back pass to the keeper and Ties took a ten point gift from his teammate. During the steeplechase, Lynn got over his penalties disappointment and totally dominated the race. But for me, my concerns were about who came second and the Dutch connections. Dutchman Otti Roethof won the hundred metres and he looked strong. As the battle for second place took shape I believed Otti looked far stronger than Ties who even seemed to injure himself as he clambered over one hurdle. For the last forty metres, it looked as if Otti could pass Ties anytime he liked. But as the home crowd cheered he didn't. I even shouted at him to get a move on. He didn't listen and Ties finished on forty-five points as well so we shared first place. Ties, a very strong competitor who never gave up, and I put him in the same category as his fellow countryman from the judo world who would also never give up. Martin Poglajen.

At the age of thirty-two, I'd become the first Britain to win the European Superstars final even if I had to share the trophy. Had the Dutch connection robbed me of the chance to win outright? Probably. But if the situation had been reversed I think I might have let a fellow British competitor beat me if it meant he could take the title. Another factor that hampered me had been the removal of the gym tests, arm dips and squat thrusts, which had been included in the previous European final. This time we had an obstacle course.

After BBC One screened Rotterdam's final the hype, which had built up after my first two appearances on Superstars, intensified even more. Everywhere I went people asked for my autograph, kids swarmed all over me, and adults congratulated me. I enjoyed this belated fame in what could have been the twilight of my career but I never lost sight of my judo roots. I knew that without them this wouldn't have happened. I owed so much to judo. I still found the time, nearly every day, for judo and coaching the youngsters at my judo club. They gave me so much pleasure and kept me grounded. Mind you if I'd started to get carried away with this Dad would have put the brakes on. But another television appearance, my third during Friday night's peak viewing time, had for certain pushed my kudos to new levels. Winning my heat, and the British final, I believed had pushed me closer to becoming a household name. Now, after sharing the European title with Ties, I think this confirmed my status and that I might not be just enjoying fifteen minutes of outside judo wonder fame. This also had a supreme knock-on effect at my judo club where more and more and youngsters turned up than ever had before. Prior to Superstars, I could measure the number of new kids each week on one hand. That changed after Superstars. I remember one week having about thirty coming through the door. Many had no idea about judo. They'd just seen me on their televisions, knew I had a club nearby, and were curious. I welcomed them with open arms and spent as much time with them as I could.

I wanted to be the first British athlete to win Superstars European title, which I hoped would be good for judo, and I did. In the same way that I wanted to be the first British athlete to win a medal at the Olympic Games and at the World Championships, I'd set these targets and my competitive spirit helped me achieve them. Plus of course, I had some great help from Mum and Dad and other family members and friends. I owed so much of my success to my dedicated team, with Dad at the top of the list. First and foremost he was my Dad. But he was also my mentor, my friend and at times a kind of tormentor at the same time.

As we know Superstars started in 1973 but now, in 1979, the British public seemed to have caught on to it in a bigger way and the viewing numbers were increasing. I'm not suggesting that this happened because of me as there were some superb competitors taking part. But I'd just won three competitions and everybody knew that I took this competition seriously and trained very hard. Plus I spoke from my heart which I think might have helped the British public identify with me. Journalist and author Norman Giller, born in Stepney in 1940, who served his apprenticeship with the Daily Express from 1964 to 1974, put it this way in his sports column.

'Giller's award for winter warmers during the freeze.

Joint first – Brian Jacks and Dickie Davies.

Brian Jacks has the screen charisma to become a cockney hero in the Henry Cooper mold and they don't make them much better than that!

His determination, infectious enthusiasm, and true grit have helped make 'The Superstars' a must viewing this year.'

42

When I announced my retirement I mentioned that a few other factors had influenced my decision and at that time I knew I'd qualified to take part in the 1979 World Superstars final scheduled to take place in Freeport, Lucaya in the Bahamas with quite a bit of prize money up for grabs. I think $40,000 for the winner. This played a big part in my decision as I wanted a piece of that. I'd also been asked to make a few personal appearances which meant a bit of money. The time had definitely arrived for me to try and start to cash in on my sporting name and hopefully my ability.

During my initial chat with Dad, before I started Superstars, he mentioned that some people didn't really consider it a real sport and the phrase 'junk sport' had been used. I totally disagreed and defended Superstars to the hilt whenever that topic of conversation came up. I said that was nonsense and that I believed Superstars had to be tougher than a decathlon. Decathlon's involved a lot of running and events like the shot put, discus and javelin. These are all about technique and they don't take anything out of you. I'd have rather done that all day long than swimming, cycling, canoeing, arm dips, and squat thrusts. That's a real test for an athlete and contestants require a wider spread of skills to cope with them. I do believe that when I arrived on the Superstars scene I upped the quality and competitiveness of the whole idea. Gone were the days when Superstars just meant a bit of light-hearted fun. I think I turned it into a bit of a phenomenon with my professional approach. I know Keith Fielding referred to me as the first professional Superstar but I just approached it with the same tactics I did with everything. I never signed a contract or anything. I just continued doing things the Brian Jacks way which seemed to create a whole new ball game with committed crowds, serious commentators, and clenched jawed competitors who wanted to win. I invested five to six hours six days a week. And as for that professional contract, I suppose I'd signed one with myself and Dad. The one that said I would dedicate myself to Superstars in the same way I had judo. It's a competition. I'm a competitor. Not only that, I'm a very good competitor. Whenever I went for something I always convinced myself that I was the best. Being a judo man helped of course as to be any good at judo you have to have speed, stamina, skill, and strength. Plus you have to be very intelligent. There is no room for dummies in judo. It's a kind of physical chess.

I got a kick from beating the best people in judo and the same buzz applied to Superstars. Even before the

European final, I received great feedback from many people in the UK. I think they saw in me, during a period of hard times and extremely cold weather, as a normal bloke getting stuck in and having a go. I know I inspired a few people. I hope I gave them a feeling which made them think if he can do it so can I. And that is one hundred percent correct. But it takes behind the scenes work. You have to train, train and then train some more. For me, this paid dividends and definitely proved the old saying:

'The more you sweat when you train the less you sweat on the day.'

With about four weeks to go before the world final in the Bahamas, I continued to push myself to the maximum. I had to as I had no idea about most of my competition and how hard they were training. I knew Lynn Davies would be there and that he would be training hard. But that was all I knew. I had to keep pushing myself. I'd already gone full on for four months and I just needed one more month of intense hard work although something didn't feel right. My energy levels dropped and I had a few aches and pains. Also, a few rashes started to appear on different parts of my body. I tried to fight on. I tried to keep training. Whatever I had I tried to train it out of me. But I couldn't. I needed to get checked and

Julie took me to the hospital. There they determined that I had shingles and a blood disorder that meant I needed complete rest for at least three weeks. I think I'd stressed my body so much during the past few months and it couldn't take any more. I knew I had to rest. I'd done too much, in a short period of time, and this put me out of the World Superstars final.

I made a total recovery and began a new phase of my life that I really enjoyed. Having announced my retirement from judo it meant I couldn't compete anymore but I still carried on at my club. However, time for me during this period of my life had now become something I needed to manage as many people seemed to want a piece of me for one thing or another. Newspapers and magazines wanted interviews. Television companies wanted me on their games shows and other programmes. I had requests to endorse sports products and to open shops. From a marketing point of view, I'd become hot. The flavor of the winter of discontent and they all wanted me in the hope that I could boost their ratings or increase their sales. The Brian Jacks brand had become synonymous with gold dust. Get me in newspapers and magazines and they would sell. Get me and people would tune into Celebrity Squares, The Golden Gold Shot, Through the Key Hole, Blue Peter, Parkinson, Magpie, and

Noel Edmonds' Multi-Coloured Swap Shop. And get me to endorse sports products and they might fly off the shelves.

This new life phase took on a whole different meaning in June as on Tuesday the 19th Julie gave birth to our son at around 7:30 a.m. You could have knocked me down with a feather. Brian Jacks, king of the dips, became Brian Jacks king of the besotted Dads as I cradled my son for the first time. I looked at him. He looked at me. And for some reason, I saw me in him. I thought I had me in my arms. It was one of the most, in fact, I think the most, extraordinary moment of my life. At the age of thirty-two, I'd thought I'd picked, or time had picked it for me, the perfect age to become a Dad for the first time. I'd travelled the World, done many things, so to become a Dad should have been a piece of cake. But no. I cried. I laughed. And when I went to get a drink I told anyone I passed that I'd just become a Dad. I wanted to shout it from the rooftops.

I found the drink I needed, and when I say that I don't mean alcohol I just felt really thirsty, in the pub next door to the hospital. I also bumped into one of my trusted Superstars training team Errol Field. Errol, what a man, I'm not really sure where to start with him. I might have become a marketing man's diamond in the rough but it was all because of Errol and one or two others who made that happen. He was my brick and he who would always be there for me no matter what time of day or night I needed him. He'd also been around the martial arts world for a long time and had opened quite a few clubs. He came from Croydon and started work as a carpet fitter which didn't really fit for him and it didn't last very long. He married a very nice girl called Vanessa and they had a son called Christopher. Unfortunately, Errol's marriage didn't last. I'm not completely sure why but I think Errol only had one real love in his life. Martial arts. He had relationships with other women and they didn't last very long either. Women, when they discovered what they were up against, moved on. They couldn't compete with his passions for judo, jujitsu, and karate. At one point he had eleven clubs in the Croydon area and he gave so much time and effort to all of them. How could carpet fitting and women fit into that lifestyle! Hundreds and hundreds of kids passed through his doors which meant he shaped a lot of people's lives. He became like an unofficial Godfather to so many of his students who always treated him with the utmost respect. In fact, a few students, who had their own children later, actually made him their child's real godfather.

We had a good chat that day in the pub about me just becoming a Dad and of course about martial arts. Errol passed on a few tips that he'd picked up with his own son plus he talked about my new responsibility. He made very good sense and I suppose he had that fatherly way about him. We stayed there until about 2:00 p.m. and neither of us touched a drop of alcohol. Many people recognised me and came over to chat and for an autograph. Of course, I mentioned that I'd just become a proud Dad!

Going back to the early days, during Superstars training just before the European final had been screened, we had a morning at Crystal Palace when Errol made it but the others didn't. This meant Errol had to work extra hard and he did. He knew he had sole responsibility to push me. We also had an American reporter with us that day as the Americans had heard I would be taking part in World Superstars and they wanted to check me out. By breakfast, Errol looked absolutely shattered. I sat down at the table and he slumped down in his chair. He looked like he might fall asleep at any moment. Breakfast arrived. Bacon, three poached eggs, baked beans, sausages, fried tomatoes, and toast. Errol opened one eye, looked at it, and made an effort to straighten up and start eating. Unfortunately, he knocked his plate and his breakfast ended up all down the front of his tracksuit.

Everyone in the cafe cracked up and the American used that incident in his story.

Julie and I had discussed girls' and boys' names as we didn't know beforehand which sex we were having. I actually threw Errol into the pot at one point but Julie didn't fancy that. In the end, Julie wanted Brian Philip Jacks but everyone called him Philip or Phil right from the start. Even Julie! I loved being a parent and Philip made us complete. He certainly changed our lives and made us very happy. By this time I'd worked a lot with children and developed a good understanding of them. I think this also helped me. Would I push Philip into judo? Certainly not! I never agreed with parents who turned up and pushed their kids onto the mat. I would let Philip develop his own interests and guide him whenever I could. If he wanted to be a pianist, ballet dancer, mechanic or a bird watcher I would help him every step of the way.

43

TOWARDS THE END of 1979 Superstars loomed large on my calendar again and I knew I had to work extra hard to defend my title. I had a similar game plan especially as I'd seen the names of the people who would be taking part in the British heats.

Competitions this season included: The British Past Masters, two heats for men, finals for the men and women, and the International final.

John Sherwood, who won a bronze medal in the Mexico 1968 Olympic Games 400 metres hurdles, totally dominated the past masters competition, winning all six of his events for a maximum score. England's 1966 football World Cup hat-trick hero Geoff Hurst came second.

There were sixteen competitors who took part in the British heats with some big names to beef up the competition. These included Somerset and England cricket all-rounder Ian 'Beefy' Botham. Scotland and Manchester United centre-forward, a man feared by many centre-backs, Joe Jordan. From the world of tennis David Lloyd who, along with his younger brother John, were two of the most successful British tennis players during the seventies.

Champion national hunt jockey John Francome who won seven jockeys titles. Boxer Alan Minter who'd won and retained his European middleweight title in July and November 1978. England's basketball player of the year in 1978 Steve Assinder. Welsh rugby union winger John James Williams, known as J. J. who won thirty caps for Wales between 1973 and 1979. Danny Nightingale, who along with Adrian Parker and Jim Fox, helped Great Britain to team gold in the modern pentathlon at the 1976 Olympic Games in Montreal. They were some of the big names I could be meeting in the final as well as Francis Morgan Ayodele Thompson. A big name if ever there was one! But he usually preferred a shorter version. Daley Thompson.

Francis Morgan, born in July 1958, which made him twelve years younger than me, already had a huge reputation as one of the world's best decathletes. In August 1978 he won gold at the Commonwealth Games in Edmonton, Alberta, Canada. A month later he won silver at the European Championships in Prague. Francis Morgan, young, six feet tall, muscular, looked a real Superstars winner in the making. A real Adonis and David Vine even referred to him as 'Mr. Muscles.' Many people believed he'd be the 1980 British Superstar Champion before the competition even started. A young fit athlete who already took part in a multi-sport event. Who could stop him?

Well, the answer in heat one turned out to be no one as he took the top spot with Danny Nightingale in second and cricketer Derek Randall back in third. This meant that joining me in the final would be the winner of the past masters John Sherwood and second-placed Geoff Hurst. From the heats Steve Assinder, J.J. Williams, Danny Nightingale and Alan Minter all came through. We would all obviously be cannon fodder for the 'champion in waiting,' the winner of heat one, and already a big favourite for the decathlon gold medal in the forthcoming Moscow Olympic Games. Francis Morgan. We didn't stand a chance. Or did we?

We gathered at the Cwmbran Stadium in South Wales, in pretty atrocious weather conditions, for Great Britain's 1980 Superstars final and it felt great to be back in the Superstars environment again, even if seven of us were there as lambs to Francis Morgan's slaughter, for Great Britain's most talented athlete. We were, however, quite a fit bunch as well as very experienced. Geoff Hurst had reached thirty-seven years of age with John Sherwood now thirty-four. I came next at thirty-three with J.J Williams now thirty-one. With four of us in our thirties, we must have looked like old age pensioners to the youthful Francis Morgan. I think it's fair to say Francis Morgan and Superstars really were a marriage made in heaven!

As I mentioned before we didn't have good weather which seemed pretty normal for Cwmbran for some reason. We also had David Vine and Ron Pickering presenting and commentating as they always did. Superstars now had a firm foothold in America, Europe and Great Britain with events taking place in all kinds of different locations. It had become a worldwide event with many fine competitors taking part. But no matter where Superstars went David and Ron always seemed to be there. They laced the competition together with their special skills and knowledge which helped make the show so popular and watchable. They seemed to know everything about sport and complemented each other so well. They were like a double act and I don't think Superstars would have been Superstars without them.

David Martin Vine. Born in Newton Abbott in South Devon and forty-three when Superstars started in 1973. He introduced the show and always looked immaculate. I think Malcolm Macdonald summed up David best when he said:

'David Vine. In big wide lapels.

Big knotted tie around a huge collared shirt.

Long hair.

Stood by the lake.

Saying welcome.'

That's how David always started the show with its familiar theme tune, Heavy Action, kicking in as soon as he'd finished his opening. John Valmore Pearson, known as Johnny Pearson, a British composer and orchestra leader who led the Top of the Pops orchestra for sixteen years, wrote Heavy Action in 1970. He didn't write it especially with Superstars in mind. How could he when the show hadn't even started and he probably thought it might be a good fit for Top of the Pops. But this music has such a strong link with Superstars than many people believe the title is Superstars and not Heavy Action.

Back to David and from the age of seventeen, he worked for the North Devon Herald, which lead to various other newspapers, before he became Sports Editor of the Western Morning News in Plymouth. In 1961 he joined Westward Television and the BBC network in 1966. He worked on BBC 2 which at that time couldn't be received in the South West and this enabled him to continue his role with

Westward. However, his Westward bosses found out, thanks to an article in the Daily Mail newspaper, which meant he had to resign from Westward. He hosted a great number of television programmes which included: Sportscene, It's a Knockout, Jeux Sans Frontieres, Miss UK, Miss World, Quiz Ball, Rugby Special, Match of the Day, A Question of Sport, Grandstand, Startshot and Ski Sunday. He acted as anchorman at the World Snooker Championships at the Crucible Theatre, Sheffield, from 1978. The first year the BBC covered the championships daily, as well as other snooker events that included the Grand Prix, UK Championship and the Masters.

I really enjoyed working with David and being interviewed by him. He made the whole interview process so easy and just kept telling me to be myself. I remember one time, just before a canoe final, he came over to me and asked me how I felt. I told him I felt great and that I would win the race in a record time. He smiled, in his own polite way, whilst Errol Field nearly fell off his seat, as he heard every word. I'm not sure what David thought, or Errol, but I kept my word and won with a record time.

Ronald James Pickering came from Hackney in the North East of London and would have been in his early forties when Superstars started. Although he worked as a commentator he also doubled up as an athletics coach which might have been his first love. He married Jean Desforges a very good one hundred metres runner. Ron studied for a diploma in PE at Carnegie College of Physical Education in Leeds and followed this up with a master's degree at Leicester University. He taught PE at Stratford Grammar School and then Wanstead County High School. Later he moved to Cardiff where he spent five years as National Athletics Coach for Wales. Guess who he met there? Yes. Lynn Davies. Ron coached Lynn and the two of them still had a special bond during Superstars. We know because Lynn said, if Ron thought he needed special help with an event, he would take him around the corner and give him some advice. A few other Superstars athletes might also have benefited from Ron's coaching ability. In 1964 Ron helped coach Team GB at the Olympic Games in Tokyo and might well have heard about my antics up that Olympic flag pole although he never mentioned it. In 1968, at the Olympic Games in Mexico, he commentated and then continued in broadcasting. Ron became the first host of BBC 's children's sports programme 'We Are the Champions' where he became known for his catchphrase, 'Away you go!' at the end of each show. Superstars soon followed.

I think it's fair to say David and Ron were sporting fanatics. They loved sport and to be given the job of hosting and commentating on Superstars must have been like winning the lottery for them and they were fantastic. With David the ultimate professional who knew exactly what he had to do and when. He had perfect timing. They were also very good friends from David's time with Westward television. This is where they met when Ron visited the West Country for a coaching session. David went to film it and liked what he saw. He invited Ron back and soon they developed their special television style. They spun off each other in a relaxed, informal but professional way, which viewers could relate to. I have to thank Ron, despite not taking me around the corner for some covert advice, for my dips fame. The gym tests were all down to his ideas. They were his baby.

Superstars had a formula that worked with David Vine, Ron Pickering, and that music all very much a part of it.

BBC One screened the United Kingdom Ferguson Superstars final on the 1st of February 1980 at 7:00 p.m.

Despite the presence of Francis Morgan, I felt quite confident of at least taking second place. Although I knew

John Sherwood would push me all the way. I'm not sure if that sounds quite right! Let me try again.

Did I fear Francis Morgan? Absolutely not! During my training at Crystal Palace, I'd seen him around a few times. I didn't know if he was stalking me or if it just happened by coincidence. I even gave him the opportunity to train with us. He accepted at first but didn't last long. I think we trained too hard for him.

John Sherwood though had made a clear statement that he'd entered to win this competition. All throughout his career he'd been a superb athlete and a great team member for his club in Sheffield where he'd turned out many times during the last ten years. However, now he'd made a decision to turn his back on that in an attempt to win Superstars as he'd given up his amateur status. This also meant he could compete in the one hundred metres sprint. When interviewed John said if he could swim better he might not have taken this step. But no matter how hard he tried his swimming didn't improve so he had no choice. I admired him immensely for taking this decision.

We began in the water with the canoe heats. Alan Minter, who ended up in the rhododendrons during heat two in Grangemouth, had been given a lane very close to the bank. He'd also trained a bit more in the art of going straight. He came up against Steve, Danny, and John. Danny won and John came second. Alan went in a perfectly straight line but didn't make the final. In my race, I eased up as I beat Francis Morgan with Geoff back in third. In the final, I came up against John who had never lost a Superstars event. Remember he cleaned up during the past masters. That changed as I powered home to win with Danny second and Francis Morgan third. Cycling came next and we had to race on a narrow tarmac path in a park beside a stream. I came up against Steve in my heat and just beat him. John rode against Danny and John made a late attack to win this one. Francis Morgan had to ride against the clock for a chance to reach the final but he missed out by point nine of a second. This meant I would ride again against Steve in the final. Steve came late but I held on. Dad, stood close to the finish line, gave me that extra special encouragement to help me over the line first.

Basketball, a new event for me, came next. Of course, I'd practiced for many hours, but I knew this would be a tough event for me. Francis Morgan looked very good and beat my time. John came on the court last and he showed great control with very clean baskets to take this event. I finished third.

For the next event, I must admit I got the hump. Being a judo player, every time I competed, I had to weigh-in. These always took place early in the morning and I planned my eating habits around them. I knew that to weigh-in at my best possible weight I couldn't eat for five to six hours before I hit the scales. I adopted this same strategy in Superstars. I weighed in. I ate. No problem for me I knew all about my diet and how best to perform. Many other sportsmen, who have to weigh-in as part of their sport, follow exactly the same routine. I actually believed I'd weighed in six kilos lighter than Francis Morgan, which I knew would be a big advantage for me. But later something happened that totally threw me. We were asked to weigh-in again and I had no idea why. After taking on a bit of food I weighed a few kilos heavier than I had before. Of course, I got the hump. I'd prepared as I normally did. I'd made calculations and written everything down in my little black book. Then they threw the curveball. After the second weigh-in, the gap between Francis Morgan had decreased to only one kilo and I knew I'd lost my advantage.

But this event had been billed as a battle between me and him and that's how it panned out as John, Steve, J.J, and Danny were soon out of the running. Geoff and Alan sat this one out. Francis Morgan lifted one hundred and twenty point five kilos. As he'd weighed in at eighty-four point five this gave him a total of twenty-eight over his body weight. For my next lift, the bar had been set at one hundred and twenty-eight. If I made it I would beat Kjell Isaksson's Superstars record. I did it for a score of thirty-six point eight over my body weight. The ways things worked out Francis Morgan had to sit, watch, wait for me to fail, and then come in. With the pressure on as I approached the bar now at one hundred and thirty-two. I felt strong. But I couldn't lift it. He came on and he smashed it up to take ten points and Superstars weightlifting record in the process. I knew that weightlifting had been part of his training programme and he'd become a clean and jerk expert. Ron Pickering described this as the best weightlifting competition Superstars had ever seen. Serious weightlifting with vein bursting lifts. How did I feel? Well, Dad had always taught me to be a good loser so outwardly I smiled and shook his hand. Inwardly I still had the hump. Ron actually said that Francis Morgan had competed in Superstars with the idea of winning the weightlifting only. But somehow I doubted that. I knew he wouldn't enter anything if he didn't think he could win. Plus he might have been fired up with my comments about Superstars being more testing than a decathlon.

We completed day one with the gym tests and for arm dips I came on last after Francis Morgan who'd managed forty-six and John thirty-eight. They were the ones I needed to beat. A few of my fans held up a banner which read they wanted to see ninety-nine plus but I set a new Superstars record with eighty.

On to the squat thrusts and here I think Francis Morgan and I conjured up, quite by chance, another Superstars classic moment that might be up there with Kevin's wobble on the bike. He came first and placed his stopwatch down in front of him on the line where we placed our hands. I couldn't understand this. For an intense minute of squat thrusts, you don't have time to look at a watch and time yourself. You have to go flat out. Stopwatch propelled he managed seventy-three. I followed him, gave him a wink as we passed each other, and put my orange down where he'd placed his watch. Orange propelled I also managed seventy-three. I think a lot of people enjoyed this moment and to this day still talk about it. John Sherwood beat us both with eighty-six to take second place in this event. At the end of day one, I led the field with forty-one points. John held second position with twenty-seven with Francis Morgan back in third on twenty-six.

As for oranges they'd been part of my normal competition routine for a very long time all thanks to Mum. Whenever she watched me compete she would always be throwing down oranges as in the early days we didn't have plastic bottles so she couldn't throw down a drink. This made oranges the next best thing and easy for her. Later I discussed eating, just prior to and during a competition, with Doctor Ken Kingsbury. He explained that when we eat blood is being used to digest food. And, if we compete with our blood being used to digest food, this means our blood is being used in two directions. So he advised that we should not eat three hours before a contest. As for drink, he said to take on the minimum needed. He talked more about the digestion system which made a lot of sense. To perform well in any sport is very difficult with a full stomach. But he also mentioned that I had the correct approach with oranges and from that point on I used to bite the top off and squeeze and suck the juice out. This helped contain my thirst and kept Mum happy as I knew she'd be watching. I'm not sure how many people followed my example but Jaffa Oranges never picked up on it and asked me to advertise for them.

Over the years few people have asked what happens after the first day of Superstars has finished and I think they might have been looking for off-camera kind of moments that might have put competitors in embarrassing situations. Maybe alcohol-related and things like that. Unfortunately, for me anyway, I normally just dined with family and friends and had early night. I think you know enough about me by now to understand that I take competition very seriously. I only had one reason for taking part in Superstars. Winning. That was it. Pure and simple winning. The thought of a night in a pub, or an all-night session in a hotel bar with my competitors, never entered my head. I always felt honoured to meet British sporting legends but that was it. We were in a competition and I behaved in exactly the same way as I had during my judo career. That might sound boring and I'm sorry if I've disappointed a few people with this revelation.

Day two and the atrocious weather continued for the start of the one hundred metres. John, who if he stayed an amateur would have sat this one out, took his place on the starting line with six others. Francis Morgan and I looked on. In the pouring rain, J.J. won with ease. John finished second and Steve third. Pistol shooting came next and we had five shots. Alan Minter, who'd now proved he could row straight, also knew how to shoot straight as he took the lead with thirty-five with Francis Morgan in second on thirty-two. Being the last to shoot I knew exactly what I had to do and I started well with two eights and a seven. The best start by anyone. But I blew it and had to settle for second place. However, this proved enough for me to win the competition with two events to go. I'd won with a total of fifty-two points and my Superstars record stood at four from four. Four competitions entered and four won.

As for my relationship with Great Britain's greatest athlete, who finished third behind John, I have to say that he left me feeling deeply disappointed and a lot of his fans. I took a coach load of kids, from my judo club, who were all looking forward to meeting him and getting his autograph. Unfortunately, Daley, let's use his real name now, refused to speak with them or sign any autographs. I didn't know if he had an axe to grind with me, which made him refuse, or if he normally behaved this way. I later discovered that this is how he behaved and it left a bad taste.

A few months later, at the boycotted by sixty-five countries Olympic Games in Moscow, he took gold in the decathlon.

44

In February 1980 I won the International Superstars final in Israel and my record now stood at an impressive five out of five. A nice feeling but just around the corner the Superstars World final loomed in the Bahamas. This would be my ultimate challenge as I faced unknown opponents, revised events, and a totally different climate. Julie, Philip, the rest of my family and my judo club, had to take a back seat as I focused on the events that could make me Superstars World champion. It totally consumed my life and nearly every thought I had related to Superstars. On top of this, I still had to juggle personal appearances and television shows. I dashed here, there and everywhere. Life had never been so hectic.

First and foremost I knew that training had to be my top priority. If I didn't put in the time I'd have no chance especially with new events and different gym tests. We, that's my fantastic team and I set our alarm clocks for the crack of dawn and began training again. During the last year, we'd become a bit of a fixture at Crystal Palace and many people, as I've already mentioned, turned up just to watch us train. They looked through windows, around doors and many times kids just sat in an orderly group on the gymnasium floor. I enjoyed these kids being there and they followed us around as we moved from one exercise to another. I felt a bit like the pied piper. I chatted to them, signed their autograph books and pieces of paper. They encouraged me to train harder. They shouted. 'Come on Brian.' They counted as I lifted weights. They cheered. They applauded. They made me smile, which certainly helped me through some pain barriers, and there was one who always shouted. 'That's tasty Bri.' They, perhaps without realising it, became very much a part of my training process. They helped push me to my limits and beyond. I had a great relationship with those Crystal Palace kids, as I did with most kids, and I hope a few of them were inspired enough to take up some kind of sport. I always asked them to watch their television screens on a Friday night if I knew I would be on. I needed them to cheer me and I'm sure they did. But there never seemed to be enough time to really interact with them, to hang out, as I would always be on my way to my next task and so on and so on. As usual, we'd spend two hours before breakfast, on the track, and in the gym. Between nine and ten we'd walk up the hill for breakfast and the kids would follow. On the way up we'd meet people who wished me well and asked for autographs. The same thing happened in the café where I signed more autographs as I ate my bacon and eggs. After this, we'd spend another hour in the gym and then an hour in the pool before lunch. Cycling followed after lunch with pistol practice and archery. I pushed myself and kept remembering Kisaburo Watanabe's words.

'The champion, who trained for three hours a day to become champion, then trained for six hours a day to stay champion.'

These words spun around in my head almost twenty-four seven. I'd won the British and European titles and now I wanted the world title as well. But there were some subtle changes I had to deal with. Arm dips were out. I knew, as did everyone else probably, that no one could touch me in this event. Could this have been why they dropped it? In came a new gym test for me called chin-ups. For weightlifting the result would now be decided by straight kilos lifted, with no allowance for body weight, providing bigger men with an immediate advantage over me. They extended the distance of the swimming and the cycling which again put me at a disadvantage with my more power packed sprinting style. Plus tennis had now come into the equation. Yes. I said tennis.

I'd never picked up a tennis racket in my life and now I had about eight weeks to learn. No doubt the Americans, and there were four of them in the final, had rackets in their hands before they could even walk. I couldn't play but I would learn. I also needed an expert and Errol came up with the answer, his uncle, Freddy Field and one of the best British tennis veterans around at that time. We met at Queens Tennis Club in West Kensington, London, and began an intensive course. We started with three hours a day and the balls ended up everywhere except on the other side of the net where they were supposed to go. They went sideways. They went backwards and to be honest with you I had no idea where the flipping balls would go. I also picked up some massive blisters on those Queens Club Courts. Most nights I had to bathe my feet in boiling hot water to try and get them ready for the next day. I'm not really sure what Freddy thought about my tennis. He never said. He just kept pushing and I had a kind of game after a couple of months with him. Not exactly serve and volley although, if the ball came back on my side of the net, I would do everything in my power to hit it even if it meant diving full length which I did many times and I had scratches on my legs to prove it. Freddy, just like all my other experts, proved a massive help. I just needed to see how my game compared with the Americans.

On Friday the 26th of May 1980 at 7:00 p.m. BBC One screened the 1980 World Superstars final which we know had taken place in the Bahamas a few weeks before. With me, there were nine other sportsmen. John Sherwood. Brian Budd the Canadian soccer player who'd turned up at the British final to check out the British talent. Of course, I wanted a crack at him and David Vine had informed me that he'd said the same about me. He'd won this event for the last two years and I knew he represented a tough challenge.

Three American football stars took their place. Charles White, Russ Francis and Joe Theismann. Racquetball champion Marty Hogan made up the American quartet. The other finalists were - Austrian skier Toni Innauer, Swiss bobsledder Eric Schaerer, Israel's water skier Moshe Ganzi and Ireland's Gaelic footballer Brendan Brogan.

There were ten events and we had to compete in seven. As usual, I dropped the running. For the third event, after seeing my competitors in practice, I had to skip tennis. The game I had wouldn't have given me any kind of chance against them. They were on a totally different tennis level to me and I would have needed a few years with Freddy, not just a few weeks, to get anywhere near them. I don't think I could have prepared any better but I knew, in this instance, I would have failed. Budd must have felt the same way as he also dropped tennis. Racquetball champion Hogan took ten tennis points. Budd won the swimming with me back in last place. That didn't go well.

Next up the gym tests and these had been built up as the big showdown between me and Budd. To stand any chance of winning this competition I had to win this event. It still annoyed me that arm dips weren't included but I just had to accept it and do my best in the pull-ups, or chin-ups, which they had instead. It didn't go well. I only managed forty-four and he pulled out forty-seven. He followed this with 114 squats to pile more pressure on me. With all the changes to this competition I knew I had to try and to think outside the box, to try and gain some kind of advantage, and for the squats, we came up with a new idea based on something South African racing driver Jody Scheckter had tried. He used engine oil on his shoes and went like a jet-propelled jackrabbit with a sliding technique. I didn't go with engine oil but I had a special pair of shoes made with plastic tops. I practiced with a sliding technique at home and it seemed to get easier and easier every time. In practice, I managed 124. However, the Bahamas hot and humid climate made this more difficult especially as we were outside. I only managed 118 to set a new record, and this gave me an overall gym test total of 162. One point more than Budd for my first ten points.

The weightlifting came down to me and Russ Francis and the new rules put him in a much more favourable position. He weighed in at 110 kilos to my seventy-seven. The script had been written so that this much bigger man should have beaten me. But he didn't. In the one hundred yard sprint Budd, desperate for his third World Superstars title in a row, came second to Brogan.

For the bike race we were split into two heats and in mine, I came up against Budd and Theismann. As I came round the track, on the outside of Budd, he must have felt I would pass him and he leaned into me. He actually nudged me and I'm sure he did it on purpose. I wobbled a bit but didn't go down, and I managed to catch him again and passed him to win the race. I celebrated, as I had before whenever I crossed the finish line in first place, with my hands off the handlebars as I punched both my arms in the air in a triumphant salute. I also backpedalled, as I had many times before, and I went flying over the handlebars. In my excitement of winning, and that moment with Budd a few seconds earlier, I'd forgotten that the Americans used a freewheel bike that braked if you backpedalled. I'd never used this type of bike before and I cursed myself as I lay on the ground all bruised and battered. I'd also banged my right knee which had been operated on again a few months before.

Budd didn't seem too concerned and maybe, when he said he wanted a crack at me, that incident on the track might have been what he had in mind.

I suppose I could have whimpered out of the competition but I didn't. In the cycling final, I finished third behind Budd in second and John in first. John looked very strong and he pushed Budd all the way in the half-mile run but just couldn't catch him. In the soccer, John managed another seven points to my one. Budd, who obviously had to sit out the soccer, came back to take ten points in the rowing and seven in the obstacle course. I finished with nothing in those events which left me in joint third place with Hogan on twenty-six points. John with thirty one finished second behind Budd who won his third successive title with fifty-eight points.

Budd was an exceptionally good athlete and a very good soccer player. He had a very good hand and eye coordination, good upper body strength, and strong legs. He worked very hard and trained for two to three months before a competition. He also had a very mean competitive edge which I'd witnessed close up that day. In the past, I'd used tactics to put people off their game, such as giving the winner's podium a quick rub with my sleeve before a final and generally playing about with crowds before a contest. I knew about kidology and messing with my opponents' brains. But he stitched me up like a kipper and for a split second, I lost my focus. The result meant I lost a Superstars event for the first time and it hurt. Julie and I stayed in the Bahamas for a two week holiday. I hope she enjoyed it. For me, I couldn't get Budd out of my thoughts. We'd had a crack at each other and he'd won. I felt sick.

Back in England, the Great British public didn't seem to mind that I'd been beaten. Work continued to flow, opening a shop, a television show, or a personal appearance in a gym to discuss fitness. Sports agents were showing quite an interest in representing me. I had calls from friends, who had friends of friends, who wanted to speak to me. Plus I had direct calls and so did Julie. One came from Bev Walker a boxing promoter who lived in Reading. He asked if I had a manager and I said I no. He asked what my thoughts were on the subject and I said I would be willing to discuss the possibility of being managed properly. Bev sounded positive as well as knowledgeable so we decided to meet the next day for lunch.

Julie joined us and I suppose we chatted for about three hours. Bev had lots of ideas and he made it clear he wanted to manage me. I'd actually been thinking about management for a while and I had a few of my own ideas related to how I wanted to proceed. I knew that having a manager would take a lot of pressure off me and that my time management would improve. At that time I just seemed to run from one job to the next. I also needed help with job selection as I never enjoyed saying no to anything. With a manager, I wouldn't have to worry about that as he would take that strain. But on the other hand, I wanted to explore every option and another idea I'd been weighing up. I wanted my own management company or part of one, so I swung the conversation that way. I explained what I wanted and he seemed quite receptive to my ideas. So much so that after a few more meetings, on the 9th of June 1980, we incorporated our own management company. Limelight (Management) Limited, with a registered office at High Holborn House. We split the company four ways with twenty-five percent each for myself and Julie and twenty-five percent each for Bev and his wife Margaret. It all seemed so easy with Julie the only person with reservations. She didn't feel comfortable with Bev and kept going on at me about his dark sunglasses. During our first lunch, Bev never removed his sunglasses. Julie thought this strange and I had to explain that we were moving into a new world where people wore dark sunglasses during lunch. She still didn't feel right about it but I told her not to worry.

This new challenge seemed perfect for me and vindicated my decision to walk away from Woolwich College even more. I had Limelight, television appearances, occasional work with Alexander Howden, public appearances and the odd columns in newspapers and magazines, all generating income. Plus I still had B and P judo which I didn't really regard as an income generator but this still gave me so much pleasure and an opportunity to give something back to judo. But Limelight now provided me with the most excitement. With my Superstars popularity, and I suppose my ability to interact with people on every level, all kinds of sports people signed up.

From gymnastics, we had Suzanne Dando who represented Great Britain in the Moscow 1980 Olympics. From football Emlyn Hughes the former Liverpool captain who played sixty-two times for England. Scottish boxer Jim Watt who became the lightweight world champion when Roberto Duran vacated his title. British Olympic swimmers David Wilkie and Sharron Davies. David who we know won gold in the two hundred metres breaststroke, in a world record time, at the Montreal Olympics and Sharron became a household name when at the age of thirteen she represented Great Britain in the same Olympics. In Moscow, four years later, she won a silver medal in the four hundred metres individual medley. Her conqueror that day, East German Petra Schneider, later admitted using drugs to enhance her performance. We had modern pentathlete Kathy Taylor, who won the women's modern pentathlon World cup in 1979, and English jump jockey Bob Champion who went on to win the Grand National on Aldaniti. These were just a few of the people who signed up during the early days and to be honest with you it amazed me how incredibly easy it was to get them on board. They must have trusted me and believed in my work ethic as I always put my heart on my sleeve and never had any hidden agendas. I wanted the best for them which obviously also meant I should do well. So I got the people in and Bev had to find them work. He really knew how to charm people, as he had me, and he did a fantastic job at finding them work. We had the perfect business model and Limelight grew and grew.

45

IN JANUARY 1981 BBC One screened the UK Superstars Challenge of Champions. All the usual favourites who'd performed well in Superstars during the past few years were there. David Hemery, John Conteh, John Sherwood, Keith Fielding, Lynn Davies, Malcolm Macdonald, and Tim Crooks. The action took place at High Wycombe.

By now everyone knew about my big three events. The weightlifting, gym tests, and the canoe where ten points were virtually guaranteed, I just had to make sure I scored well in the swimming, basketball, and crossbow. But I didn't. I just managed third in the swimming and nothing in the other two. David took swimming, John basketball, and Keith the crossbow. This put me on the back foot and under pressure for my big three. Lynn, my main contender in weightlifting, had to sit it out with a back problem. I won and with the adrenalin pumping, I tried to beat Thompson's record. I failed.

In the gym tests, I managed another record-breaking performance in the arm dips. Before I started I saw a banner in the crowd that said something about one hundred and one arm dips. I felt quite good and with my counter, Emil Grygar ready to count, I decided to go for it and pushed out one hundred and another record. In the squat thrusts, I managed one hundred and three to take that event. This is how Emil Grygar recently described his part that day:

'It was an honour to support Brian on that day way back when. My little claim to fame. Ha. It makes my grandkids chuckle, and others, whenever they find the clip on YouTube. Or I send them the link! I feel like I too am part of history. It's a nice feel. Brian is, in his way a National treasure. He epitomizes British-ness to the fullest. As for that day, I counted and he performed. It felt so great, to be so close, as his right shoulder came down on my left fist. I could taste his body heat. He knew he was good but he didn't do anything to let his opponents know. Mind you, by this stage, most of Britain must have known. But he remained humble. When he passed a previous contestant's score that was relevant, he smiled. A winning smile! Brian Jacks. King of the dips. And my grandkids have nicknamed me the great 'King counter of the dips.'*

In the canoeing, Keith won my heat but that fired me up for the final where our positions were reversed. Worryingly though it provided another seven points for him and he still had four events to go. With only an eight-point lead I knew I had a problem especially as he had a very good chance of picking up ten points in each of those events. But instead of picking up the remaining forty points he only managed thirty-one to finish with fifty-one and take the title. The second day completely belonged to Keith he finished with thirteen points more than me back in third. Lynn finished second. For the first time on British soil, I'd been beaten. I, like John, now needed to decide if I would continue to compete.

The Superstars feeling, the buzz, lasted for three years. By the time of the 1981 Challenge of Champions, I felt burnt out. I couldn't compete anymore at the level I wanted to which for me meant the end. I never competed in anything just to be in it. I had to win and I turned down many requests to return. I spoke with Dad. He and Mum had been with me every step of the way. They and the rest of my family had provided me with great support and travelled thousands of miles to watch me. It helped, especially abroad, I remember during a cycling event in Israel when I had to dig deep cycling up a hill. I didn't think I would make it. Then I heard my support and this lifted me again. From somewhere I found more power. I called it family power and it helped to pull me over the line many times. Dad put me on the right road by making me complete four hundred arm dips a day and my overall training also put me on a completely different level. People might have thought I was mad but I didn't care. I did it because I loved to win. Dad had taught me how to win and that I couldn't win every time. I always knew what I had to do and I planned everything down to the finest detail. I had a plan plus Dad's words always ringing in my ears. 'Fail to prepare. Prepare to fail.'

There is no doubt, no question, that Superstars changed my life. But it also changed the lives of other people as they became inspired just by watching me on television and they started judo or another martial art. Here's one.

Brian. Used to watch you big man on Superstars! That's why I took up judo in the first place. Did it for three years and started doing judo again two years ago on my fiftieth birthday. Now I'm a blue belt and a silver medallist in the British Masters in 2016. You have so many admirers. My friends, lots of players, grew up watching you on Superstars. All the best. Peter Harvey.

46

Having now retired from Superstars didn't mean life became any less hectic. Bev continued to work his magic and I, plus our clients, were kept very busy. We really were a marriage made in heaven. With all my television work, personal appearances and my judo club I didn't have a lot of spare time, which suited me as I always liked to be kept very busy. I had a full plate and didn't think I could take on any more responsibilities. But something came up in April 1981. In front of a full house at Crystal Palace, during the British Championships, I took my bow as Charlie Palmer announced me as judo's new British Team Manager with a three year contract. I didn't really have to go through a long drawn out interview process as they wanted me as did most of the British judo world. Many people believed, and some even wrote, that this had been inevitable for years. Another marriage made in heaven and I took over from joint managers Dave Starbrook and Tony Macconnell. There were rumours that they got the hump over this and even comments floating around related to industrial tribunals. I didn't believe any of this and remained great friends with both of them.

I managed to juggle everything, without dropping any balls, and I had some good players at my disposal who responded to my no-nonsense management style. They knew I liked a laugh and a joke. But on the mat, they had to perform. I'd been coached by some serious people in the past and I tried to bring different qualities from each of these coaches. People like Dad, Ted Mossom, Trevor Leggett and Kisaburo Watanabe to name but a few. Obviously, TP played his part in my judo education and I used quite a few of the things I picked up from him. I've already mentioned that he was a very clever man and he wanted his students to become overall better people. I remember Ray Ross telling me a story one time about how he used to turn up with a copy of the Daily Mirror newspaper under his arm. TP didn't approve and he insisted that Ray switched to the Daily Telegraph. And, not only that, he had to learn three new words a day from this paper. Ray did and at the end of the week, TP would test him on his new vocabulary. I don't think I changed reading habits but I hope I inspired them to improve in everything they did and not just judo. I'd had my judo club for many years and taught in a few schools and colleges. I think I had a good grounding in understanding how to get the best out of people and I made sure I used all this with my new position as team manager. I had a good idea about who the best players were as I'd trained many of them and they knew me very well. In those days we didn't have the internet which meant no e-mails or Facebook for communications and of course mobile phones hadn't taken over. So to communicate I used the good old telephone landline system and the post office. With my squad, based all over the UK, communication costs were high but I didn't care about this. As Britain's team manager, I knew I had to show I cared for my players and I telephoned them regularly to find out how they were and discuss any problems they had. We needed to bond as a team and I put every effort into making sure this happened. A bit like creating a manual WhatsApp or Facebook group which today is a very efficient method of bringing a group of people together and keeping them informed about what's happening.

I had people like Arthur Mapp, Densign White, Neil Adams, Christopher Bowles, Gavin Bell, and Peter Middleton. Neil had the most talent and as I mentioned previously we met at the Budokwai a few years before when I hadn't impressed him with my special Budokwai initiation! This generated a bit of tension between us but I knew he was a remarkable player and Britain's best chance of winning a medal at the World Championships held in Maastricht, Holland early in September 1981. He had a good draw, not easy, but I knew this gave him a chance. Japan's Jiro Kase, who I believed would be his toughest opponent, had been drawn on the other side which meant they could only meet in the final. Kase looked to have a more difficult set of opponents.

Neil seemed inspired in all of his contests and in many people's eyes he must have been favourite for the gold. Kase, on the other hand, looked out of form and appeared to struggle against his. Somehow, with typical Japanese doggedness, Kase clawed his way to the final where he would face Neil who'd breezed his way through. A few seconds before the final I stood with Neil who I thought appeared quite nervous and in a zone where I didn't want him to be. He also seemed worried. I knew I had to do something drastic so, just before they called his name, I slapped him around his face as hard as I could. This totally confused him and he put his fists up as if he wanted to have a go at me. We were eyeball to eyeball and that tension between seemed likely to boil over. I held his wrist and told him to get out there and fight him. Not me. He did and he gave Kase no chance as he became the first Britain to win a gold medal in the World Championships. It also confirmed his standing as a truly great champion on the world stage. He made us all proud and gave me so much pleasure. Would he have won if I hadn't slapped him? Probably.

His win put British judo on a high and I began looking at plans that would put us in a really strong position for the 1984 Los Angeles Olympic Games. I set things up with a few people to check out talent in different areas of the country, like a scouting network, and we communicated by landline telephones on a regular basis as I did with the players. Most days I would spend a couple of hours speaking with people in places like Birmingham, South Wales, Liverpool, Newcastle, Scotland, and Ireland. I didn't think twice about it. I just did it. I needed everyone to understand the importance of the journey we were on and I needed all the players to feel wanted. If they had problems I wanted to know about them. I'd been around a while and I believed that I knew how to find the answers to everything or that I could wing it if I had to. Moving into 1982 I felt confident about the future of British judo with me at the helm. Even though there were committees they knew my style. Charlie Palmer actually knew me better than most and fully understood how I loved to work alone. All my life I'd worked this way and that would never change no matter what I did.

But in January I received official notification about a BJA meeting that apparently I needed to attend. I called Charlie who assured me it was just a normal year-end procedure meeting, to go over a few numbers, and to discuss a few plans for the New Year. Right up to the last minute I tried to get out of it but I couldn't and I found myself sitting around an oval table with a bunch of people who didn't know that much about judo. A position I'd never enjoyed. Don't get me wrong, they were all important to judo. They loved the sport but they just couldn't do it. Although I always appreciated the time and effort they put into organising competitions.

When I arrived I made the usual jokes that I'd made with the same people for many years. Over the years they'd smiled back and made their standard replies which I'd expected. But not this time! Tension filled the air and you could have cut the atmosphere with a knife. For some reason, I felt like I might be in the doghouse and the reason soon became clear. They interrogated me about my £420 telephone bill. They wanted all the details about the calls I'd made. Who I'd called? Why I'd called? And how long each call had taken? I did my best to keep my rising irritation under control and explained that as team manager I needed to communicate with my players and my unofficial team of regional scouts. They wouldn't have it. They wanted details of every call. I said I wouldn't do it. They said I had to and I walked out of the meeting. Colin McIver soon took over as team manager and I couldn't help thinking they'd primed him for my job before that meeting. That marriage made in heaven ended up on the rocks.

I really enjoyed meeting people from different sports. Especially Henry Cooper. I loved him, as did Dad, and he introduced me to the Royal Variety Club Golf Society early in the 1980s. This became a massive part of my life. The society is actually a spin-off from the Royal Variety Club which started in 1912. Fifty-four years later the Golf Society thanks to Sir William Heygate Edmund Colborne 'Billy' Butlin. The South African born entrepreneur whose name became synonymous with Butlins holiday camps which first opened in 1936. He turned holiday camps into a multimillion pound industry and introduced Butlins Redcoats. His frontline staff at Butlins camps responsible for taking care of customers and entertaining them. This is where careers began for people like Jimmy Tarbuck, Des O'Connor, Ted Rogers, Jess Conrad, Michael Barrymore, Jimmy Cricket and quite a few others. Tarby and Jess have both dedicated a lot of their time to the golf society. Sir Billy got things started and when he died in 1980 his wife Shelia took over. Our aim and I'm still a member of the society as I write, is to provide Sunshine Coaches to schools and care centres looking after disabled and disadvantaged children. I'm certain over a million pounds has been raised since I started my association with this group and I'm proud to be a member.

With Limelight things were getting better especially, as we moved into 1983, and signed one of the greatest young football talents around at that time. Charles 'Charlie' Nicholas from Glasgow, Scotland. At the age of twenty-one, many people regarded him as the most exciting prospect in British football. The next big thing and he had the looks, talent, and the world at his feet. I might still have been quite marketable myself but 'Champagne Charlie' as some people referred to him, belonged in a different league. He'd just signed for Arsenal for a fee of £750,000 which made him the second most expensive export from Scottish league at that time. There were reports that he'd also become the highest paid footballer in Britain.

Things were still going well a year later. My family life, my judo club, and especially Limelight. I began thinking that I might be able to retire in 1990 at the ripe old age of forty-four.

Not long later I had a call from the Manager of Barclays Bank and he wanted to see me. I asked him what for but he said it would be best if we spoke face to face. At that particular time, I knew Bev had taken a vacation so there was no point in trying to contact him. When I arrived he didn't look happy and it felt like my final meeting with the BJA again. At that one, you could have cut the atmosphere with a knife and the same applied here. Another interrogation! He said Limelight owed £57,000 in taxes and that we were £40,000 overdrawn. I couldn't believe it. I asked the manager to show me one cheque that I'd personally signed. He couldn't. I never signed anything and left all that in the hands of Walker.

We were in a bad position and I needed to work out how to play things. I didn't want to just confront Walker so I decided to do some investigations. Obviously, I didn't know where to start so I did, what I always did, when I needed help with something. I contacted an expert. In this case, forty-five year old private detective Mr. Chris Lee who worked for Magnum Investigators in Surrey. I also went to see a solicitor called Brian Marsden. We soon discovered that Walker had been made bankrupt many times, and we decided to pay him a visit where he lived in the wing of a Sussex manor house. We arrived at 7:00 a.m. but apart from a few heated exchanges we couldn't get anything out of him and he denied all knowledge of any wrongdoing. When I asked what he'd done with the money he just opened his hands in a kind of who knows and who cares gesture. Well, I certainly cared as the company owed me a lot of money. After a chat with Mr. Lee, I agreed to let him go full steam ahead with his investigation and very soon the whole story made front-page news in British newspapers. There were reports of how Walker brokered deals that meant secret payments were made to Daley Thompson, from cosmetics giant Faberge, that questioned his amateur status and could have forced him out of the 1984 Olympic Games. Neil Adams also got caught up in this mess. For me, another marriage made in heaven ended on the rocks.

47

AS MUCH AS the fall out with Walker hurt work continued to pile up and in 1984 I met Colin Deaton from Chesterfield in Derbyshire. Colin had a successful scrap metal business. In his youth, he'd been one of England's top junior international table tennis players and he'd represented England on many occasions. His workload meant he had to abandon table tennis but during his spare time he coached and put a lot of effort into promoting the sport and motivating others to play. In 1957 he coached at one of Butlins holiday camps and he set up the Colin Deaton Table Tennis Academy.

Colin invited me to his house to discuss holiday camps as, at that time he engaged all kinds of people to work in these places, and he'd opened a company called 'Colin Deaton's International World of Sports Limited.' He had many contracts at places like Butlins, Pontins, Haven, and Warners. Deaton put in teams of wrestlers to entertain holidaymakers plus numerous other sportsmen from all different sports. People like Ray Rearden from snooker, Bobby Moore from football, and even the famous champion racehorse Red Rum who won the Grand National in 1973, 1974 and 1977. Deaton wanted me to give it a go. He said I could perform forty-five minute judo demonstrations at two or three camps a day. He made it sound great and it meant I would be doing something I loved, in a relaxed environment, and being paid a salary with expenses.

Deaton even described how he'd motivated people in the table tennis world in his earlier years and suggested that I could do the same for judo, which I'd already done with Superstars, and that this could be an extension of that. He said that hundreds of people, each week, would see me and that the benefits for British judo would be enormous. I went away from that meeting with a big smile on my face. I spoke with Dad and he agreed to help. I wrote a demonstration programme, that Dad and I practiced, and we went to see the BJA to explain exactly what we would do. I asked them for a van to carry mats and other equipment. I said I would advertise on the van with some kind of sign that said: 'Brian Jacks Sponsored by the BJA.' This van would be seen by thousands of people at the camps and hundreds of thousands of others as we drove across the country. I knew we would have morning shows in places like Cornwall, followed by an afternoon show in Devon, and evening show in Bournemouth. I'd been booked for twelve slots a week so this provided great exposure for me and the association. Definitely a win, win opportunity for British judo.

Obviously, this meant a lot of driving and some very early morning starts. We used to wake up at 4:00 a.m. to make sure we were at our first location on time, with our mats set up, and ready to go. Hundreds of people watched each demonstration and people from the crowd always had an opportunity to take part. Basically, we were there to put smiles on people's faces and make them laugh with a light-hearted judo demonstration. We achieved that. But at the same time, I wanted to send the message that all types of people could take part in judo. So I did. I had my stage and I tried to educate them about judo in a very funny way. I enjoyed this experience so much and I met so many interesting people from sport, entertainment, and people staying at the camps. After each show, I would stay to sign autographs and I would never leave until I'd signed for the last person. Sometimes this meant we left late for our next appointment which meant we had to find ways to make up time and there may have been times when I used unorthodox driving methods. Such as using the hard shoulders of motorways. I remember one time being stopped by a police patrol car. Errol, in the little van with me at that particular time, begged me to say nothing. But the officer recognised me and ended up giving us a police escort all the way to our next appointment.

In common with Superstars, I had a reliable team with me all the time. Dad, Errol, David Wilkinson and my son Philip even worked the last season with me which was absolutely fantastic. During my four years working the camps I met thousands and thousands of people and had a wonderful time. The crowds who watched really seemed to enjoy themselves and we liked nothing more than to interact with them rather like pantomime. Kids and adults came up on to the stage and were given the chance to hold me down. I played with them and even let some of them think they might hold me down the required thirty seconds. I loved the camps and they provided me with a perfect platform to give something back to judo. I mentioned before about the win, win situation for me and the BJA. Or, I should say, it should have been but the BJA turned down me down right at the beginning. To this day I still really believe they missed out on a fine opportunity to publicise judo. We were at ten to twelve camps every week and could have been performing in front of 50,000 people a month. Their negative response annoyed me and my relationship with them, which had at times been strained over the years, led to my involvement with other associations such as the British Judo Council where I met a couple of guys from Kent called Nobby and Martin Clarke. We got along very well together, did a few training courses, and I helped them with coaching as well. This might not have pleased the BJA.

To this day people still send me pictures taken with them during this period of my life and I receive many e-mails and Facebook messages. This one came in recently:

'Hi Brian. I don't know if you remember me but you used to call me the 'Welsh Champion.' My name is Steve Holmes and we talked a lot at the British championship at Crystal Palace. I got a lot of great memories of you. One them you fighting the German champion for a tracksuit which you won. But I never will I forget the time I came to see you at Minehead Butlins with my family you invited me and my family to have a meal with you and Bobby Moore. Your meal went cold because people wanted your autograph you kept saying sorry to me and Bobby Moore because of signing all the autographs. Then you said to one of them would you like to have Bobby Moore who was captain of the England football team when England won the world cup and we got Steve the Welsh champion. So they got mine and Bobby as well. But 1 lady wanted your autograph for her son and you said where is he? She said he was outside. He is disabled and we can't get him in. You said come on Steve and we went outside and carried him in his wheelchair. He and

his family were over the moon. You are a great man Brian. From a friend Steve Holmes.'

Being on the road sometimes meant strange things happened and one of these included forty-seven year old Mavis Wollerton from Darfield Village in South Yorkshire. We were on our way to Wombwell High School and we stopped by a pedestrian crossing near St. Michaels RC School, St1yford Road, Low Valley to ask Mavis for directions. Mavis, the local lollipop lady, poked her head into the car to answer my question. I actually sat in the passenger seat as we had someone else driving. Mavis provided us with the information we needed and we pulled away. But as we did Mavis's crossing patrol coat somehow got entangled with our car's rear bumper and as we accelerated down a village street we dragged Mavis behind us. We didn't hear anything and I think she might have been too stunned to scream. We dragged her about thirty yards before the buttons on her white plastic coat burst. At that point, we noticed something had gone wrong and we helped her get to the hospital where we found out she'd broken her shoulder. It left me totally shocked and it could have been a lot worse. I sent Mavis flowers and she told me some friends of hers had joked that she'd fallen for Brian Jacks. A few newspapers picked up the story and there were headlines like 'lollipop lady Mavis lolli

– bopped' and 'Brian Jacks knocks out lollipop lady.' They might have even suggested that I was driving but I've already mentioned that someone else had the wheel that day. It was a freak accident on a wet, windy and dark early evening that could have been so much worse.

On another occasion, a few of us were in the car again, with me at the wheel this time, just outside Birmingham and we'd stopped at some traffic lights. A woman with bags of shopping in both her hands started to cross the road. As she stepped off the curb she noticed me but she continued walking. By the time she'd reached the middle of the road, something must have clicked in her brain. She stopped, turned, faced me and smiled. I smiled back and she moved her arms up and down as if she might be pushing out a few dips. As she did her shopping bags broke and her shopping ended up all over the road. Fruit and cans of drink were rolling down the road. Eggs smashed and all kinds of other groceries just lay there. Even though the traffic lights had changed I had to jump out of my car to help her pick it all up and the bloke stopped behind me didn't get angry. He just casually got out of his car and started taking pictures!

With a positive end to the eighties, I looked forward to the next decade and felt upbeat with everything in my life especially Philip who I had a really developed special relationship with. He'd become the most important person in my life and we were like very good mates. However, I had an early hiccup when Julie and I broke up. I thought we had a marriage made in heaven but it ended on the rocks and she moved out. I took care of Philip and later I began a relationship with Laura Perry and she eventually moved in with us. We'd been together for about eight years when one day I received a telephone call from Chris Metas. He said Laura had been to see him regarding arranging a secret wedding and she made him swear he wouldn't call me. Obviously, as soon as she left, Chris called and told me all about it. But I went through with it and a year later we were on the rocks as well. In both cases, my relationships with these women broke down and we went our separate ways. These things happen and we just have to get on with our lives.

Philip and I discussed judo quite a few times, and I even coached him to a very good level. I entered him in competitions, under another name, and he did okay. I also presented him with his black belt as he never had any problems when he met other black belts on the mat. But he gave up as I don't think his heart was in it. If anyone asks him he sometimes says that I might have been a tough act for him to follow and that might be partly true. Plus he also saw the supreme effort I'd made and the injuries I'd suffered. Maybe he didn't fancy taking that road. I didn't mind. I'd always said that I'd support Philip in whatever he wanted to do and it seemed that cars were his thing.

Mum passed away in 1996, which was obviously a sad time for all of us, especially Dad who'd been with Mum for more than fifty years. She'd been the glue that had kept us together and we were completely lost without her.

48

I still had the lease for the B and P Judo Club building and no one had bothered me for more than twenty years. I did my own thing, my way, and it worked. I didn't have committees or meetings. I just did it until one day a young lady turned up from Bromley Council brandishing her Health and Safety business card. I thought her visit might be a joke at first, but no, Miss Prim and Proper was the real deal. I had a small refrigerator and she pointed to it and said what's that? Stunned I replied it's a refrigerator what do you think it is? She ticked something on her clipboard and then asked what's in it? I said a pint of milk. She then asked how cold is it? I said what the pint of milk? She made a note on her clipboard and said that the refrigerator had to be a certain temperature. I told her that I'd had it for twenty years and no one had ever complained that the milk was too hot or too cold. She said that the past didn't matter and I had to get it right from now on. I got the hump, unplugged the refrigerator, and carried it outside. Now we didn't have a refrigerator anymore and I politely asked her to leave. She didn't and I think she had the hump now as well. I followed her into the men's toilet and she looked at the sink with two taps. A red one and a blue one. She asked what that meant. I said that red meant hot and blue meant cold. She asked how hot the hot water was. I said what kind of stupid question is that? She said I needed to put a sign on the wall that confirmed how hot the water was. I said don't be so stupid and do you need a sign to say how wet the water is? She made one more note on her clipboard and left.

The next day a van turned up with four men and they were all dressed in white protection suits from head to toe. They wanted to perform an asbestos test. Now I'd had the freedom of Bromley since 1983 and I knew a few people on the council. For my lease, I'd always dealt with John Whitman so I called him. I said John they want to do an asbestos test on my building and I hope they find some so I can sue you. John called off the test.

Miss Prim and Proper, turning up like that, really depressed me. I didn't like the way rules and regulations were taking over. I know health and safety is very important and I always made sure my students had a safe environment to work in. I had a formula that worked but she seemed more interested in my refrigerator and the temperature of my hot water. At this point, I realised that the time might have arrived for me to try something different. From a personal point of view, the nineties had been a testing decade for me and I came up against some challenges that I'd never faced before. Dad helped me a lot and he always provided me with sound advice. He too had to learn how to handle some difficult circumstances which he did very well. He even spent time in hospital for a cartilage operation and I went to see him every day. I remember one time I went he said. You'll never guess what happened today? I said what Dad? Well, last night the breakfast lady pushing her empty trolley came to see me with her breakfast menu. As she passed it to me I thought she recognised me as she looked embarrassed. I looked at her ring finger and noticed a ring on it. It shocked me and I was quite taken aback. But I regained my composure, ordered a bacon and egg sandwich, and she walked away. Now, Brian, I've never discussed this with you before, but back when I was eighteen I met this girl and fell in love with her. I even bought her a ring and I'm one hundred percent sure that was the ring. Anyway, I got called up and eventually posted to the Scilly Isles. But I'd fallen head over heels in love with her and I wrote to her every day for three years but I never received a reply. Now I've seen the ring again on her finger. She must have loved me all that time as well.

This amazed me. I always believed that Mum was the only love of his life. I said, Dad, what happened next? He looked at me and I looked at him. I'd never seen that look on his face. Slowly he replied. She delivered my sandwich this morning, without the ring on her finger, and you'll never guess what was in the egg and bacon sandwich? I said, Dad. The ring? He, with the same sombre look on his face, replied. Don't be so stupid Brian. It was egg and bacon!

Dan status update: On the 22nd of November 1994 I received my eighth Dan.

The Dips. They were tough and my body cried out in pain!

Squat thrusts and the orange moment!

With Lynne Davies. One of my toughest opponents.
Being interviewed by the immaculate David Vine.

With Daley Thompson being interviewed by the
incredibly knowledgeable Ron Pickering

Stage 5

SAT IN MY OFFICE

49

SAT IN MY office, located about a ninety minute drive from Thailand's capital city Bangkok, and close to Pattaya City, my reasons for settling in Thailand spring to mind and I have to confess. It all started by accident.

Early in 1972, whilst flying back to London from Tokyo, we had to make an unscheduled landing at Bangkok's Don Muang airport due to some kind of electrical fault. Originally we were advised that the delay would only be for three to four hours. But a short time later we found out that we'd be there two nights. We were transferred to a hotel. Bored in my room I decided to go in search of a coffee and I found a bar on the ground floor. The barman there thought I might have been American and in Bangkok for some much needed rest and recuperation from the Vietnam War. We had a good laugh as I explained my real story and he explained a few things about Bangkok. As we chatted a young Thai lady approached and asked if she could sit next to me. I agreed and the three of us started chatting. I explained to Nid, the young lady's nickname, exactly why I happened to be staying at this hotel. She, like most people, thought I looked American but once she understood my predicament she asked me if I'd like a tour of Bangkok with her and I agreed.

Outside where we found a taxi and I climbed in the back. Nid sat in the front and she chatted with the driver. We had a great time and visited the Golden Buddha, Reclining Buddha, Royal Palace and many other interesting places that included a famous market called Chatuchak. That evening I brought her and the driver a nice meal. They dropped me back at my hotel and as they were about to leave I asked Nid if there were any good beaches nearby as I fancied a day relaxing on the beach. She said there were but suggested it might be more interesting if we visited a place called Pattaya. I agreed and we arranged to meet up the following morning at 6:00 a.m.

Well, I have to say I wish I'd never agreed to this. The roads were absolutely horrendous. I'd never imagined that a road system could be so bad. Plus the local drivers seemed to have no idea what they were doing. They just kept stopping, pulling out and turning right and left without giving any signals. The roads themselves were full of potholes, in some parts flooded, and in others parts just missing. Our driver, once we actually hit a stretch of open road where he seemed to know what he was doing, would suddenly slam on his brakes as the road suddenly disappeared down some massive crater. I think the journey must have taken five hours and there were times when I seriously doubted if I'd make it out of this trip alive. Or at the very least sustain some kind of serious injury that would put me out of Munich.

But when we arrived we had a wonderful day. We spent some time on Pattaya's pristine beach, with its clear and clean water, before we had a very nice lunch in a seafood restaurant. We spent the day there and this was my accidental introduction to Pattaya which I liked very much. In a way, Pattaya reminded me of Tokyo in the early sixties when it didn't have that many buildings and a lot of people sold food, and all kinds of other products, from carts on the street. Both Bangkok and Pattaya had the same kind of roughness that I enjoyed about Tokyo.

Due to other many other commitments, I didn't get an opportunity to return to Thailand until the end of 2001. At this point, Thailand's draw on me became more and more powerful. It's difficult to explain but if you can imagine a gigantic vacuum cleaner, with your name on it trying to drag you in, then that's how it felt. Prior to this, I'd resisted as I had big plans that didn't include Thailand. But not so much now and I felt Thailand's full power and knew it would be hard to resist. My life had felt like a book and most of the time I'd enjoyed the chapters. But now things had happened in my life that I didn't like or want to be involved with. I needed a fresh start and a new challenge.

During my absence, Thailand had changed and the roads were now in much better shape than they were back in 1972. Then Thailand could have been classified as a third world country. But not in 2001. Pattaya had also moved on in a big way. It no longer resembled a sleepy fishing village. Hotels, shopping malls, restaurants, entertainment venues, housing developments, condominium resorts, new roads and a whole lot more had happened. Although the one thing that attracted me before, people cooking on the streets, had remained. It amazed to see this still going on. Often these mobile food vendors rode motorbikes, with their equipment and food fixed to their vehicles in many different ways, and they parked outside restaurants selling the same things they were making, but for twenty percent of the restaurant price! There were also a lot of open markets that reminded me again of how things used to be in Tokyo. This time I saw a lot more of Pattaya and even though it had expanded so much, I enjoyed my time there. I really believed the next chapter of my life had begun. But I hadn't gone all in yet as I still had business to deal with in Great Britain.

Time moved on and I bounced between England and Thailand on a regular basis until one day I met a young lady called Doo quite by chance during Thailand's 2003 New Year celebrations. Thailand's New Year is at a completely different time to the rest of the world and actually happens in April. Doo agreed to have lunch with me the following day. I suppose we spent two hours together and she left a great impression on me. She'd recently turned twenty-five, came from a place called Chanthaburi, which is in the east of Thailand and close to the Cambodian border. She had a four year old daughter called Pop who she took care of with her mother. She said her local husband had died about three years before in a motorcycle accident. She also said she'd only been in Pattaya about two months and that she didn't really like it. For the next month we saw each other on a fairly regular basis and sometimes she stayed over with me and at other times she went home to a rather shack-like house where she lived with her mother and daughter. We shared a lot of moments together and Doo really helped to make this new chapter of my life complete.

During 2003 she came to England with me for three months but it didn't go well as I think she missed her daughter. She seemed to lose her sparkle that first attracted me to her. She also lost weight. Back in Thailand, she picked up again and we went back to enjoying life as we had before. Although her weight seemed unstable, she coughed a lot, and sometimes she had trouble breathing. I took her to the Pattaya Memorial Hospital where they appeared to give her a complete medical examination. They took x-rays, blood samples, and gave her a bunch of pills to take morning, noon and night. I tried to ask the doctor, and Doo, what was wrong but didn't get a proper answer which frustrated me.

Prior to meeting Doo, I'd purchased some land about five miles outside the main central Pattaya area in a place called Nurn Plub Wahn. I had this dream about owning horses and I wanted to get a few dogs as well. I'd always loved animals and thought this would be a good idea. I just needed to get down to business and build something. But with one thing or another I didn't get back to my land for about a year and when I eventually did a lot of the jungle, that had originally attracted me to the area, had been cut down. All kinds of building projects were in progress. Housing estates, condominiums, hotels, shops, and restaurants. This totally ruined my plans for a nice country house with stables for my horses. Pattaya appeared to be stretching out and pulling Nurn Plub Wahn in. I needed a plan B to keep my dream alive and fortunately, I found it about ten minutes further on from my original plot of land where a small derelict house sat on a large plot of land. My vision returned and I could see myself building a larger house and restoring the derelict house which still had good foundations. The wasteland next door looked perfect for horses. I immediately bought it and began building.

We finished and Doo and I moved in halfway through the year. The future looked great. Doo seemed perfectly happy although she continued to cough a lot and her weight still seemed very unstable. Philip came to stay twice in 2003. A short stay mid-year and for a month at Christmas. He didn't seem in the best of spirits as his relationship with his girlfriend had broken down. I suggested that he came to stay with me for a while which he did in 2004. It felt great having Philip, then twenty-five, with me. Even though I knew he still felt a bit down about his break up we managed to have some fun.

At the beginning of December, we were rocked by news that Doo had been rushed to the Pattaya Bangkok International hospital and admitted to intensive care. I couldn't see her and we had no idea what was going on. Eventually, a doctor explained that Doo had a severe tuberculosis condition and they were doing their best to help her. I didn't know what to do. My new dream world seemed to be falling apart just as it had taken off. After a month of doing their best doctors realised there was nothing they could do and she passed away early in 2005. This devastated me and again I needed the support of Philip and a few others.

50

AS YOU CAN imagine 2005 didn't start too great for me. I'd done all I could for Doo but at the age of 27 her body had just shut down. It felt such a shame for someone so young.

I still had Philip with me and we were both in periods of our lives when we needed to move on. For me, I couldn't have wished for a better person to share my moving on time with. Philip might say the same about me. We were a lot younger back then and I, very probably, a bit madder than I am now. Even at fifty-eight I still felt like a youngster. Maybe I had a younger kind of outlook on life for my age. On my left shoulder, I have this cheeky mischievous and sometimes outrageous monkey. On my right shoulder, I have this intense, serious and focused monkey. They are both very competitive, should never be dared, and I think my left monkey has probably enjoyed more exposure in Thailand that he did anywhere else in the world. But I didn't have a normal teenage life when compared to most teenagers, and I missed out on my happy twenties. I don't mean I didn't feel happy during that period of my life it was just that I had to focus on different things. Between the ages of thirteen to nineteen I only ever trained. I never went to parties, pubs, discos, nightclubs or anything like that. I focused on judo, always went to bed early, and lived my life more or less in the same way, up until I finished Superstars. Train, sleep, compete and then again and again and again for about twenty-five years. Yes, I deviated slightly when I managed a couple of West End clubs but that didn't stop me training. Plus I needed to do that to put food on the table to help me train. So for me, my fifties, equalled my teens plus happy twenties, all in quite a short space of time.

How did Philip and I move on? Well, I think it's fair to say we partied a bit although not for quite a few months after Doo passed. We partied in Pattaya which is one of the best places in the world to do this. At night it's a party town and one night, around midnight we were in a place called the Walking Street where they had this Neapolitan ice cream parlour that served all kinds of different flavoured delicious ice creams. Philip and I, plus an old friend who also happened to be staying at my house at the time called Chris Clifford. Well the three of us, walked away from this Neapolitan ice cream parlour each with a big tub of ice cream, and into the Jacuzzi Go-Go Bar. Built into the centre of the stage they had a Jacuzzi where two scantily clad girls, who were probably in their late twenties, splashed around with the bubbles. On one side of them, there was an empty sofa. Originally we'd found a place to sit on the side of the bar where we sat eating our ice cream. After about five minutes Philip dared me to sit on the empty sofa right next to the Jacuzzi. Left monkey stepped straight in and I soon found myself sat on the sofa still eating my big tub of ice cream. Obviously, I had a close-up view as the girls splashed around in the Jacuzzi. But sitting there must have been some kind of special place and a signal to the girls. One of them jumped out of the Jacuzzi, ripped my shirt off. I carried on eating my big tub of ice cream. The second girl then undid the button on my shorts which immediately dropped to the ground. I continued eating although this exposed another problem. My total lack of underwear left me in my birthday suit eating my big tub of ice cream, in front of a packed crowd. The manager stood at the bar had a look of complete horror on his face. He came running over with a big towel to try and cover my privates. Now suitably attired, the Jacuzzi girls pulled me into the Jacuzzi with them where I sat and continued to eat my big tub of ice cream. They were not happy with this. They took the ice cream tub from me and placed it on the side. They wanted me to interact with them but I only had one thing on my mind. Eating my ice cream. They tried but nothing they could do turned me on. Philip and Chris were in hysterics, pure pantomime, and the crowded bar seemed to enjoy it as well. We had a few moments like this but we never looked for any trouble. Just some fun that I'd missed out in my younger days.

During my relationship with Doo, we'd met a girl called Lek, a friend of a friend, who became our friend. I'd always liked Lek, as a friend, from the first day I saw her. She had the right kind of personality that I always liked in a lady. Not too pushy and not too shy, although she did have a certain innocence about her. By chance, I met her again and we'd shared a few lunches and dinners. We got on well and after about six months I persuaded her to move in with me. She came from a small village called Chai Nat, which is in Sing Buri close to Ayutthaya, and about eighty-five kilometres to the north of Bangkok.

I'd now been based in Thailand for four years and although content with the life I felt I needed something else to do. Philip, who'd arrived for a one year visit in 2004, looked like he might be staying longer. Dad also came out to see me now and again and during one of his visits the three of us were having a chat about my land. I could have sold it but it now seemed that quite a few foreigners had discovered Nurn Plub Wahn and some, like me, had settled in long term. Whilst others, keen to avoid the hustle and bustle of Pattaya, were now spending their vacations in and around this area. I thought it might be a good idea to try and provide a cost-effective place for people to stay. Dad and Philip agreed and we decided to build an apartment block. Other people had noticed the trend and were ahead of me. A few blocks had already been built along with some hotels. I had a look around with Philip and made a few notes about the types of places that were available. Lek also spent a few days doing her own research. I wanted to find out what these places offered as I wanted to beat them on price and quality. Some of the apartment rooms I saw were way too small with not enough room to swing a cat. I couldn't live in such a tiny space so I knew immediately that my rooms had to be bigger. I drew up some plans, we completed all the red tape which took a lot long longer than I anticipated, and then we broke ground with a formal ceremony with eight monks from the local temple. At the start of any building project in Thailand, it's a tradition for a group of monks to attend. The locals believe they will bring the project good luck.

During construction we faced many challenges and the luck I had, that the monks prayed for on the first day, came from having Philip around. He was my project manager and I don't know where I'd have been without him. Lek as well proved a great help keeping the Thai side of things under control, as did as Nam, Philip's new girlfriend. They were all outstanding and we managed to open in January 2008. Well, that's when our first customers moved in and we were about eighty percent complete although it still looked like a bit like a building site. As per our plan we ended up with sixty-four rooms all with plenty of space for swinging cats.

Getting the apartment open early in January 2008 meant a great weight off my mind as I needed to get back to England. I'd heard that Dad hadn't been too well. It was great to get back and see him but clearly, something had gone wrong. I stayed with him every day and it was so sad to watch his health deteriorate. On the 25th of February Dad passed away. I was devastated but I knew Dad would expect me, as his eldest child, to keep everything together and get on with life. I can assure you it wasn't easy. I had Christine Wildman with me at the hospital on the 25th and she wrote this.

'Unfortunately, Albert became very ill and I went to see him in the hospital. I was so glad that I did as, fortunately, I was one of the few people that had the privilege of spending time with him at the hospital. I was so fortunate to be able to give Brian some support when this lovely man

passed away. Brian was so lucky to have had such a wonderful man to be his father. Everyone in the judo world remembers Albert as he attended all the judo championships to give support to Brian.

I arranged 'A Service of Thanksgiving and Celebration' for the Life of My Dad. Albert Thomas Jacks. My Dad. My coach. My mentor. My friend. Sometimes my tormentor. But, most of all, the best Dad a son could ever have. Philip, Errol and I all read tributes. I called mine 'My Dad – Our Dad.' Philip's 'My Grandad -The Letter,' and Errol's 'My Friend Albert.'

Philip's letter:

'Written on 3rd of March 2008 at 6:55 p.m. The evening before I fly back to Thailand. By Brian Philip Jacks:

Grandad I just wanted to let you know you meant so much to me even though I didn't see as much of you as I would have liked as I've lived the other side of the world with Dad in Thailand. I am sorry I couldn't be here with you today but as you know we have a lot going on and I have to be here to take care of the animals and the building site. Dan the builder sends his regards to you. I am also really sorry I didn't get back in time to see you in the hospital before you passed away. I arrived back a day too late. Dad did tell me you were a lot happier knowing that I was on my way back.

I just wish I got back that day earlier so I could give you a kiss and a cuddle and told you I loved you.

I will never forget the good times we had together when you used to tell me stories about the old days. And when we used to go to the sweet shop together to buy a cheeky ice cream and when we used to go to Brick Lane for our bagels. We would stand there, eat them, and have a good old chat. You would always have a crafty cheesecake before we came back home. I never told anyone about it by the way.

I will really miss the days but never forget them.

I also remember when I called you last year and pretended I was in Thailand then I turned up one hour later with Mum on your doorstep. The look on your face was great. You were so happy to see me. I will never forget that look.

Nam misses you a lot and sends her love to you. She remembers the time you and Ann came to visit us in Thailand. And we all went out for a Chinese meal and you had a sugar attack. It was as though you were drunk and you chased Nam around the car and kept kissing her. And then you told her to stop kissing you. She got very confused as you were the one kissing her.

You did make us all laugh and there is so much more I remember about that holiday when you kept me laughing all the time.

I was always happy when you were around and things will never be the same.

My Mum also sends her love to you and she was so happy to visit you in hospital.

Make sure you eat as many cakes, sweets, and ice creams as you don't have diabetes anymore and the good thing is no one can moan at you.

Send my love to Nanny and give her a big kiss from me.

I will never forget you. Love forever.

Philip and Nam xxxx

P.S. Mark, Ash and the rest of the boys from Thailand send their regards. Also little Chris. I had a pie and mash but it didn't taste the same because you were not there.

Love you.

Just let me explain a few points from Philips letter. Later in life, Dad developed diabetes which meant he had to be careful what he ate. But he just couldn't resist a piece of cheesecake whenever he had the chance. Ann came into Dad's life after Mum passed away and became his partner. Errol and Dad were great friends and became closer when I left England. At least once a week they would meet somewhere for dinner. Errol reminded me recently about a time Dad picked up a hitchhiker in his own car.

Driving home one day Dad noticed a hitchhiker standing by the side of the road with a judo bag down by his feet. As a rule, Dad never picked up hitchhikers but the judo bag made him stop. He thought a judo player would give him a chance to have a chat about judo. The hitchhiker dropped his judo bag on the back seat and it made a hell of a noise. Dad tried to be friendly with him but he didn't seem to respond. Dad then asked him what he had in the bag and the hitchhiker said mind your own business. Dad didn't really like his attitude and stopped by the side of the road to let him out. He got out, gave Dad the big bad middle finger, and stormed off. Dad drove home and when he got there noticed the judo bag still on the back seat. Errol couldn't believe it and asked Dad what was in the bag. Dad replied. Mind your own business!

51

BACK IN THAILAND, we finished the apartment and we felt quite pleased with our work. We'd created a low rise, three-story building, with very nice accommodation at an affordable price. Philip's one year in Thailand had now stretched to more than four and he decided it was time for him to return to the UK to get his career back on track. Nam, from Nakhon Ratchasima Province also known as Khorat in North East of Thailand, returned with him. They seemed very happy together and it pleased me that Philip had found a new love in his life. Lek and I took our seats in our apartment's office and we began the next stage of our careers as apartment owners.

In England Philip and Nam seemed to be getting on fine. Philip, back working with cars, loved his job. He also took his relationship with Nam to the next level. They were married on the 2nd of June 2010 in a London registry office. Unfortunately, I couldn't make it but it did make me think about Lek and on the 16th of January 2011 we were married in Bangkok at a hospice with twelve other couples. Lek wanted to do this as it meant all the money went to charity to help thermally ill monks. On the 22nd December 2012, Philip and Nam were married in traditional Thai style in

Nam's home province. Many people from my apartments made the journey and we all had a very enjoyable day.

52

THAT'S THE STORY of my life so far and as I've said before I'd have liked to have called this book 'I did it for my Dad.' By that, I don't just mean my book. I mean my judo career and Superstars which Dad helped me with so much. He set my training programmes. He trained with me whenever he could. He came to watch me fight. He was on the mat with me every time I went out to fight. Not literally on the mat but I felt his strength. And the same applied to Superstars. He would always be there to provide me with encouragement and more strength for each of the events. I had this intense desire to win because I really wanted to win. But at the same time, I really wanted to make Dad proud. Not just Dad. Mum as well. She was magnificent. She held everything together and she provided the steadying, grounding influence that I needed throughout my career.

Why did I take so long to write my autobiography? Well, I wanted to live a good part of my life first, and I think 70 might be a good part of my life, plus it's for my wonderful son, his beautiful wife, and their amazing new daughter, my first grandchild, Millie. Millie, if you're reading this, Grandad loves you even though he might be a long way away. You, entering this world on the 22nd of August 2016 at 5:12 p.m., are the joint first best things that have ever happened to me. You share that honour with your Dad.

But you did create a bit of a 'Rocky Horror Show' moment for me. Philip and Nam have a French bulldog called Rocky and when Nam went into hospital to give birth I took care of Rocky. I'd done this a few times and we got on well. Rocky knew that when I whistled he had to come. Just like many other dogs I had. I had whistle and voice control which they all respected, until this day, about an hour before Millie's birth when I took Rocky out to the park. Philip said don't let him off his lead. Philip always said that. In fact, he said it twice. I always ignored him and this time I ignored him twice. Rocky had a good run and after about twenty minutes I whistled for him to come to me. He didn't. He ran to another corner of the park. I walked towards him and when I got near he ran to another corner. I couldn't believe it. I kept whistling, walking and running and he kept waiting and then running off to the other corners. This went on for about an hour and totally wore me out. When I eventually got him home I had to go straight to the hospital and I felt absolutely shattered.

Maybe Rocky knew that Millie had arrived and that he might have to play second fiddle to her for a while! And I have to say, as Millie approaches her first birthday, she is getting on fine and into everything. Philip and Nam are wonderful parents and I'm so pleased for them.

With Lek. The love of my life and making my life complete.

Philip and Nam on their Thai wedding day.

Millie, just checking Facebook, with Mum Nam.

Printed in Great Britain
by Amazon